Subversion in the Fiction of Jean Rhys, Angela Carter and Michele Roberts

A Thematic and Stylistic Study

Richa Goyal

ATLANTIC

PUBLISHERS & DISTRIBUTORS (P) LTD

Published by
ATLANTIC
PUBLISHERS & DISTRIBUTORS (P) LTD

7/22, Ansari Road, Darya Ganj, New Delhi-110002
Phones : +91-11-40775252, 23273880, 23275880, 23280451
Fax : +91-11-23285873
Web : www.atlanticbooks.com
E-mail : orders@atlanticbooks.com

Branch Office
5, Nallathambi Street, Wallajah Road, Chennai-600002
Phones : +91-44-64611085, 32413319
E-mail : chennai@atlanticbooks.com

Printed in India at Nice Printing Press, A-33/3A, Site-IV, Industrial Area, Sahibabad, Ghaziabad, U.P.

Preface

This book entitled *Subversion in the Fiction of Jean Rhys, Angela Carter and Michele Roberts: A Thematic and Stylistic Study* scrutinizes the thematic and stylistic subversion of established premises about gender on which western philosophy, myths and religion are based. The three contemporary British women, whose works have been selected for analysis, together span almost a century of feminist theorizing about the status of women in society and the means of constructing pathways for women's liberation.

Though women have been writing subversively for centuries now, both within and without patriarchal enclosures, the literature of subversion in its contemporary flagrant exterior is chiefly a product of the failure of the British counterculture and sexual revolution to liberate women from the straitjacket of over-determined media images. The colonization of women's identity through external determination of their roles within the social matrix and the entrapment of their bodies within the male gaze are the chief concerns of these writers as they undertake the responsibility of setting women free.

The book opens with a justification for the endeavours of the feminist women writers to subvert the gender status quo and an illustration of the misogynistic belief systems on which the treatises written by giants like Plato, Aristotle, Rousseau and Descartes rest. A study of western psychoanalytic thought and literary canon is also carried out to reveal similar somatophobic, phallocentric and misogynistic attitudes. An examination of the works of Freud, Lacan, W.B. Yeats, William Shakespeare, Charles Dickens, Alexander Pope, etc. is done through the gender lens in order to bring to fore dichotomous portrayals of women who are depicted as wearing either halos or horns.

Rhys's postmodern novel, *Wide Sargasso Sea,* is scrutinized through post-colonial and post-structural paradigms to underscore Rhys's subversive stance about the linking of race and gender with madness, the concept of unitary self, enlightenment dictums of reason and progress, the reliability of memory and the logocentric postures about God and Truth.

A close study of Angela Carter's speculative novels and re-written folklores and fairy tales showcases her theoretical dialogue with female fetishizing, engagement with the concept of woman-as-sign and unveiling of sexism present in fairy tales intended for the social conditioning of young children. The main intertexts are the tales collected by Charles Perrault, ancient Greek myths, and oral folklores. An examination of Carter's conceptualization of "a moral pornographer" throws light on one of her strategies used to aid the process of "demythologizing".

Somatophobia in Catholic religion, the search for a feminist utopia, valorizing the body and articulating its presence through "writing in the feminine" are the key features of Michele Roberts's novels. Re-defining both masculinity and femininity through a revision of Biblical myths, stories about female saints collected in *The Golden Legend* and the Gospels written by the male followers of Christ is also central to Roberts's writing.

The narrative strategies employed by the three writers for supporting their aim of subversion have also been examined. The study reveals the writers' ingenuity in using lexis, syntax, semantics, graphology, tone, genre, form, narrative voice, silences and intertextuality as means of deconstructing ideological mansions. The texts abound in ambiguities, aporias and multiplicities which invite the reader to co-create meaning. Nevertheless, the meaning remains elusive which makes resolving the textual tension difficult for the reader.

Richa Goyal

Abbreviations

Impossible Saints	:	IS
Nights at the Circus	:	NC
The Book of Mrs Noah	:	BMN
The Bloody Chamber	:	BC
The Infernal Desire Machines of Doctor Hoffman	:	IDH
The Magic Toyshop	:	TMT
The Passion of New Eve	:	PNE
The Secret Gospel of Mary Magdalene	:	SG
Wide Sargasso Sea	:	WSS
Wise Children	:	WC

Contents

1
Introduction

The Post-war British society found it difficult to sustain "an authoritative whole picture" (Head 9) of Britain as a result of the process of decolonization and the rising spirit of post-nationalism. Under such circumstances, the subversive currents of the countercultural revolution of the 1960s made Britain a breeding ground for experimental literary forms. The Welsh, Scottish and the Irish writers in Britain had started fracturing the outmoded belief systems of the British high culture and got acceptance in the mainstream alongside the modern avant-garde writers who were overhauling the literary norms with new trends.

Though the counterculture brought a dramatic shift in the post-war British society, revamped the traditional family unit rooted in marriage and destabilized the economic dependence of women on men (Head 9), it failed to bring equality for women. Therefore, feminist writers started using literature to protest and interrogate the validity of the social, political and cultural norms related to gender status quo. They began writing subversively to draw attention to gender discrimination and female identity. The feminist writers believed that "the personal is political" and used subversive literature as a means of critiquing and restructuring the power relations within the microcosm of society and family. A study of the rise of women's movement in the West, the synergizing of feminism with postmodernism and the literary tools used for feminist subversion would offer insights into the motivating factors for the creation of subversive literature by the contemporary British women writers.

Feminism, which is a subversive movement, started as a movement in the nineteenth century by the middle class white women in North America and Western Europe. As the movement gained complexity, it spread to the third world and amalgamated the cultural and racial aspects with women's political liberation. The first wave of the feminist movement which according to Patricia Waugh dates from "1830 to 1920" started with a struggle for women's suffrage and was marked by the works of Mary Wollstonecraft (*A Vindication of the Rights of Women*, 1792), John Stuart Mill (*The Subjugation of Women*, 1869), and Virginia Woolf (*A Room of One's Own*, 1929) who provide a critique of patriarchy and of women's subordinate position in society. During the first wave of feminism in the West women also fought for the right to education, right to equality at work, property rights and the rights to reproduction and contraception.

Flora Alexander notes that "the aim of universal suffrage was achieved in Britain in 1928, and it was in the "1960s that equal rights and opportunities for women became once more a matter of widespread and lively concern" which gave birth to the second wave of feminism (1-2). The second wave started from 1960 and took up more radical revision of areas like cultural theories, psychoanalytic criticism and the structure of the western languages. Waugh notes that the attempt to "examine the underlying causes of sexual discrimination was an invaluable starting point for feminists wanted to progress beyond the demand for civil rights and educational opportunities that had characterised the first wave" (Waugh 320).

A variety of feminist theories flooded the literary world post 1970s and made feminism a much more diverse movement than it was during the first wave. The key points of interrogation by the contemporary feminist writers are the master narratives of the western civilization, the literary canon and the androcentric bias in western languages. Contemporary feminist literature by British women writers also appropriates psychoanalytic, post-structuralist, Marxist and myth criticism for the purpose of equality and deconstruction of woman-as-sign. It also synergises with a bunch of theories subsumed under the umbrella term of postmodernism and draws from its intolerance for political and cultural inequalities. Postmodernism distrusts the ideologies of Humanism, History, Religion, Progress etcetera on which the West depends, and feminism uses this antagonistic attitude for challenging the patriarchal ideology which oppresses women and minority groups. Ihab Hassan defines the postmodernist attitude thus: "We deconstruct, displace, demystify the logocentric, ethnocentric, phallocentric order of things" ("Making Sense" 445). By asserting that "the truths of history are ideology-bound, teleological and positional," (Salat 32) postmodernism also supports the feminist agenda of questioning the historical master narratives which project unrealistically idealised or demonized portrayals of women. Though a few feminists like Nancy Miller state that postmodernism "forecloses the question of agency" (106) for women by deciding that the author is dead, there are others like Craig Owens (*The Discourse of Others*), Andreas Huyssen (*After the Great Divide*) and Linda Hutcheon (*A Poetics of Postmodernism*) who believe that postmodernism and feminism have real affinities because of their common aims of undermining the master narratives and making space for pluralism, ambiguity, marginality and difference.

A detailed study of the works of the feminists who aim at subverting the myths created by the ideological bases of the Western society shows that the tools of subversion used by them are: deconstructing the image of woman as the "angel in the house" Patmore (*The Angel in the House*), uncovering the basis of misogyny in Western philosophy, interrogating the notion of the unitary and gendered self, reclaiming the female body in writing, psychoanalytic re-conceptualization of women, projecting homosexuality as normal and even desirable, searching for a new anti-phallic language and finding new ways of assessing literature written by women.

When the feminists turned their focus to the cultural and social discrimination against women they realized that women equally participate in their own subjugation. This could be illustrated through John Berger's famous statements about self-objectification by women in *Ways of Seeing*:

> Men look at women. Women watch themselves being looked at. This determines not only most relations between men and women but also the relationship of women to themselves. The surveyor of women in herself is male: the surveyed female. Thus she turns herself into an object—and most particularly into an object of vision: a sight. (47)

This tendency towards self-objectification among the British women in the Victorian era could be viewed in the works of Jane Austen, Charlotte Bronte, Anne Bronte, Elizabeth Gaskell and George Eliot. Male writers like George Meredith, George Gissing and Henrik Ibsen also explored the subordinate and falsely idealized status of women in society through their works. Feminists like Virginia Woolf in her work *A Room of One's Own* stressed upon the need of individuality and private space for women while asserting that women should free themselves from the fear of patriarchal judgement. Woolf believes that if women want to write it is imperative for them to kill the angel in the house before it kills her.

One finds that there are two opposite attitudes to women in the traditional British literary canon. One is excessive reverence and the other is excessive denigration and demonization. This type of dichotomy is glaringly visible in the Western mythology where the virginal chastity of Mary stands in contrast to the sin of Eve. One finds a dualistic pattern in Western literature where the idealized projections of men's desires in the forms of the Madonna, the Muses and the "angel in the house" exist in total contrast to the uncanny projections of men's fears in the forms of Eve, Pandora, Medusas and the Furies. However, the feminist critics also identify those male writers such as William Shakespeare, Henrik Ibsen and George Bernard Shaw who rose above the sexual biases of their times in their portrayal of women characters.

Feminists have also brought to the notice of academicians and readers the fact that men in all ages have governed the inscription of religious, political, moral and artistic knowledge whereas women have remained restricted to childbearing and family. Therefore, in order to understand the basis of misogyny in western culture it is imperative to study the writings of those men who were responsible for constructing the various knowledge systems on which the western culture stands. For example, Plato, the classical Greek philosopher and mathematician, placed women between men and brutes on the ladder of spiritual evolution and states in *Timaeus*:

> He who lived well in his appointed time was to return and dwell in his native star, and there he would have a blessed and congenial existence. But if he failed in attaining this, at the second birth he would pass into a woman, and if, when in that state of being, he did not desist from evil, he would continually be changed into some brute who resembled him in the evil nature which he had acquired.

It is important to note that Plato was the founder of the Academy in Athens, the first institution of higher learning in the Western world. Aristotle was another influential Greek philosopher whose writings were the "first to create a comprehensive system of Western philosophy", encompassing morality and aesthetic; logic and science; politics and metaphysics ("Aristotle"). His works depict women as a deformity of nature and as defective men. According to him procreation happens because of men because it is the male element that brings life to the inert female element (*On the Generation of Animals*). The presence of misogyny in Western knowledge systems could also be viewed through the fact that women were seen as prone to madness (Showalter, *The Female Malady*), and the word hysteria is derived from the word 'hystera' in Greek which means the womb.

The Genevan political philosopher, Jean Jacques Rousseau, who revolutionized the world with his influence on the French and the American revolutions, suggested that women should be confined to the domestic sphere. Rousseau advised that all the education of women should aim at catering to the needs of men at different stages of life. They should learn how to love, protect, console, care for and please men. Rousseau also declared that "a woman should never, for a moment, feel herself independent, that she should be governed by fear to exercise her natural cunning, and made a coquettish slave in order to render her a more alluring object of desire, a sweeter companion to man, whenever he chooses to relax himself" (qtd. in Wollstonecraft *A Vindication of the Rights of Women*).

Rene Descartes, the seventeenth century French philosopher, deemed the father of modern philosophy, also believed that the human self is split into two parts, the mind and the body. Women according to him are associated with "res extensa" that is the machine like corporeal substance and men are associated with "res cogitans" that is the power of intelligence and the site of selfhood (Price and Shildrick 2). One can find in these philosophers hatred for corporeality of the bodily processes, especially those related to reproduction, and admiration for the powers of the intellect. The body, its needs and desires, appear to these philosophers as impediments in the way of spiritual growth which leads to somatophobia or fear of the body. Women are perceived by them as incapable of rising above their bodies due to their reproductive processes and are therefore considered unpredictable, dangerous and unclean. This serves as the logic behind the establishment of the semantic associations of the signifier "man" as active, dominating, rational and creative; and of "woman" as passive, meek, emotional and conventional, based on the sexual and reproductive processes of both the sexes.

The second generation of French feminists like Helene Cixous, Luce Irigaray and Julia Kristeva, reclaim the body as the pride of womanhood. They promote the different-but-equal philosophy and deconstruct the mind-over-matter ideology. They celebrate the body, reject any of its limiting definitions promoted by biological determinism and give importance to it in the estimation of women's identities. Irigaray also challenges the defining of female sexuality by male parameters. She believes that men and women are biologically and psychologically different, and if women want to liberate themselves from the rule of the male sex they have to start celebrating their oneness with nature and the body. Her work called *The Sex which is not One* inspires questions like: Is a woman's pleasure in sexual relationship related only to "lack" where the desire is endlessly deferred in search of a penis? She negates the Lacanian concept of lack and asserts that desire is rather a result of the "wonder-full excess between the sexes". Cixous, with the other French feminist thinkers like Kristeva and Irigaray, inspires the women writers to focus on the female body, women's feelings and desires. Cixous asserts in *The Laugh of the Medusa*:

> Woman must write herself: must write about women and bring women to writing, from which they have been driven away as violently as from their bodies—for the same reasons, by the same law, with the same fatal goal. Woman must put herself into the text—as into the world and into history—by her own movement. (250)

Cixous says that writing is an act which would "realise the un-censored relationship of woman to her sexuality, to her woman-being giving her back access to her own forces" and she motivates women by saying "write yourself: your body must make itself heard" ("Sorties" 103). Deconstructing the notion of gender these new feminists reconceptualise the body as a transformative organism which evades categorization. The male/female dichotomy is rejected by them in favour of a multiplicity of differences. In their radically subversive philosophical tradition body becomes a palimpsest inscribed with events with nothing essential and fixed. These feminists are proud of their bodies and its functions. It gives them their power instead of being their weakness. They are not ashamed of their bodily functions and jealously guard the uniqueness of their bodies from the incursion of biotechnology as prescribed by Shulamith Firestone in *The Dialectic of Sex*. Firestone suggests the use of contraception and abortion as well as the reproductive technology of in vitro fertilization to free women from their biologically determined position.

Another important mode adopted by the feminist theorists for undermining the patriarchal authority is deconstruction of the notion of an essential and stable self. The Enlightenment humanism that is based on the concept of a conscious, rational and autonomous self is destabilized by the feminists in favour of a more flexible subject who remains in a state of flux. The concept of an essential gender identity is deconstructed in feminist works like *The Second Sex* (1944) by Simone de Beauvoir, *Sexual Politics* (1970) by Kate Millet and *Gender Trouble* (1990) by Judith Butler. Simone de Beauvoir contradicts biological determinism in her influential work, *The Second Sex* (1949), by following a constructionist approach. She asserts that unlike sex, gender is a cultural category which is constructed through the process of socialization. She deals with the myths about women, propagated by men, and an unjust resultant treatment of women as the "other" to the norm that is man. According to Patricia Waugh the work of de Beauvoir is "heavily influenced by existentialism which denies the existence of a pre-ordained human nature, and emphasises the freedom and responsibility of each person to create him or herself as a growing individual" (321). Millet works through Marxist, psychoanalytic and literary criticism in order to prove that gender is a construct. Going a step further, Judith Butler asserts that not only gender but even sexual identity is a fictional construction, and it is a result of repeated gendered actions. Julia Kristeva in *Revolution in Poetic Language* prescribes fluidity of identity for women who are monologically inscribed by history. She envisions an outburst of the bodily drives or the semiotic that would defy singular identities. Kristeva provides a contradiction to the construction of a unified subject by what she calls "subject-in-process/on trial". Her notion of the semiotic *chora,* which is a site of negativity and the repressed, also challenges the unitary subject of the symbolic order.

Psychoanalytic criticism is another major area of feminist enquiry that has promoted a subversive approach to gendering. Sigmund Freud, who founded the psychoanalytic school of psychiatry, theorized phallocentric views about human sexual development as exemplified by his theories related to castration anxiety in boys and penis envy in girls. Alexander notes that "Freud has been of particular importance in giving currency to the ideas about female psychological development that explain it in terms of lack and negativity, or of not confirming to the norm derived from males" (4). Freud also postulates that "women have little sense of justice because of the predominance of envy in their mental life" (qtd. in Fitzpatrick-Hanly 134-5). Jacques Lacan, the famous French psychoanalyst and philosopher, also theorizes about the psycho-sexual and linguistic development of the child on the basis of the Freudian concept of castration complex. The French feminists attack both Freud and Lacan for grounding their theories on patriarchal assumptions. Among the feminist thinkers who oppose Freud's theories for being conservative and deterministic are Nancy Chodorow, Jean Baker Miller and Carol Gilligan. Nancy Chodorow contradicts Freud's stance by asserting that a child's sense of self or ego first develops in relation to the mother and as the first "other" for girls is like them, so their sense of self remains more flexible. Being more accommodating throughout their lives they are morally superior to boys (*The Reproduction of Mothering*). Jean Baker Miller in her work *Toward a New Psychology of Women* and Carol Gilligan in *In a Different Voice* stress the fact that women should subvert male aesthetics by including the undervalued qualities of relatedness, empathy and nurturance in their writings.

Kate Millett uses the premise, "the personal is political", to discuss the political nature of heterosexual relationships in *Sexual Politics* (1969). She argues that all the aspects of society and culture function on the basis of sexual politics, as a result of which, women internalize their inferiority which slowly becomes psychologically rooted. Millett also critiques the manipulation of power in society by men and analyses the works of male literary writers like D. H. Lawrence, Henry Miller and Norman Mailer, to study the way men create a cultural hegemony by portraying women as submissive sexual objects. Luce Irigaray in *When Our Lips Speak Together* and Mary Daly in *Gyn/Ecology* propose the promotion of autoeroticism and homosexuality for women in order to undermine the phallocentric beliefs. Alexander observes that "lesbianism has become much more visible, and some women see it as a desirable political stance, rather than simply a matter of personal preference" (6). Mary Daly is the most radical of the American critics, also advocates homosexuality and recommends women to "wildize" themselves (Gyn/Ecology). Irigaray suggests that women should use their marginalized position as a source of deconstructive power. They should become subversives by refusing to be a part of the mainstream ideology. Judith Butler, another American queer theorist, undermines heterosexuality in *Gender Trouble* by saying that sexuality instead of being inherent is a cultural construction and a political choice. Adrienne Rich also engages herself with the heterosexist assumptions of literary studies and unravels a tradition of lesbian writings in *Of Woman Born.* Helene Cixous in "*Sorties*" prescribes bisexuality and rejects the repression of homosexuality in female aesthetics which she calls "the pitiless repression of the homosexual element" (93). Along with the encouragement provided by these theorists, the "legalization of homosexual acts in 1967" (Head 113) also strengthened the independent tradition of gay and lesbian writings in the contemporary British literature.

Another important tool for the construction or deconstruction of history, culture and gender is language. Feminism fractures the symbolic order through deconstructing language itself. Deborah Cameron and Robin Tolmach Lakoff demonstrate in their works *Feminism and Linguistic Theory* and *Language and Woman's Place* respectively the male bias encoded in linguistic conventions. Felman states that "western metaphysics is based on the totalitarian principle of so-called logocentrism" (118) and it could also be found in discourse at the level of vocabulary and syntax. The dominance of logic, fixity of classifications and maintenance of objectivity make the western languages phallocentric. Kristeva in *Revolution in Poetic Language*, Cixous in *The Laugh of the Medusa* and Irigaray in *When Our Lips Speak Together* also criticise the western languages for being male-dominated. They endeavour to establish a woman's language that resists being appropriated by the phallogocentric language. Cixous uses the term *ecriture feminine* for the language of women which draws from the pre-linguistic and unconscious stage of mother-child unity. For her writing in the feminine means placing feminine consciousness at the centre of language in order to inscribe the female self in writing. Such a language would subvert the fixity of signification and would be open up to a free play of meanings. Irigaray prescribes fluidity, diversity and multiple possibilities in the structure of language. Julia Kristeva suggests that the "symbolic" should give way to the revolutionary unsystematized signifying process of the "semiotic", so that breaking free of the law of the father becomes possible. Flora Alexander comments on the revision of patriarchal theology by feminists like Mary Daly and Sara Maitland and notes that "in the face of irrational hostility" women have suggested that "the male language and imagery used in worship should be supplemented by female terminology" (3).

For feminist writers, apart from writing as women, being read as women is also important. Dale Spender notes in *Women and Literary History* that there are "one hundred good women novelists of the eighteenth century and together they were responsible for almost six hundred novels" yet they have "all disappeared" (18). She questions: "How is it that we have come to lose this knowledge about many good women novelists?" "How have we come to lose it so completely that its one-time existence does not even register, so we are blissfully unaware of what has been lost?" (19) Feminists reveal that women have faced not only the lack of opportunities but also the lack of acceptance, and this could be exemplified by the fact that women literary writers like the Bronte sisters, Mary Anne Evans and even the contemporary writer Joanne Rowling had to use masculine *nom de plumes* for being accepted by their readers. Alexander observes that "even today, when bookshops are amply stocked with literature by women and about them, and with specialist material from feminist publishing houses" it is still that "women's writing receives less critical attention than it is given to men's writing" (7). To make the women writers visible Elaine Showalter in *A Literature of their Own* (1977) conceptualises "gynocriticism" as a critical framework for assessing the literature written by women. She tries to recover the female literary tradition and calls for a new set of criteria for evaluating women's literature based on their field of experience and individuality.

Feminist scholars have re-read the works of those women whose contribution to literature has been slighted by male academicians, for example, George Sand, Elizabeth Barrett

Browning, Elizabeth Gaskell, Christina Rossetti, Harriet Beecher Stowe and Sindonie-Gabrielle Colette. Their works have been re-evaluated by feminist critics through the gynocritical standards. Some female writers who have been completely overlooked like Margaret Cavendish (1661-1717), Aphra Behn (1640-1689), Lady Mary Wortley Montagu (1689-1782), Charlotte Perkins Gilman (1860-1935), and a number of African-American writers such as Zora Neale Hurston (1891-1960) have also been made visible. Bonnie Kime Scott observes the invisibility of women writers in the modern era and states that "modernism was unconsciously gendered masculine" as "the inscriptions of mothers and women, and more broadly of sexuality and gender, were not adequately decoded, if detected at all "(187).

The contemporary British women writers such as Beryl Bainbridge, Eva Figes, Dorris Lessing, Muriel Spark, Fay Weldon, and Jeanette Winterson employ all the above mentioned tools to create subversive literature which spreads destabilizing ideas, deconstructs patriarchy and allows difference and diversity. Jean Rhys, Angela Carter and Michele Roberts also belong to this cadre of subversive feminist writers. The literature of subversion by these writers is an assertion of their freedom to disagree with the status quo, construct and remap perception, reality and truth.

Ella Gwendoline Rees Williams or **Jean Rhys** (1890-1979) was a Creole of West Indian origin. She was born in Roseau, Dominica on 24 August, 1890. Her father William Rees Williams was a doctor who immigrated from Wales in 1881, and her mother Minna Lockart Williams was a white West Indian. Her maternal grandfather who was a Scot had settled on a plantation in Dominica in 1824. She had an unhappy childhood during which she remained unloved by her mother and went through painful incidents like the burning of her house by the plantation slaves and sexual abuse by a relative. The depressive state of her father and the surrounding hostility made Ella a lonely girl full of fear and mistrust.

She went to England at the age of sixteen in 1907, but she was never able to bring herself to like England which remained a cold, friendless place to her forever. In England she studied dramatic art and worked as a choir singer. She married the Dutch poet Jean Lenglet and went to Paris with him in 1919, where she gave birth to a son and then a daughter. The son died of pneumonia within three weeks of his birth. The couple lived a poor life in Paris till 1925 when Lenglet was arrested for theft. After this, her daughter went under the care of the state and she met Ford Madox Ford, the English writer and critic, whom she looked up to for guidance and instruction. Under Ford's patronage, Rhys published her first collection of short fiction in 1927, called *Left Bank and Other Stories* which was promoted by Ford with a long preface. Ford, her mentor and lover, was the one who suggested that she should use a pseudonym to get her works published and gave her the name Jean Rhys, derived from the names of her father and husband. She published two more volumes of short fiction including *Tigers are Better Looking* (1968) and *Sleep it Off, Lady* (1976), this time without Ford's help. According to Joy Castro, "her relationship with Ford, beset by multiple tensions, ended badly, and following their stormy break, Rhys dropped out of the Paris literary scene altogether" (8).

In 1927, Rhys became involved with Tilden Smith, a gentle Oxford graduate who worked as a British literary agent. Tilden Smith supported the literary talent of Rhys for almost two decades, and this proved to be the most fertile period of her growth as a literary writer. She produced her first novel *Quartet* in 1928, followed by others. *After Leaving Mr Mackenzie* came in 1930, *Voyage in the Dark* in 1934 and *Good Morning, Midnight* in 1939. Meanwhile, she got a divorce from Jean Lenglet. In 1934, she married Tilden Smith, and the couple lived together till Tilden Smith's death in 1945. By then Rhys had become an alcholic. In 1947, Rhys married Tilden Smith's cousin Max Hamer who was involved in illegal activities and was an alcoholic too. She stopped writing, and all her earlier books went out of print. Then came a long silence in her literary career, resulting from her psychological ill-health and the conditions created by the First World War. Castro observes:

> Made increasingly paranoid by poverty and alcoholism, Rhys provoked frequent altercations with her neighbours and in 1949 was arrested and incarcerated in a prison

> hospital for psychiatric evaluation. Released on probation, Rhys continued her destructive pattern of heavy drinking and assault, and she spent the next several years under the frequent supervision of the British justice system. (8)

In 1950, Max Hamer went to jail for larceny, and Rhys spent her years in poverty living in cheap accommodations. Rhys regained public acclaim in 1956, with her radio production of *Good Morning, Midnight.* During her stay in London from 1957 to 1966, she kept working on *Wide Sargasso Sea.* She suffered a heart attack in 1964. Max Hamer died in 1966, and that was the year Rhys published *Wide Sargasso Sea* which won the WH Smith Literary award in 1967. All her books were then published by Penguin in paperback between 1967 and 1973. Her collection of short stories *Tigers are Better Looking* and *Sleep it Off, Lady* appeared in 1968 and 1976.

Alfred Alvarez called her "The Best Living English Novelist" in *New York Times Book Review* in 1974. In 1978, she received CBE for her services to literature. Her unfinished autobiography *Smile Please* was published posthumously in 1979. A collection of her letters called, *Jean Rhys: Letters 1931-66* edited by Francis Wyndham and Diana Melly came in 1984.

Jean Rhys is well known for bringing the issues related to the psychodynamics of women under patriarchy to the fore. The Rhysian world presents the feminine modes of experience, thinking, feeling and perceiving oneself and the world. Rhys's narratives have female protagonists, and mostly these women live on the margins of the society as mistresses to wealthy men. Her works bring to the centre the voices of those women who struggle for survival in the men's world. The dejection endured by her characters is based on the traumatic experiences of Rhys in her relationships with men. Joanne Shattock notes that writing was a means of "ordering life" for Rhys through which she tried "writing out" unhappiness (357). She always believed in writing about the self, and in an interview with Hannah Carter said: "If you want to write the truth you must write about yourself. It must go out from yourself. I don't see what else you can do. I am the only real truth I know". Rhys suffered from alcoholism just like her female protagonists. She, like Antoinette of *Wide Sargasso Sea*, also faced the stigma of racial hybridity. Rhys's personal dreams also find expression in the novel through Antoinette's dreams. The distrust of England, an unhappy marriage, traumatic love relationships, and the loss of child are all motifs drawn from her own life. Joy Castro says: "One pleasure of being a reader or scholar of literature now is that theory and criticism have at last caught up with the challenging work of Jean Rhys. A writer of tremendous originality and wit, she explores her melancholy subjects with heartbreaking grace". (8)

While Rhys contributes significantly to the literary canon by bringing into focus the hidden spaces of female psyche, **Angela Olive Carter** (1940-92) re-orders and displaces the male literary canon by undermining the master narratives of the Western civilization through mimicry and satire. Angela Carter was born in Eastbourne, England on 7th May, 1940 and her father was a journalist of Anglo-Scottish origin. Like Jean Rhys, she was closer to her father and had a problematic relationship with her mother, Olive Stalker. Carter moved to Yorkshire during the Second World War where she lived with her maternal grandmother who used to work as a chambermaid before her marriage. This class shift that she experienced in her family made her realize at a very young age that human identity is ever changing. In 1959, she worked as a journalist like her father. After studying English literature at the University of Bristol, she taught at various universities in the USA, Australia and England.

In 1960, Angela married Paul Carter whose second name she kept throughout her life. Their relationship lasted for twelve years. This was a very fertile period of her literary career during which she wrote six novels. Carter lived in Bristol for much of the 1960s. Her three novels called *Shadow Dance* also known as *Honeybuzzard* (1966), *Several Perceptions* (1968) and *Love* (1971) are set in Bristol and together make the Bristol Trilogy. The bohemian protagonists of the Bristol Trilogy represent the countercultural changes in the British society during the 1960s. *The Magic Toyshop* (1967), which won John Llewellyn Rhys Memorial Prize, "established her as a leading practitioner of the magic realism school" (Joanne Shattock 91). *Heroes and Villains* (1969) imaginatively creates a post-apocalyptic world and mocks at the cultural changes happening in the British society during the 1960s. *The Infernal Desire Machines of Doctor Hoffman,* also known as *The War of Dreams* (1972), is an allegory of the struggle between reason and imagination.

In 1969, Carter won the Somerset Maugham Award for *Several Perceptions* and used the money to fly to Japan, away from her husband, where she stayed for two years. Her experiences in Japan are recorded in the collection of short stories *Fireworks: Nine Profane Pieces* (1974). Japan contributed to Angela Carter's radicalization as a fiercely feminist writer. After her stay in Japan she visited the United States, Asia and Europe and spent a decade as a writer in residence at various universities including the University of Sheffield, Brown University, the University of Adelaide and the University of East Anglia.

In 1977, she married Mark Pearce who was eighteen years younger than her, and had a boy, her only child. The same year she produced her seventh novel called *The Passion of New Eve. Nights at the Circus* and *Wise Children* followed in 1984 and 1991 respectively. *Nights at the Circus* won the James Tait Black Memorial Prize for literature in 1984. The book was also short listed for the Booker Prize in the same year. At the age of 51 she died of lung cancer on 16 February, 1992.

Angela Carter was a prolific writer. Apart from novels, she also produced collections of short stories called *The Bloody Chamber* (1979) which won the Cheltenham Festival of Literature Award, *Black Venus* (1985), *American Ghosts and Old World Wonders* (1993) and *Burning Your Boats* (1995). She also contributed many articles to the *Guardian*, *Independent* and *New Statesman* which are collected in *Shaking a Leg: Collected Journalism and Writing* produced in 1997.

Two of her fictional works were adapted as films called *The Company of Wolves* (1984) and *The Magic Toyshop* (1987). *Come Unto the Yellow Sands* (1985) is a collection of four radio plays. *The Curious Room: Plays, Film Scripts and an Opera* (1996) is a collection of her dramatic works, screenplays for film adaptations, radio scripts and a libretto for an opera of Virginia Woolf's *Orlando*. *The Holy Family Album* is a controversial television documentary. As a writer of fiction, she also wrote many children's books like *The Donkey Prince* (1970), *Miss Z, the Dark Young Lady* (1970), *Comic and Curious Cats* (1979), *Moonshadow* (1982) and *Sea-Cat and the Dragon King* (2000). At the time of her death she was writing a sequel to Charlotte Bronte's *Jane Eyre* depicting the life of Adele Varens, Jane's stepdaughter.

Her non-fictional works apart from journalism include *The Sadeian Woman and the Ideology of Pornography* (1978), *Nothing Sacred: Selected Writings* (1982) and *Expletives Deleted: Selected Writings* which was posthumously published in 1992.

Carter was very interested in fairy tales, which she used to make statements about the notions of gender, culture, history, truth and reality. She translated many fairy tales by Charles Perrault which are collected in *The Fairy Tales of Charles Perrault* (1977) and edited many anthologies of fairy tales like *Sleeping Beauty and Other Favorite Fairy Tales* (1982).

The works edited by her include *The Virago Book of Fairy Tales* (1990), *The Second Virago Book of Fairy Tales* (1992), *Wayward Girls and Wicked Women: An Anthology of Subversive Stories* (1986) and *Angela Carter's Book of Fairy Tales* (2005).

Angela Carter made her mark so prominently in the field of literature that in 2008 *Times* ranked Carter tenth, in their list of "The 50 Greatest British Writers Since 1945". Today her works are an important part of the British canon and are included in the curriculum of many universities. As noted by Jeff Vander Meer, Carter was also the co-founder of Virago press for women along with Carman Calil. This press intends to provide a platform to women writers for articulating their anger, desires and fears. Carter bluntly states her intentions thus:

I suppose I am moved towards it by the desire that no daughter of mine should ever be in a position to write BY GRAND CENTRAL STATION I SAT DOWN AND WEPT, exquisite prose though it may contain. (BY GRAND CENTRAL

STATION I SAT DOWN AND TORE OFF HIS BALLS would be more like it). (qtd in Sage 33)

In an article that Salman Rushdie wrote on Carter's death for New York Times, he calls her a great writer who never received her due fame in Britain. He asserts that "she was not placed where she belonged—at the center of the literature of her time, at the heart". He also expresses his regret that a rare and bewitching writer like Carter died before she was granted her place in the literary pantheon.

Michele Brigitte Roberts (1949), an Anglo-French novelist, short story writer and poet, also re-visions the myths about women through highly experimental prose. She not only deconstructs old myths but also creates new myths to replace the old ones. The main targets of her subversive strategies are patriarchy and Catholic religion. Roberts is an Emeritus professor of creative writing at the University of East Anglia. She is also the Chairperson of the British Council advisory panel. Along with this, she keeps broadcasting and reviewing books. Her latest book, *Ignorance* came in 2012. She lives in London and in Mayenne, France.

Roberts has written fourteen novels, three collections of poems, four collections of short stories, one collection of essays and one memoir and was awarded the *Chevalier de L' Ordre des Arts et des Lettres* by the French government for her contribution to Arts in 2000. Her first book *A Piece of the Night* came out in 1978 and won Gay News Literary Award in the same year. She was also awarded the WH Smith Literary Award in 1993 for her novel *Daughters of the House,* and the book was also shortlisted for the Booker Prize in 1992. Michele Roberts was also selected a Fellow of the Royal Society of Literature in 1999.

Michele Roberts was born in Hertfordshire, England on May 20, 1949. Her father was an English Protestant and her mother was a French Catholic. Michele was bilingual from childhood as she grew up in both France and England. She read English Language and Literature at Somerville College, Oxford and then spent two years studying to become a librarian. She then worked in Bangkok as a librarian for the British Council during 1973-

74, but she had to leave the place due to the destruction caused by the Vietnam War.

While doing part-time jobs for earning a living, she used to write at nights and got involved with a writers' group. Roberts started making sufficient money from writing after *Daughters of the House* was shortlisted for the Booker prize in 1992 and won the WH Smith Literary Award in 1993. This allowed her to give up her part-time jobs and pursue a writing career freely. In the seventies, she lived in a commune which followed feminist and libertarian ideas with political purposes. During her stay with the commune she faced a tug of war between her love of solitude and the impulse to be a part of a bigger commune (*Paper Houses*). Her life in the 1970s was marked by a radical, bohemian existence, communal living, free love and the socialist feminism of the time. She had multiple sexual relationships both heterosexual and lesbian. *Paper Houses,* which came in 2007, is a memoir of her life since the 1970s.

Roberts also worked as a poetry editor of *Spare Rib* in 1974 and editor of *City Limits* magazine in 1981-83. From 1995-96 she was a research fellow at Nottingham Trent University where she later worked as a visiting professor in writing for several years. She married twice and has two stepsons. She never had a child of her own though she wanted one by her painter husband Jim Latter. She states in an interview to Linda Richards:

> In later life when I met the man I'm now with who I love very much, I wanted to have a child. And then I discovered that, because of some stupid birth control I'd been given, I'd been made infertile and I couldn't have babies. I kept having miscarriages instead. And it was incredibly sad. I don't mind, but I think the consolation is that I have stepsons and I brought up my niece partly. And books, of course, are like babies.

In her writings Roberts takes distant and unfamiliar setting varying from the Old Testament to a Hobbesian future and deploys Gothic, Lesbian and Catholic motifs to deal with the contemporary issues related to women. In novel after novel, she interrogates the concept of female chastity and rubs the surface of female stereotypical figures to show the real women underneath. She draws a lot from psychoanalytic criticism to bring out the hidden secrets of her characters. One of the major influences on Roberts is the work of Colette. Sharing commonalities with Doris Lessing and contemporaries like Sara Maitland and Alison Fell, she writes of female sexuality, the pleasures of cooking and critiques the mortification of flesh practised by the Catholics. Roberts's novels are mostly inspired by the urge to write about the dangerous aspects of Catholicism, the religion she was supposed to follow.

Ignorance (2012), Roberts's latest novel, is an exposition of religious hyprocrisy and an interrogation of bourgeois morality. With the backdrop of World War II, it depicts how day-to-day realities change during difficult times through a portrayal of the lives of two young women. *Delusion* (2008), is an examination of women's relationships with both men and other women. The book also showcases an ambivalent attitude towards religion. Its four main characters extend over ancient Egypt, Victorian England and contemporary London. Her most well-known book, *Daughters of the House* (1992), set in occupied France, is a story of two female cousins. It is based on the memoirs of a modern saint called "The Little Flower". The story deals with the pubescent fantasies of the two cousins, their bourgeoning sexuality, their old intimacy turning into antagonism and the revelation of a few secrets.

Piece of the Night (1978) is a semi-autobiographical work that alternates between past and present exploring the themes of religion, lesbian feminism and family. *The Visitation* came out in 1983. In this novel a modern woman called Helen communicates through dreams with women from Greek mythology. *The Wild Girl* (1984) republished as *The Secret Gospel of Mary Magdalene* in 2007 is a rewriting of the much maligned character of Mary Magdalene and the concepts of Christianity established by the male Christian leaders. *The Book of Mrs Noah* appeared in 1987, and in this novel too she re-works some Biblical myths, especially that of Mrs Noah in the Old Testament through feminist paradigms. *In the Red Kitchen* (1990) deals with Victorian ideals, spiritualism, psychoanalysis, ghost stories and murders. Women and houses are important in Michele Robert's works as sites of domesticity and female labour. They also serve as symbols of female fears and fantasies. *Flesh and Blood* (1994) is very experimental, as it tells tales within a tale moving backward in time.

Impossible Saints (1997) is a collection of biographies of imaginary female saints and the realities of their sexual and religious lives. These stories show how religion and sexuality complement rather than negate each other. *Fair Exchange* (1999) is a fictional depiction of the lives of Mary Wollstonecraft and William Wordsworth during the French Revolution.

The Looking Glass (2000) is based on the life of a French poet called Mallarme and his philandering with various women. It uses a multi-perspective narrative which talks of women's domesticity and passions, memories and desires. The protagonist is a poet called Gerard, and his female lovers find their voices through diaries, letters and stories. *The Mistressclass* (2003) is a story of two sisters living in London and their changing relationship with a man. *Reader, I Married Him* (2005) is the story of Aurora who serial kills her husbands.

Michele Roberts produced three collections of poetry - *The Mirror of the Mother: Selected Poems 1975-1985* (1986), *Psyche and the Hurricane* (1991) and *All the Selves I Was: New and Selected Poems* (1995). Her poems explore the various faces of femininity and are rich in religious imagery and classical myths, which are used to re-imagine mother-daughter relationships.

Her short stories are collected in *Tales I Tell my Mother: A Collection of Feminist Short Stories* (1978), *More Tales I Tell My Mother: Feminist Short Stories* (1987), *The Seven Deadly Sins* (1987), *The Seven Cardinal Virtues* (1990), *During Mother's Absence* (1993) and *Playing Sardines* (2001).

Roberts also wrote a play called *The Journeyman* which was first performed in 1988. *Food, Sex and God: On Inspiration and Writing* (1998) is a collection of essays by her. Her works as co-editor include *Cutlasses and Earrings* (1977) and *Mind Readings: Writer's Journeys through Mental States* (1996).

Michele Roberts is a feminist writer who believes in connectedness and finds talking to friends extremely pleasurable. Though she faced problems in her relationship with her mother who was a devout Catholic, she tries to reconcile with her through her writings. Many of her works are an exploration of a daughter's search for the lost connection with her mother. Michele Roberts loves the common fair of human life, and she keeps roaming around London, observing and taking notes, glimpses of which are sprinkled all over her books. A detailed description about the French countryside and cuisine is also found in her works which shows her attachment to her mother's culture. Her language is characterized by poetic sensuousness and her writings radically subvert the traditional style of storytelling. Roberts is boldly experimental both in her life and in her writings. As a professor of creative writing she asks her students to be free and not to be scared of creating a mess.

A comparative study of the subversive works by Jean Rhys, Angela Carter and Michele Roberts reveals three different approaches for interrogating and re-writing the master narratives of the Western literary canon with the aim of liberating women from both false ideological stigmas and idealizations.

According to Dominic Head, the strong articulation of feminist concerns became manifest in the fiction of the 1960s and the 1970s, but the era post 1990s saw the emergence of post-feminism and a re-evaluation of feminism's oppositional stance due to a positive change in the reality of gender relations. He observes a drift towards a more inclusive projection of human rather than women's rights and says that "in a climate of post-feminism the explicit critique of patriarchy has become an anachronism, as more complex and self-conscious gender identities are taken for granted" (Head 105). Many critics today assert that a re-assessment of feminism and its objectives is needed, especially with reference to the successes of feminism and the economic changes that have come about in British social life.

Critiquing the relevance of feminism today Richard Bradford notes that since the mid 1990s "the political and ideological subtext of gender difference has been treated as a redundant obligation and an encumbrance" (9). He adds that as Woolf's room is available today, quality in an artistic production is more important than adherence to a cause.

Considering the views of critics like Head and Bradford some pertinent questions that arise in the mind of a student of subversive literature today are: Is feminist subversion relevant today? What is the direction of women writers' quest? Are they searching for some kind of utopia? Are the tools used for subversion too lethal? Is there a streak of misandry in subversive literature by women? Would misandry reverse the aim of subversion by strengthening the case for misogyny?

In this book all the three novelists under consideration are analysed individually in a comparative perspective so as to highlight their characteristic thematic preoccupations and different artistic merits. Chapter 2 engages in a detailed study of Rhys's *Wide Sargasso Sea* and her subversion of Charlotte Bronte's *Jane Eyre* from postcolonial perspectives. The argument involves Rhys's interrogation of the racial prejudices in *Jane Eyre*, her rupturing of the assumptions about madness analysed through the psychoanalytic framework provided by Melanie Klein, the deconstruction of the notion of a unitary self, the mangling of the Enlightenment doctrines and re-writing of certain scenes in *Jane Eyre*. The chapter also analyses the critical perspectives of postcolonial, poststructural and feminist critics like Edward Said, Homi K. Bhabha, Gayatri Chakraborty Spivak, Karl Miller, Judith Butler, Kristeva and Gilbert and Gubar.

Chapter 3 scrutinizes the various ways in which Carter in her speculative fictions and short stories has subverted the master narratives of western culture including the Enlightenment myths, the myth about female liberation and the unreal projections of women as Mother Goddess and the mystical femme fatales. Theorists like Mikhail Bakhtin, Michel Foucault, Julia Kristeva, Toril Moi, Judith Butler, Jean Baudrillard and Donna Haraway are discussed to explicate Carter's attitude towards gender and its performance.

Chapter 4 discusses Roberts's critique of somatophobia and misogyny in the Catholic religion and patriarchy. Three of Roberts's fictional works are selected to study her subversion of Biblical and Catholic myths, her search for possible utopias and her wish to reconcile with the lost mother. The discourses of feminists like Adrienne Rich, Helene Cixous and Luce Irigaray are taken up to examine Roberts's views on homosexuality and female creativity.

Chapter 5 is a comparative study of the narrative techniques deployed by Rhys, Carter and Roberts for subversion of patriarchal paradigms. It analyses how the style used by the three women writers at the levels of lexis, syntax, semantics and genre appears to be based on the notion of the *ecriture feminine* contributed by French feminists and the theories of poststructuralists like Roland Barthes thereby opening up the texts to reading and interpretation of ambiguity, multiplicity and difference.

WORKS CITED

Alexander, Flora. *Contemporary Women Novelists: Modern Fiction*. New York: Edward Arnold, 1989. Print.

Alvarez, Alfred. "The Best Living English Novelist". *New York Times Book Review*. 17 March 1974: 6-7. Print.

Aristotle. *On the Generation of Animals*. Trans. Arthur Platt. eBooks@ Adelaide. The University of Adelaide library. 25 Aug 2010. Web. 10 May 2012.

"Aristotle." *Wikipedia: The Free Encyclopedia*. Wikimedia Foundation, Inc. 22 July 2004. Web. 20 July 2011.

Beauvoir, Simone de. *The Second Sex* trans. and ed. H.M. Parshley. Harmondsworth: Penguin 1982. Print.

Barker, Paul. "The Return of the Magic Storyteller". *The Independent on Sunday.* 8 January 1995.

Beer, Gillian. "Representing Women: Re-presenting the Past". Eds. Catherine Belsey and Jane Moore. *The Feminist Reader*. London: Macmillan Press, 1997. Print.

Berger, John. *Ways of Seeing*. Penguin Group, 1972. Web. 7 Jan 2012.

Bradford, Richard. *The Novel Now: Contemporary British Fiction*. USA: Blackwell Publishing, 2007. Print.

Butler, Judith. *Gender Trouble: Feminism and the Subversion of Identity.* London: Routledge, 1990. Print.

Cameron, Deborah. *Feminism and Linguistic Theory*. New York: Palgrave, 1985. Print.

Castro, Joy. "Jean Rhys". *The Review of Contemporary Fiction* 20.2 (2000): 8. *Questia*. Web. 22 Jan. 2011.

Chodorow, Nancy J. *The Reproduction of Mothering: Psychoanalysis and the Sociology of Gender*. Berkley, Los Angeles, London: University of California Press, 1978. Print.

Cixous, Helene. "Sorties: Out and Out: Attacks/Ways Out/Forays". Eds. Catherine Belsey and Jane Moore. *The Feminist Reader*. London: Macmillan Press, 1997. Print.

——. "The Laugh of the Medusa". Trans. Keith Cohen and Paula Cohen. *New French Feminisms*. Ed. Elaine Marks. New York: Schockin, 1981. Print.

Daly, Mary. *Gyn/Ecology: The Metaethics of Radical Feminism*. Beacon Press, 1978. Web. 12 Mar 2012.

Felman, Shoshna. "Women and Madness: The Critical Fallacy". Eds Catherine Belsey and Jane Moore. *The Feminist Reader*. London: Macmillan Press Ltd., 1997. Print.

Firestone, Shulamith. *The Dialectic of Sex: The Case for Feminist Revolution*. New York: William Morrow and Company, 1970. Print.

Fitzpatrick-Hanly, Margaret Ann. "Feminism as Facilitation and Resistance: the Question of Penis Envy." Canadian Journal of Psychoanalysis Vol 2 (1994): 29-45. *Questia*. Web. 20 July 2010.

Freud, Sigmund. *The Ego and the Id*. Ed. James Strachey. New York: W. W. Norton and Company, 1989. Print.

Gilligan, Carol. *In a Different Voice: Psychological Theory and Women's Development*. USA: Harvard University Press, 1982. Print.

Gramsci, Antonio. Ed. David Forgacs Lawrence. *A Gramsci Reader: Selected Writings 1916-1935*. London and Wishart, 1999. Print.

Hassan, Ihab. "Making Sense: The Trails of Postmodernism". *New Literary History*. 18.2, (1987). Print.

Head, Dominic. *The Cambridge Introduction to Modern British Fiction 1950-2000*. UK: Cambridge University Press, 2002. Print.

Irigaray, Luce. *The Sex which is Not One*. Trans. Catherine Porter and Carolyn Burke. Ithaca: Cornwall University Press, 1985. Print.

——. "When Our Lips Speak Together". Trans. Carolyn Burke. *Signs* 6.1 (1980): 69. *JSTOR*. Web. 2 Jan 2011.

Jones, Ernest. *Sigmund Freud: Life and Work Vol 1: The Young Freud 1856-1900*. London: Hogarth Press, 1953. Print.

Kristeva, Julia. *Revolution in Poetic Language*. New York: Columbia University Press, 1984. Print.

Lacan, Jacques. *The Seminars of Jacques Lacan*. Web. 18 May 2012. http://www.lacan.com/seminars1.htm.

Lakoff, Robin Tolmach. *Language and Woman's Place: Text and Commentaries*. Ed. Mary Bucholtz. Oxford: Oxford University Press, 2004. Print.

Lyotard, Jean-Francois. *The Postmodern Condition: A Report on Knowledge*. Trans. Geoffrey Bennington and Brian Massumi. Minneapolis: University of Minnesota Press, 1984. Print.

Meer, Jeff Vander. *The Scriptorium*. <http : // www.thermodernword.com/scriptorium/carter.html-125k>

Mill, John Stuart. *The Subjugation of Women. Modern History Sourcebook*. Fordham University. Web. 25 May 2012.

Miller, Jean Baker. *Toward a New Psychology of Women*. Massachusetts: Beacon Press, 1976. Print.

Miller, Nancy K. *Subject to Change*. New York: Columbia University Press, 1988. Print.

Millet, K. *Sexual Politics*. New York: Doubleday, 1969. Print.

Patmore, Coventry. "The Angel in the House". *The Victorian Web*. Web. 17 May 2012. <http://www.victorianweb.org/authors/patmore/angel/>

Plato. *Timaeus*. Trans. Benjamin Jowett. *The Internet Classics Archive*. Web. 10 Aug 2012.

Price, Janet, and Margrit Shildrick. *Feminist Theory and the Body-A Reader*. New York: Routledge, 1999. Print.

Rhys, Jean. Interviewed by Hannah Carter. "Fated to be Sad". *Guardian*. 8 Aug 1968. Web. 2 July 2010.

Rich, Adrienne. *Of Woman Born: Motherhood as Experience and Institution*. 1977. *History is a Weapon*. Web. 17 May 2012.

Roberts, Michele. Interviewed by Linda Richards. *January Magazine*. Web. 23 Jan 2011.

——. Interviewed by Linda Richards. *January Magazine*. Web. 23 Jan 2011.

——. *Paper Houses: A Memoir of the '70s and Beyond*. London: Virago, 2007. Print.

Rubin, Andrew N. "Edward W. Said". *Arab Studies Quarterly*. Vol 26. 2004. Print.

Rushdie, Salman. "Angela Carter, 1940-92: A Very Good Wizard, a Very Dear Friend". *New York Times*. 8 Mar 1992. Web. 3 Dec 2010.

Sage, Lorna. "Death of the Author". *Women in the House of Fiction: Post War Women Novelists*. London: Macmillan, 1992. Print.

Said, Edward. *Orientalism*. London: Penguin Books, 1978. Print.

Salat, M.F. "Sub-versions and Contra-dictions". Ed. Shirin Kudchedkar. *Postmodernism and Feminism: Canadian Contexts*. Delhi: Pencraft International, 2005. Print.

Scott, Bonnie Kim. "The Gender of Postmodernism". Ed. Dennis Walder. *Literature in the Modern World: Critical Essays and Documents*. 2nd ed. Oxford: Oxford University Press, 2004. Print.

Showalter, Elaine. *A Literature of Their Own: British Women Novelist from Bronte to Lessing*. London: Virago, 1978. Print.

Spender, Dale. "Women and Literary History". Eds. Catherine Belsey and Jane Moore. *The Feminist Reader*. London: Macmillan Press, 1997. Print.

Shattock, Joanne. *The Oxford Guide to British Women Writers*. Oxford: Oxford University Press, 1994. Print.

Showalter, Elaine. *The Female Malady: Women, Madness and English Culture 1830-1980*. London: Virago, 1985. Print.

"The 50 Greatest British Writers since 1945". *Times*. 5 Jan 2008. Web. 21 July 2011.

Waugh, Patricia. *Literary Theory and Criticism*. New Delhi: Oxford University Press, 2006. Print.

Wollstonecraft, Mary. *A Vindication of the Rights of Woman with Strictures on Moral and Political Subjects*. London: Joseph Johnson, 1792.

Woolf Virginia. *A Room of One's Own*. London: Penguin, 1945. Print.

2

Women, Madness and Colonization: Jean Rhys's Postmodern Novel

Is it in Myself.

What is?

All. Good, evil, love, hate, life, death, beauty, ugliness.

And in everyone?

I do not know everyone. I only know myself.

And others?

I do not know them. I see them as trees walking.

(Rhys, *Smile Please* 161-2)

The novels of Jean Rhys are marked by the fact that all their protagonists are women put in circumstances that Rhys herself had to go through in her life. Helen Carr notes that "like many modernist writers, Rhys had used her life, in all its painful rawness, as the material from which she formed her fiction" (3). Rhys knew that to turn autobiographical material into a novel is not an easy task as "a novel has to have a shape and life does not have any" (*Smile Please* 10).

From the margins of the late nineteenth century English society and the mainstream literary world Rhys wrote as a woman who had known the ills of being emotionally and/or economically dependent on a man, both within and without wedlock. Her protagonists know the pain of not belonging, of being left alone in a sea of selfish and unsympathising people and of belonging to a culture that is patriarchal and thus maddeningly partial. Rajni Walia observes that "Rhys's work is modern in its sensitive portrayal of the loneliness of modern life, which has been drawn into the vortex of the feminine self" (34).

Her protagonists keep warring against their existential predicaments and continue their desperate search for some meaning in life, and fail. Her novels are intensely pessimistic and thickly painful. All her women protagonists seem to be one woman during different stages of adjustment with self and society. This view is supported by Rajni Walia according to whom Rhys's first four novels form a quartet of their own due to "the likeness in the psychological and emotional make-up of the female protagonists" (35). These women are victims of emotional trauma, "a deeper sense of pain and loss" (Linnet 437) which makes them "paranoid-schizoid" (Simpson 113). Acute chronic depression at times leads them to a split of ego or dissociated identity disorder and fatal dementia. Addiction to alcohol or substance only makes their condition worse. Like these fictional women Rhys was also an alcoholic and lived as an expatriate in London and Paris. Linnet notes that some critics view Rhys's characters' "consistent passivity as evidence of innate weakness and lax morals" (439); whereas, she herself is of the opinion that their passivity is "a result of trauma" found in people "who have actually been helpless in the face of previous threats" (Linett 439). Zeikowitz concludes that this traumatization of Rhys's heroines into immobility and silence is a result of an extremely forceful masculine economy.

Jean Rhys wrote the first four of her five novels between the two World Wars and fell into a long silence after 1939. *Wide Sargasso Sea* came during the second phase of her writing career in 1966 and got her worldwide acclaim. The main themes in *WSS* are rootlessness of people in an alien culture, the hypocrisy of those who command social power, and injustice done towards women and children by men and adults respectively.

Rhys also subverts the conservative roles of victim and victimizer and portrays both of them being assaulted by the powerful emotions that shape their perceptions as well as the resulting behaviour. The tragic tension in her novels is maintained not by virtue and vice but by the unconquerable dead seas of silence which do not let individuals meet at psycho-spiritual planes. The conventions of the society also add to this isolation of individuals from each other. Therefore, if the weak suffer from scarcity and moral degradation, the powerful suffer from self-alienation.

Rhys's first novel *Quartet* (1929) paints the psychoscape of Marya Zelli who, after her husband's imprisonment, lives with an art dealer Heidler and his wife Louis. Her affair with Heidler causes her immense anxiety and pain. According to Simpson the psychological subtext of the novel shows the Oedipal longings of Marya, which make her fall for a father figure (67). Her increasing dependence on Heidler makes him recoil. While Marya's is still suffering from the pain of rejection, her husband comes back from prison, gets to know about the affair and tries to assault her.

After Leaving Mr Mackenzie (1930) narrates the life of Julia Martin who tries to maintain her psychological balance in a selfish world governed by patriarchy. Julia depends on men for sustenance, and the men use her for resolving their inner conflicts. This novel concentrates more on the identity crisis that Julia faces rather than on a failed love relationship. She visits her ailing mother for solace but gets no help. Julia's heart gets heavier with grief, and she grows intensely hostile and suspicious of the world.

Anna Morgan of *Voyage in the Dark* (1934) is ten years younger than Marya and Julia and has had a West Indian childhood. She works as a choir girl and has her first and tormenting affair when quite young. Rhys takes the description of Anna's childhood in Dominica, experiences of school in London, job as a chorus girl, beginning and end of an affair, abortion, heart break and humiliation from her own life. A psychoanalytic reading of the work shows that like Marya, Anna's pre-Oedipal longing for intimacy with her mother remains insatiate. Simpson asserts that though Anna's story depicts her entery into adult femininity through affairs with various men, "beneath the text is another story, one that records a child's powerful and consuming need for her mother" (21). The absence of mother during her childhood makes her susceptible to harm and with age she becomes more and more aware of her vulnerability.

Sasha Jensen of *Good Morning, Midnight* (1939) tries to come face to face with her own demons. She, the oldest of all Rhysian women, is in her forties and lives in dingy rooms in Paris. Earning money through men has become more difficult due to her fading looks, and the ennui and desolation of life has made her addictive to drugs and alcohol. *Good Morning, Midnight* is the last of four novels written by Rhys during the first phase of her writing career and is also the most mature of them. The tone is more detached and contemplative. Many sections of the novel consist of dreams and hallucinations during which the deeper Oedipal longings of Sasha come to the fore.

Antoinette Cosway of *Wide Sargasso Sea* is also a woman living in a patriarchal society, but life is more difficult for her than for any other Rhysian heroine. Her tragedy is the larger tragedy of the English Creoles in the Caribbean. The novel is an agonising portrayal of what it is to inhabit the liminal racial identity in a multiracial setting. Maggie Humm describes *WSS* as "Rhys's most complex novel of border crossing in relation to colour" (66).

WSS was earlier called *Le Revenant,* which means the ghost. Later Rhys chose to select the present title which has been taken after the name of a sea in the North Atlantic Ocean, between the West Indies and Azores, called Sargasso Sea. The title problematizes the issue of racial and gender biases which keep two individuals in a state of mutual fear and suspicion thus negating any possibility of a healthy relationship between them.

> The *Wide Sargasso Sea* of the title appears symbolic of the unsurpassed wide gulf separating the two cultures, as well as the parallel male and female perspectives and dichotomies, which receive the most extensive exploration through the Antoinette-Rochester relationship. (Walia 51)

Rhys, a descendant of a Scottish slave owner from her mother's side, spent her childhood in Jamaica after the abolition of slavery. She had to face the unacceptance of both the natives and the English, due to the prevalence of racial tensions amongst them. Rhys depicts the same "emotional desolation" (Walia 34) and the longing to be accepted through the life of Antoinette Cosway, the first Mrs Rochester, taken from Charlotte Bronte's classic *Jane Eyre*.

Jane Eyre has drawn a lot of critical attention including both praise and blame of writers and critics. The book has also evoked responses related to gender and search for identity, and it is both loved and condemned by the feminists. Angela Carter states: "Of all the great novels of the world *Jane Eyre* veers the closest towards trash" (Carter *Expletives Deleted*, 162). Michele Roberts adapted Jane's proclamation "Reader, I Married Him" to a raging "Reader, I Murdered Him", and made it the title of one of her novels. Jean Rhys finds the portrayal of Bertha Mason, the first Mrs Rochester, shocking. In a letter to Francis Wyndham she describes that after reading *Jane Eyre* she "was vexed at her portrait of the 'paper tiger' lunatic, the all wrong Creole scenes, and above all by the real cruelty of Mr Rochester" (Rhys "Selected Letters", 139). She feels surprised that a writer known for her strong feminist characterization of Jane could be so unjust in her portrayal of poor Bertha brought from the Caribbean and caged by her husband in the attic of a large Victorian manor. Rhys recreates a life for this poor figure in order to fill the gaps in Bronte's text and to find out why she would burn her house and kill herself. She wants to find out the secret which the prim and proper surface of civilization hides.

WSS gives the narrative power to Bertha Mason, whom Rhys renames Antoinette Cosway for the purpose of defamiliarization, and shows the readers that the fixity of meaning in a deterministic novel like *Jane Eyre* comes at the cost of a voice which is muted. Helen Tiffin calls *WSS* a "canonical counter discourse" and defines canonical counter discourse as a strategy in which a writer takes up the assumptions of a British canonical text and subverts the text for postcolonial purposes. Such a discourse challenges the over-determination of identities by the politics of imperialism.

WSS is a highly subversive novel and rewrites many deterministic concepts which lead to improper conceptualization of norms related to gender and race. Madness is one such concept which in colonial discourse is linked with the female sex and the colonised races. Madness and sanity are also perceived as mutually exclusive. This view is supported by the attitudes developed during the age of Reason in the West or the Western Enlightenment. Michel Foucault argues in his work *Madness and Civilization* that madness, which has the power to point out the limits of social order, is silenced by reason. Foucault also depicts madness as located in society and culture rather than in mind or body. Some of the Victorian psychoanalytic theories also propound that women are prone to mental instability which should be regulated by using repressive techniques such as clitoridectomy (Showalter *The Female Malady*).

Modern psychology has developed new perspectives about madness and has revealed that the most important causes of madness are injury, stress, abuse and the neglect of children during their developmental years. It views madness an ailment related to the mind which is curable. An understanding of its symptoms and the development of a new vocabulary such as depression, stress, dissociated identity disorder, obsessive compulsive disorder have helped in the development of a scientific attitude towards madness.

Rhys not only undermines the false Victorian assumptions about madness as "a female malady" but also questions its association with the Creoles by re-visioning the character of Bertha. She underscores the irrationality behind the apprehension of the West Indian Isles as madness inducing and describes them as a place of beauty and freedom. She shows in *WSS* how it is the paranoia of Edward Rochester that makes him suspicious of the wild and beautiful Dominica.

A close look at Charlotte Bronte's classic is needed to understand the colonial bias in *Jane Eyre* which overshadows its feminist cause. In *Jane Eyre,* Bertha is shown as having been locked for almost ten years in the attic room of Rochester's house. The questions that such a delineation of Bertha's character raises are: Is it possible for any normal human being to remain sane after being caged and supervised like an animal for ten years? Bertha is described as having a "pigmy intellect" and "giant propensities" resulting from a nature "the most gross, impure, depraved" (*Jane Eyre* 311). She is not only treated as an animal but also as some supernatural incarnation of evil by those who know her. She is described by them as "the foul German spectre-the vampire" (*Jane Eyre* 258), "a demon", "a hag", "an Indian Messalina" (*Jane Eyre* 283), and "a witch". She stands for sexual excess and represents Freud's "id" (*The Ego and the Id*) and Kristeva's "abject" (*Powers of Horror*) which patriarchy tames and persecutes.

A further enquiry about the motifs in *Jane Eyre* reveals that all of Rochester's un-English mistresses are "often by nature, and always by position, inferior" (*Jane Eyre* 316). Being women from countries other than England, they become subject to his derogation. Celine is French; Clara, German; Giancinta, Italian; Blanche Ingram, Angrian. Adele, who is just a child, also shows defects in her personality inherited by her French mother, which according to Rochester should be corrected by the English education. Jane too is being compared to a Hindu and an African slave when she tries to challenge the repressive status quo.

The characterization in *Jane Eyre* is based on biological determinism as the physical traits of the characters which are a product of their genetic makeup are seen as expressions of their inner self. Such an attitude could also be found in the works of other Victorian novelists, most notably Charles Dickens and Thomas Hardy. Rochester's vanity surfaces in *Jane Eyre* when he pushes his locks back to impress Jane with his broad forehead, a physiognomic proof of his higher principles and refined tastes.

Jean Rhys's *WSS* appropriates the notions of race, class and gender while writing the reasons behind Antoinette's eventual dissociation of identity. She shows that Antoinette's psychological ailment is not an inevitable result of her being a Creole but is socially induced. Rhys makes the reader look deeper for finding out that Antoinette's madness is acquired and not genetic. According to Edward Rochester, "Bertha Mason is mad; and she came of a mad family;—idiots and maniacs through three generations!" (*Jane Eyre* 265). Jean Rhys shows that the reason for Antoinette's abnormality is childhood stress and neglect by her only parent, Annette. The book is divided into two parts. The first part shows the unsuccessful relationship of Antoinette with her mother which leads to improper identity formation, and the absence of a father figure which leads to the lack of confidence about having a successful relationship with any member of the opposite sex. The second part deals with Antoinette's estrangement from her husband and her final dissociation of identity.

Object relations theorists like Melanie Klein are important for analysing Rhysian narratives. The paranoid-schizoid position is explained by Melanie Klein in *Notes on Some Schizoid Mechanisms* as an ailment which in its advanced stage causes the splitting of ego and results in a dissociated sense of identity. Antoinette in the end sees herself in the mirror as "other", due to the dissociation of the different aspects of her identity which fail to cohere and strike a balance.

An understanding of the perceptions, desires, frustrations and terrors of the earliest existence is also given by Melanie Klein in *Early Stages of the Oedipus Conflict* and Ronald Fairbairn in *The Repression and the Return of Bad Objects*. According to Melanie Klein's object relations theory, a child's growth starts through its relation with the external objects, the first of which is the mother. Rejection by objects of need create childhood trauma that has a great impact on the relationships that the child, as an adult, forms. In Antoinette's case, her mother Annette has always been detached and apathetic towards her which serves as a source of maladjustment in her adult life. Annette is depicted as a mother who "repeatedly fails to mirror Antoinette's attitudes and behaviour and who thereby demonstrates how a child's sense of her own reality might be steadily eroded (Simpson 116). Thus Antoinette always finds herself split and fragmented. Her search for an identity keeps travelling from Tia, to the garden and pool in Coulibri and to Christophine, a kind of surrogate mother.

Being a Creole, she is rejected by the English who consider her prone to genetic madness and is hated by the Jamaicans among whom she grows up as a "white cockroach" and a "white nigger". According to Simpson, Antoinette's childhood experiences are full of unloving, threatening objects placed in a powerful position which make her anxious for her own safety. Annette "holds the place of the withholding mother of Klein's 'bad breast'" and Christophine represents "the giving mother of the 'good breast'". These "radically opposed maternal presences" reflect the "paranoid-schizoid quality of Antoinette's experience" (Simpson 115).

After failing to identify with her mother and friends, Antoinette depends on her husband Rochester for the consolidation of her fragmented self. Rochester also fails her because he is a paranoid man himself. Unsure of his father's love for him, he finds himself trapped in marriage with Antoinette whom he does not understand. Antoinette's mental health starts degrading continuously after she hears Rochester making love to Amelie, the black servant girl. This experience of abandonment makes Antoinette furious with Rochester because she fears that her childhood dejection would be repeated in the form of her husband's behaviour.

The thwarted attempts at a successful marital relation drive her to identity dissociation. Such individuals according to Christopher Bollas "lose faith in love and loving" and in them "hate establishes itself as the fundamental truth of life" (129-30). In order to attract the attention of the object from which love is expected such individuals start showing mad rage as anger which is at least life affirming. According to Bollas, their primary aim becomes "to be cathected by a parent, even to the point of becoming a reliable negative self-object for him or her... as their true dread is that of being unnoticed and left for dead" (130). Similarly, Antoinette fills herself of rage which is a substitutive emotion for emptiness and coldness and "she behaves as a wounded child who has become an assailant in reaction to repeated experiences of neglect and loss" (Simpson 117). Her expression of rage speaks of her disappointed hopes and unfulfilled needs. The novel shows how all expressions of anger need not be negative even if the cultural edicts make us see them in such a light. Unfortunately Antoinette's fury leaves Rochester colder than before.

The text makes use of mirrors to suggest Antoinette's search for psychic unity which she never attains. "Long ago when I was a child and very lonely I tried to kiss her: But the glass was between us—hard cold and misted over with my breath" (*WSS* 180). The Lacanian sense of security, as discussed in "The Seminars of Jacques Lacan", which comes when one identifies with one's specular image, never comes to Antoinette. Antoinette keeps on longing for an imaginary unity and laments its absence when she talks of the destruction of the garden of Coulibri where the tree of life grew.

Apart from the failure of finding proper objects to relate with, another reason for Antoinette's undetermined sense of identity is her over determination as "white nigger", "white cockroach", "beke", "Marionette" and "Bertha". These multiple signifiers try to fix her in contradictory identities. She fights with fixities so that she can maintain her interest in both the Miller's daughter and Tia at the same time. One can observe that when the fluidity of the subject is marred, the free movement through borders is hampered and when the subject is gripped at different poles simultaneously madness creeps in due to the repeated splitting of self in fixed binaries. Likewise, if the subject restricts oneself to one side then also the self remains unrealized because there is a sense of lack. Free dialogue is needed to give agency and confidence to the subject. Nidesh Lawtoo notes that "Bakhtin's dialogic principle calls for a non-hierarchical and non-teleological relationship where opposites do not dissolve in a unifying synthesis, but are engaged in a process of negotiation instead".

Thus, madness in Antoinette's case is not genetic as Daniel Cosway makes Rochester believe, but it is a result of the inability to make the fragments of her personality cohere. Simpson observes:

> The madness that others will condemn in Antoinette is that of a person who refuses the choice of self deception, and in

> this respect she demonstrates same potential agency and is more sane that those others of her narrative. (Simpson 126)

The text also interrogates the meaning of "sanity" and takes a long hard look at Rochester's personality in this regard. Rhys reproaches the conventional sanity as nothing but an assertion of absolutism:

> Even if she had wept like Magdalene it would have made no difference. I was exhausted. All the mad conflicting emotions had gone and left me wearied and empty. Sane. (*WSS* 171-2)

Rhys shows that in the conventional sense "sanity" is repressive and can lead to actual madness. Antoinette gets mad only when Rochester tries to straitjacket her within the patriarchal codes. There are moments when Edward Rochester finds himself drawn towards the mystery and loveliness of Jamaica, but it makes him uncomfortable. The reinstatement of the imperial bias according to which both Antoinette and her island are evil is called a return to "sanity" by him.

WSS is a highly deconstructive work which also challenges the most cherished of all unities, that is, the unity of character. A cultural study of the traditional western literary canon unravels many colonial and patriarchal master narratives which depend on the dichotomous epistemology of the "self" and the "other". This Anglican episteme is based on the premises taken from various religious texts like the Bible. The conception of the unitary model of the "self", is conceived within the Old Testament where man is created in the image of God and placed in paradise. Adam lives in a pure state of grace uncorrupted by any negative influence before his Fall. Both Satan and Eve who seduce him represent the subalterns. Satan incarnates evil because he falls from the esteem of God, and Eve is a gendered subaltern created not directly in the image of God but from the rib of Adam to serve as his companion. Thus the world is divided into dual forces of good and bad, and all that exists is categorised hierarchically in binaries viz. day and night, man and woman, occidental and oriental, high and low, mind and body, self and other, where the first term in every set is celebrated and the second denigrated. These binaries of western logic are mutually exclusive and jointly exhaustive. For centuries many thinkers, aesthetes, philosophers, religious gurus have adopted the same binary *weltanchauung*. In the twentieth century, the binary logic and syllogistic logic proposed by Aristotle have been replaced by fuzzy logic which deconstructs the fetishization of boundaries, thus emphasizing unity and inclusion rather than creating difference and exclusion.

Modern psychoanalysts have contributed largely to the undoing of mind/body dichotomy. Freud deconstructs the notion that rational ego is completely independent of the bodily desire in *Three Essays on the Theory of Sexuality*. His theories have brought a radical shift in the way human personality is viewed and conceptualised. For example, Freud talks of the tripartite structure of the human psyche and not of a single homogeneous self. Human beings, according to Freud, are innately split in between the ego, id and superego. It is wrong not only to segregate them into high and low, but it is also fallacious to think of them in strictly unisexual terms (*The Cambridge Companion to Freud*). His illustration of the formation of gender identities during the post Oedipal crisis forms the basis of contemporary psychoanalysis including Jacques Lacan's resistance to western humanism. Lacan deconstructs the paradigm of an essentialist self by illustrating Descartes' cogito thus: "Cogito ergo sum, Ubi cogito, ibi sum" (Lacan *Ecrits*, 182) which means: I think therefore I am, where I think, there I am.

The postcolonial critics like Edward Said in *Orientalism* and Homi K. Bhabha in *Nation and Narration* have discussed that the "self" is a fictional identity constructed by the colonisers who project the darker instincts of their unconscious on the "other" which is the colonised. In most of the literature of the colonial era, it has been observed that the colonised subject is presented in very bleak terms as the one who is violent, mad, sexually voracious, insensitive and lacking emotional control. Thus reality is totalised, essentialized and reduced by the colonial paradigms. Having fully comprehended the essentializing and reductive tendencies of the unitary model of the human self, the postcolonial critics explore the means that perpetrate such thinking and simultaneously undo them. In the language of postmodernism the term "subject" is commonly used to represent the self which rather than being autonomous is subjected to various social, discursive and ideological forces.

Discussing the fetishization of boundaries, Karl Miller asserts in *Doubles* that there is no such thing as character. The most loved of all unities, the unity of character, has been deconstructed by the modern critical thinkers. Whether it is Simone de Beauvoir's constructionist view of human personality as elucidated in *The Second Sex*, Judith Butler's performative theory as described in *Gender Trouble*, Foucault's view of human sexuality as explicated in *The History of Sexuality*, Sedgwick's contribution to Queer theory in *Between Men* or Marxist and new historicist criticism of unitary subjectivities, the post structural paradigm of decentring the subject is strengthened by all of them. They present the subject in a state of psychological tension because of the ever changing relationship between the so called "self" and "other".

"Doubling" (Miller) and pairing of opposites is a motif used by the women writers of the twentieth century to deal with the themes of freedom and individuality. "Doubling" is used by them in a subversive way to write about the socially unacceptable feelings and behaviours. Sandra Gilbert and Susan Gubar in *The Madwoman in the Attic* also discuss the use of "doubling" as a woman writer's way of subverting the conventions about gender. Rosemary Jackson in *Fantasy: The Literature of Subversion* discusses the contribution of "doubling" in creating subversive fantastic literature. These postcolonial writers use the technique for showing the permeability of the boundaries separating the colonizer and the colonized. They create characters which belong to different genders, races or classes, show the apparent differences and then deconstruct the very differences to reveal the basic similarities beneath the surface.

Rhys also deconstructs the fixity of the boundaries separating the colonial or Creole "self" from the Creole or the colonized "other" respectively in *WSS* by creating textual doubles. It blurs those ideological, social, moral and psychological boundaries between people who are segregated by race, class and gender and whose identities are compartmentalized in rigid hierarchical structures. A comparative study of Edward Rochester's character with Sandi's, Antoinette's with Tia's and Antoinette's with Rochester's would explicate the process which Rhys uses to challenge the notion of a stable character. She also deconstructs the Manichean set of opposites constructed by Bronte in form of Bertha and Jane by presenting Antoinette as an intertextual double to Jane Eyre.

Rhys's Antoinette is similar to Jane in the circumstances she faces in life including poverty, social humiliation and repressive religious schooling. Like Jane, Antoinette has a loveless childhood that sharpens her longing for love. Both Antoinette and Jane are sad and lonely at heart and are scared of animosity from the people whom they love. Both feel isolated in the patriarchal world, and both in their own ways try to resist Edward Rochester's commodification of their bodies and minds. Jane objects to the pretty clothes which Rochester tries to make her buy, and Antoinette objects to the new names that Rochester tries to give her. Drawing parallels between Antoinette and Jane, Michael Thorpe observes that "both heroines grow up fatherless and emotionally threatened by those who take charge of them; they live much within themselves and in their imaginations, made fearful by emotional and physical insecurity" (176). They become introverts because of maltreatment and find relief in dreams and fantasies. Thorpe also finds similarities between Bertha's suffering at Thornfield Hall and Jane's agonies in the "red-room" where Aunt Reed confines her.

Doubling in *WSS* not only crosses the boundaries of stereotypical Victorian femininity but also that of gender and race. Antoinette is similar in many ways to Rochester and even to the servant girl Tia. Even the villainous Daniel Cosway, the coloured half brother to Antoinette, is not as different from Rochester as he appears at first sight.

WSS initially stresses the opacity of the boundaries that separate a white English male from a Creole woman. When Edward sees Antoinette for the first time he associates her with the natives who are mysterious and unmistakably other.

Rochester says of Antoinette, "Long, sad dark alien eyes. Creole of pure English descent she may be, but they are not English or European either" (*WSS* 67). Edward, who is proud of being English, resists falling in love with his Creole wife whom he sees with suspicion. One can draw a parallel here between the otherness of a colonised land and the otherness of women. One also finds that this "other"-ness is just a discursive formation imposed on Rochester by the colonial paradigms, and the text gives instances when Edward empathises and finds a response in his heart for both the wilderness of the island and Antoinette. Finally he rejects Antoinette saying: "Vain silly creature. Made for loving? Yes, but she'll have no lover, for I don't want her and she'll see no other". (*WSS* 165)

According to Simpson, Rochester projects his own malign instincts on Antoinette as a way of disavowing them. He sees her as an embodiment of everything that is to be feared. Her becoming lustful, uncontrollable and murderous "is an expression of his own responses that have been rejected from his sense of himself so as to be more safely lodged in a perceived other" (Simpson 121). But Rochester is similar to Antoinette because of his existential angst that makes him as vulnerable as her. Rochester also has not resolved his pre-Oedipal longings and nurtures a grudge against his father who holds tightly to the English Inheritance Law. Like Antoinette, he too is a rejected child, alone in a strange land, afraid of being hurt and exploited. It is his fear which makes him unable to love though he keeps longing for it: "She had left me thirsty and all my life would be thirst and longing for what I had lost before I found it" (*WSS* 172). His housekeeper says, "I knew him as a young man. He was gentle, generous, brave. His stay in the West Indies has changed him out of all knowledge. Don't ask me to pity anyone who has a hand in it" (*WSS* 177-8). Even Christophine does not have a completely bad opinion of Edward as a person: "The man not a bad man, even if he love money, but he hear so many stories he don't know what to believe." (*WSS* 114) Helen Carr notes that "The Rochester figure is no simple brute: he too like Antoinette loves, hates and raves...He is a study in the process of repression: Antoinette opens herself to the repressed. (87-88)

Both Antoinette and Rochester are victims of the English patriarchal law. If Rochester is denied his rights to patrimony by his father due to "primogeniture", Antoinette becomes a *femme covert* when her brother gives all her patrimony to Rochester as dowry. If Antoinette is paranoid and suspicious of new people and places, Edward is no less so. Antoinette's fear of and apathy towards England and her disbelief in God are no more fatal to their relationship than Edward's suspicion of the lush green island whose beauty and uniqueness he fails to accept. He is afraid of getting overwhelmed by the Caribbean excess. "Everything is too much ... Too much blue, too much purple, too much green. The flowers too red, the mountains too high, the hills too near" (*WSS* 70). Both Edward Rochester and Antoinette Cosway live a life of denial where they fail to understand the true nature of their desires and the destructive influence they can have on their partners. Both of them are highly egocentric and their common failing is the inability to love and appreciate difference.

Carole Angier's comments on the male-female equation in the Rhysian world to show the falsehood underlying the victor/victim dichotomy in human relationships:

> For the first time Jean Rhys faces the possibility that the 'bewildered English gent' loved and suffered too: that not only Anna and Julia loved and suffered, but Walter, Jeffries, and Mr Mackenzie, and Neil James too. She no longer divides the world into strong and weak, with the strong exploiting the weak and getting off scot-free. (101)

If there is a villain in the story who intends harm it is Daniel, the coloured cunning bastard child out to avenge himself on the innocent for the wrong done to him. Daniel is oppressed by rejection and isolation, fear and distrust like Edward Rochester. According to Angier, Rhys is trying to demonstrate "that it is through weakness rather than strength that cruelty and hurt enter the world" for the strong characters like Aunt Cora and Christophine are kind (102). She further states that "rejection and fear make people, according to their natures, angry and violent (like Antoinette), envious and bitter (like Daniel), or cold and cruel (like Rochester) (102). A close reading of the text shows that Rhys has characterised Daniel as a person full of vengeance more than of mindless evil. Both Daniel and Edward are proud and cannot take rejection. Rochester, the decent English gent, proves no better than the unscrupulous Daniel when he sleeps with Amelie just to give vent to his rage. Simpson notes:

> [B]y novel's end Rochester himself is very much like Daniel-embittered, deceitful, exploitative of not only "Bertha", the wife he has renamed and imprisoned, but by implication also a manipulator of the Jane of Bronte's text, the fiancée to whom he will lie as he tries to claim her. (Simpson 125)

Another pairing done by Rhys in *Wide Sargasso Sea,* to speak about the possibility of friendship between those divided by the racial borders, is of Tia and Antoinette. Tia is a typical poverty-stricken black child who steals Antoinette's dress and money. Antoinette and Tia part because of their racial prejudices. Antoinette becomes a passive medium for the perpetration of the colonial discourse when she calls Tia a "cheating nigger", and Tia becomes a similar medium of the colonised people's blind ire which sets out to punish all the Creoles without discrimination. Both of them share the pain of separation from their alter ego. After having hurt Antoinette, Tia stands with tears in her eyes and Antoinette with blood on her face looking at each other as in a looking glass.

> When I was close I saw the jagged stone in her hand but I did not see her throw it. I did not feel it either, only something wet, running down my face. I looked at her and I saw her face crumple up as she began to cry. We stared at each other, blood on my face, tears on hers. It was as if I saw myself. Like in a looking glass." (*WSS* 45)

Sandra Drake calls the scene as "one of the most painful scenes of the book, apparently of brutal rejection of white by black" and observes that the "little girls are equally hurt" (204). Drake comments that Antoinette and Tia are "not simply in a relation of ego and alter-ego – but the same person" (204). In the end Antoinette sees Tia as a part of her lost self which she desires to redeem.

Through these textual doubles Rhys tries to show that there is no hierarchy, no mutually exclusive binaries and no dichotomously fixed characters. Human beings are subjected to the circumstances of their lives, yet they keep on changing, and their character cannot be determined by the assumptions about their race, class or gender.

Apart from deconstructing the notion of a unitary and stable subject, *WSS* also follows many other tenets of post-structuralist thought. The text is full of aporias which make the search of a fixed meaning futile. Rhys creates ontological doubts and questions the existence of any transcendental signified which is treated as self-sustained, be it the notion of God, Truth or Real.

Nietzsche proclaimed in *The Gay Science* that God is dead. The death of God according to him leads to the absence of any coherent and objective truth. The optimism of Bronte in *Jane Eyre* and her impeccable faith in God stands in sharp contrast to the dark pessimism of Rhys. Rhys rewrites the concept of "the beneficent God of this earth" (*Jane Eyre* 405) who "sees not as man sees, but far clearer: judges not as man judges, but far more wisely" (*Jane Eyre* 405). Rhys contradicts Bronte's assertions and denies the existence of God as an omniscient, benevolent and omnipotent presence. Antoinette's existential angst and apathy is in contrast to Jane's faith in God as the moral energy behind the force of human feelings. Antoinette believes that even if God exists, He is equally absurd and makes no difference to the injustice prevalent in world. Rhys shows how Antoinette's life in the convent does not lead her to self-actualization but is restrictive and inhibiting. All the references to God in *WSS* serve only to heighten the tone of painful sarcasm. God is presented as a patriarch who seconds the cause of men in maintaining their supremacy over women. Thus, only male characters in *WSS* believe in God. Rochester has impeccable faith "in the power and wisdom of my creator (*WSS* 127)."

By the end of the eighteenth century, it was realised that the gamut of human knowledge is not based on any unitary Truth but is a product of the limited perceptions of the human intellect. There is no privileged position from which one can view truth objectively as one is a part of the structures one chooses to study. To emphasize the complexity of unravelling one Truth, Rhys directs the readers look at the same event from different points of view, all of them contradictory. Christophine's assessment of Annette's and Antoinette's characters is entirely different from that of Rochester's. Antoinette and Edward have different ways of perceiving truth and reality. Antoinette struggles painfully to make Edward understand and to make him see her version of truth but fails. When Antoinette says that her mother died when she was a child, she refers to the metaphorical absence of her mother from her life. According to her there are two types of death, "the real one and the one people know about" (*WSS 128*). Antoinette tells the truth to him "as she knows it" but Rochester does not believe her. What seems real to one is just a dream for the other. For example, England is not real but is like a cold, dark dream for Antoinette. For Rochester everything about West Indies is unreal including his wife because the other reality threatens him.

WSS shows that one's dependence on memory for trying to get at the Truth can also be misleading. Like Truth and Reality memory is also subjective. One fact can be encoded in multifarious ways in the minds of various people, and the reproductions of the same fact based on memory can be extremely distorted. So any form of self-righteousness, howsoever convincing, is only a trap. For example, Daniel says to Rochester, "Give my love to your wife—my sister" (WSS 126) and Rochester recollects Daniel's words as: "Give my sister you wife a kiss from me. Love her as I did—oh yes I did" (WSS 158).

By subverting the patriarchal belief systems, Rhys creates space for women and their experiences in her writing. She creates pairings of women to interrogate whether or not meaningful relationships between women are possible. Rhys's characters have surrogate mother figures to help them survive the agony of loss. Antoinette has Christophine, and Anna (*Voyage in the Dark*) has black Francine. These are women of the real world with the power with which to challenge the establishment. Rhys introduces Christophine in *WSS* as Klein's "good breast"

("Notes on Some Schizoid Mechanisms") who partially fills the vacuum created by Antoinette's mother, "the bad breast". Christophine challenges patriarchy, interrogates the imperial motives behind Rochester's marriage with Antoinette, subverts assumptions about madness and even chides Antoinette for being excessively dependent on Edward. She is a strong woman who has developed her own strategies of survival in the man's world. She resists all forms of domination, values her culture, refuses to treat the whites as belonging to a superior race and is the only one to fully appreciate the plight of Antoinette.

Rhys's subversion of *Jane Eyre* also involves reconceptualising a few episodes from *Jane Eyre* in order to sensitise the audience to the vulnerability, humiliation and pain of Antoinette. The last scene is very artistically framed by Rhys in *WSS*. It is a revision of the episode from *Jane Eyre* which shows Bertha's burning of the Thornfield Hall. The motive given by Rhys for Antoinette's desperate act redeems her. The act is shown not as the negative destructive rage of a maniac but as an attempt of an encaged human being to be free. It is her search for an identity; her revolt against imprisonment, humiliation and misunderstanding. The fire is an assertion of her will. Antoinette is not thinking about harming Rochester or his mistress, she is thinking about how to avoid "the man" (*WSS* 190) who hates her.

The loss of her identity which is a result of the long imprisonment in the cold dingy attic room is sensitively shown in the following lines in which she is not able to recognize her mirror image and longs for Christophine to give her some proof of her identity:

> It was then that I saw her—the ghost. The woman with streaming hair. She was surrounded by a gilt frame but I knew her. I dropped the candle I was carrying and it caught the end of a table cloth and I saw flames shoot up...I called help me Christophine help me and looking behind I saw that I had been helped. There was a wall of fire protecting me. (*WSS* 188-9)

Antoinette burns the house and seemingly takes a leap out of language, dry logic and patriarchy, in order to get united with Tia. The text dwells on the motif of wings to speak about Antoinette's need to be free from the restrictive patterns in her life. Her action, which in *Jane Eyre* is shown as an unholy suicide attempt resulting in death, is depicted in *WSS* as a jump into freedom and peace.

WORKS CITED

Adjarian, M M. "Between and Beyond Boundaries in Wide Sargasso Sea". *College Literature*. 22.1 (1995) *Questia*. Web. 30 Jan. 2011.

Angier, Carole. *Jean Rhys—(Lives of Modern Women)*. New York: Viking, 1985. Print.

Anzaldua, Gloria. *Borderlands: The New Mestiza*. San Francisco: Aunt Lute Books, 1987. Print.

Aristotle. *On the Generation of Animals*. Trans. Arthur Platt. eBooks@ Adelaide. The University of Adelaide library. 25 Aug 2010. Web. 10 May 2012.

Bakhtin, M.M. *The Dialogic Imagination: Four Essays*. Ed. Michael Holquist. Trans. Caryl Emerson and Michael Holquist. Austin and London: University of Texas Press. 1981. Print.

Beauvoir, Simone de. *The Second Sex* trans. and ed. H.M. Parshley. Harmondsworth: Penguin 1982. Print.

Benjamin, Jessica. *Shadow of the Other: Intersubjectivity and Gender in Psychoanalysis*. New York: Routledge, 1998. Print.

Bhabha, Homi K. *Nation and Narration*. London: Routledge, 1990. Print.

Bollas, Christopher. *The Shadow of the Object: Psychoanalysis of the Unthought Known*. New York: Columbia University Press, 1987. Print.

Braithwaite, Edward Kamau. *Contradictory Omens: Cultural Diversity and Integration in the Caribbean*. Kingston, Jamiaca: Savacou Publications, 1974. Print.

Bronte, Charlotte. *Jane Eyre*. Noida: Mayoor Paperbacks, 1987. Print.

Butler, Judith. *Gender Trouble: Feminism and the Subversion of Identity*. London: Routledge, 1990. Print.

Carr, Helen. Jean Rhys. Plymouth: Northcote House Publishers Ltd, 1996. Print.

Carter, Angela. Expletives Deleted. London: Vintage, 2006. Print.

Derrida, Jacques. "Of Grammatology as a positive Science". *Of Grammatology*. Trans. Gayatri Chakravorty Spivak. Baltimore and London: Johns Hopkins University Press, 1976. Print.

Drake, Sandra. "Race and Caribbean Culture as Thematics of Liberation in Jean Rhys' Wide Sargasso Sea". *Jean Rhys: Wide Sargasso Sea—A Norton Critical Edition* ed. Judith L Raiskin. New York and London: W.W. Norton and Company, 1998. Print.

Fairbain, W. Ronald D. "The Repression and the Return of Bad Objects". *An Object-Relations Theory of the Personality.* New York: Basic Books, 1954. Print.

Foucault, Michel. *Madness and Civilization: A History of Insanity in the Age of Reason.* Trans. Richard Howard. New York: Vintage, 1988. Print.

——. *The History of Sexuality.* Vol 1. London: Penguin, 1990. Print.

Freud, Sigmund. *The Ego and the Id.* Ed. James Strachey. New York: W.W. Norton and Company, 1989. Print.

——. *Three Essays on the Theory of Sexuality.* Trans. James Strachey. New York: Basic Books, 1962. Print.

Gilbert, Sandra and Susan Gubar. *The Mad Woman in the Attic: The Woman Writer and the Nineteenth-Century Literary Imagination.* New Haven: Yale University Press, 1979. Print.

Hermans, H.J.M. and Kempen, H.J.G. *The Dialogical Self: Meaning as Movement.* San Diego: Academic Press, 1993. Print.

Humm, Maggie. *Border Traffic: Strategies of Contemporary Women Writers.* Manchester and New York: Manchester University Press, 1991. Print.

Kafka, Franz. *The Metamorphosis.* New York: Bentam Dell, 1972. Print.

Klein, Melanie. "Early Stages of the Oedipus Conflict". Contributions to Psycho-Analysis, 1921-1945. London: Hogarth Press, 1950. Print.

——. "Notes on Some Schizoid Mechanisms". 1946. Developments in Psycho Analysis. London: Hogarth, 1952. Print.

Kristeva, Julia. *Powers of Horror: An Essay on Abjection.* New York: Columbia University Press, 1982. Print.

Lacan, Jacques. *Ecrits: A Selection.* UK: Tavistock Publications, 1977. Print.

——. *The Seminars of Jacques Lacan.* Web. 18 May 2012.

Look Lai, Wally. "The Road to Thornfield Hall: An Analysis of Jean Rhys's *Wide Sargasso Sea*". Ed. John La Rose. *New Beacon Reviews: Collection One.* London: New Beacon Books, 1968. Print.

Lawtoo, Nidesh. "Hybridity, Dialogism and Identity in Jean Rhys's *Wide Sargasso Sea* and Tsitsi Dangarembga's *Nervous Conditions*". *Portals: A Journal in Comparative Literature.* San Francisco State University, 2010. Web. 10 June 2010.

Linnet, Maren. "New Words, New Everything: Fragmentation and Trauma in Jean Rhys". Literary Criterion, July 2006. Print.

Miller, Karl. *Doubles: Studies in Literary History*. Faber Find, 2009. Web. 30 Mar 2012.

Naipaul, V.S. *The Enigma of Arrival*. London: Penguin Books, 1987. Print.

Nietzsche, Friedrich Wilhelm. *Beyond Good and Evil*. Trans. Marion Faber, Oxford: Oxford World's Classics, 1998. Print.

——. *The Gay Science*. Trans. Walter Kaufmann. New York: Random House Inc., 1974. Print.

Phillips, Caryl. *Cambridge*. New York: Vintage International, 1991. Print.

Plasa, Carl ed. *Jean Rhys: Wide Sargasso Sea—A Readers Guide to Essential Criticism*. New York: Palgrave Macmillan, 2001. Print.

Rhys, Jean. "Selected Letters". Ed Judith L. Raiskin. *Wide Sargasso Sea: A Norton Critical Edition*. New York: W.W. Norton and Company, 1999. Print.

——. *Smile Please*. London: Andre Deutsch, 1979. Print.

Rhys, Jean. *Wide Sargasso Sea*. London: Andre Deutsch Limited, 1966. 6th impression 1983.

Said, Edward. *Orientalism*. London: Penguin Books, 1978. Print.

Sedgwick, Eve Kosofsky. *Between Men: English Literature and Male Homosocial Desire*. New York: Columbia University Press, 1985. Print.

Shelley, Mary. *Frankenstein; or, The Modern Prometheus*. Ed. Susan J. Wolfson. New York: Pearson Longman, 2007. Print.

Showalter, Elaine. *The Female Malady: Women, Madness and English Culture 1830-1980*. London: Virago, 1985. Print.

Simpson, Anne B. *Territories of the Psyche: The Fiction of Jean Rhys*. New York: Palgrave Macmillan, 2005. Print.

Spivak, Gayatri Chakravorty. "Three Women's Texts and a Critique of Imperialism". *Critical Inquiry*. 12.1 (1985) 243-261. JSTOR. Web. 14 Se 2011. http://www.jstor.org/stable/134346

Thorpe, Michael. "The Other Side: Wide Sargasso Sea and Jane Eyre". Ed Judith L. Raiskin. *Wide Sargasso Sea: A Norton Critical Edition*. New York: W.W. Norton and Company, 1999. Print.

Tiffin, Helen. "Post-Colonial Literatures and Counter—Discourse." *The Post—Colonial Studies Reader*. ed by Bill Ashcroft, Gareth Griffiths and Helen Tiffin. London: Routledge, 1995. Print.

Walia, Rajni. *Women and Self: Fiction of Jean Rhys, Barbara Pym and Anita Brookner*. New Delhi: Books Plus, 2001. Print.

Woolf, Virginia. "*Jane Eyre* and *Wuthering Heights*" The Common Reader. Ed Andrew Mc Neillie. London, New York, San Diego: Harcourt Brace and Company, 1925. Print.

——. "Women and Fiction". *Virginia Woolf: Women and Writing*. Ed. Michele Barrett. London: Women's Press, 1979. Print.

Zeitkowitz, Richard E. "Writing a Feminine Paris in Jean Rhys's Quartet". *Journal of Modern Literature* 28.2 (2005) 1-17. Indiana University Press. Web. 1 Aug 2011. <hyyp://www.jstor.org/stable/383171.>

3

Demythologizing Master Narratives: Angela Carter's Speculative Novels and Short Stories

> If a number of academic theses devoted to an author were to be taken as a reliable measure of the author's relative importance, Carter would emerge as the single literary giant of the period. (Head 4)

Angela Carter's writing is marked by a fine blend of fantasy, practical wisdom and theoretical ideas. Carter is famous for her speculative novels which are greatly influenced by the works of British new wave science fiction writers like J.G. Ballard and Michael Moorcock who use the genre innovatively to represent dystopian modernity and the psychological impact of technological advancement.

The main purpose of Carter's speculative novels like *The Infernal Desire Machines of Doctor Hoffman* and *The Passion of New Eve* is to undermine and deconstruct the projection of woman-as-sign. Her collection of short stories called *The Bloody Chamber* also revises the fairy tales to reveal the repressive image of women projected in them. Her works challenge the master narratives of the Western civilization in a postcolonial fashion and weaken the claims of all forms of fundamentalism and fanaticism including the extreme practices of radical feminism.

The Infernal Desire Machines of Doctor Hoffman (1972) was the first of Carter's three speculative novels, the other two being *The Passion of New Eve* and *Nights at the Circus*. *IDH* falls under the category of theoretical fiction and is packed with theoretical repertoire of the 1970s. Carter tells Lorna Sage that this was her favourite novel and "there are passages in *IDH* that still give me enormous pleasure" (Sage "*A Savage Sideshadow*", 56). The title of the novel recalls Deleuze and Guattari's statements about the nature of desire and sexual drives in *Anti Oedipus* (1972). The term "desiring machines" was coined by them to emphasize that desire is produced by the social machinery, instead of being a product of "lack" as postulated by Freud and Lacan (*The Seminars of Jacques Lacan*). Deleuze and Guattari underscore the subversive nature of desire and its resultant suppression by the societies that value order and cultural hegemony.

Carter once declared "I am in the demythologising business" (Carter *The Sadeian Woman*, 5). One of the Enlightenment myths is that reason leads to human progress, and Carter deconstructs this myth by presenting Desiderio, the protagonist of the novel and blind follower of Minister, as suffering from intense boredom. The determination police of the Minister also "looked as if they had been recruited wholesale from a Jewish nightmare" (*IDH* 22). Linden Peach comments that "the reference to the Holocaust is a reminder of the fact that rationality played a key role in the design of the Holocaust, of the concentration camps and of the gas chambers". (105-6)

Doctor Hoffman desires to bring a realm of uncertainty to the city governed by the Minister. He is a megalomaniac scientist who topsy turvies the social structure of the world by creating the "desire machines" which generate "eroto energy" for the cause. His War which he calls "great war" tries to erase the boundaries that separate one object from the other. The dividing line between the animate and the inanimate worlds is also blurred. One can find in the city phenomena like "morning with ears" and objects like "flowers that are heard and not seen" and "pineapples with the colour and texture of strawberries and taste of caramel". Sarah Gamble illustrates that "Hoffman's vision of the possibility of actualising any of the imagination's imaginings threatens Desiderio's city, where empirical reality is usurped by the manifold, unstable and ever-changing concretisations of fantasy" (*The Fiction of Angela Carter,* 75). The war in the book is a metaphysical war between patriarchal imposition and feminine amorphousness.

Doctor Hoffman, both a master scientist and a philosopher, tries to turn the city through his experiments into a place where the limitations of space and time are subverted. Sally Robinson compares the epistemological revolution in the novel with the postmodern condition in which "culture's master narratives are losing the power and authority to order experience and, conversely, in which 'experience' is no longer considered the ground of epistemological certainty" (*The Anti-Hero as Oedipus*, 108). Taking his theoretical framework from Derrida, Hoffman aims at liberating desire and rewrites the COGITO thus: "I Desire Therefore I Exist" (*IDH* 272). Hoffman aims at liberating the unconscious from the social fictions and cultural myths. The Doctor also emphasises individuality and suggestively his name is also taken from one of the German Romantic authors called Ernst Theodor Amadeus Hoffman (1776-1822). Hoffman wants to de-sublimate the psyche and free the unconscious from the transcendental element that is God. All structures and stabilizing notions, including the notion of language, are attacked by Hoffman. Kath Filmer notes that "subversiveness and the sense of the particular run right through *The Infernal Desire Machines*", and the work is "constantly metaphysical or at least abstract in its reach" (149). He further states that "only in this novel do we have a war which is not a physical but a mental one, whereby Hoffman is trying to de-stabilise order, empiricism and priori notions of reality, by liberating each phenomenon into a mutating mass of alternating forms" (149).

The peep show, which represents Hoffman's views about the world, depicts random changes in the pictures which represent the many simultaneously existing worlds governed by no fixed set of rules. Dr Hoffman, the adversary of the Minister, asserts "reason cannot produce the poetry disorder does" (*IDH* 206). Here Carter refers to the conflict between the powers of imagination and reason present in Plato's *Republic*. It subverts the myth entertained by Plato that indulging the imagination is destructive. According to Carter, imagination and desire have immense creative potential and can be used as sources of energy. Linden Peach explains the use of Platonic ideology in Carter's text and asserts that "in Plato's *Republic* the poets compete with the philosopher-king as Hoffman competes with the Minister of Determination; threatening the stability of the state by appealing to the irrational desires and the unruly appetites" (100).

Carter wittily explicates in the novel that excessive dependence on either logic or imagination leads to phallocentricism. Peach notes that in the course of the novel, rationality and imagination are shown as coming together to further the means of human abuse. The love pens used to fuel the "desire machines" contradict the Doctor's claims about establishing a realm of complete liberation. Doctor Hoffman's "desire machines" are least emancipatory as they restrict desire by binding it to an ongoing sexual act maintained by inhuman doses of hormones:

> All along the mirrored walls were three-tiered wire bunks. In the ceiling above each tier of bunks, were copper extractors of a funnel type leading into an upper room where a good deal of invisible machinery roared with a sound like rushing water but the noise of the machinery was almost drowned by the moans, grunts, screams, bellowing and choked mutterings that rose from the occupants of those open coffins, for here were a hundred of the best-matched lovers in the world, twined in a hundred of the most fervent embraces passion could devise. (*IDH* 213-14)

Though the Doctor claims to liberate the world with his methods, he fails to let his daughter Albertina grow freely. The libratory schema of the Doctor is presented as similar to the political dissention of the counterculture which, according to Sarah Gamble, had metamorphosed into an inarticulate hooliganism, and, thus no longer functioned as a valid vehicle for protest. Robinson also elucidates the colonial paradigms of the Minister's and the Doctor's approaches:

> The Minister, a representative of 'logical positivism' speaks for a humanist epistemology that cannot countenance

> contradictions in its systems. The Doctor speaks for a post-humanist epistemology where contradictions rule and where rationality has been put radically into question. Yet, the two systems are quickly seen to be complicit in the same ideological agenda: they both position Man as an imperialist subject whose desire gives free reign to exploitation and domination. (*The Anti-Hero as Oedipus*, 110)

Sarah Gamble states that the revolution fails to take place not because Desiderio murders Hoffman but because the choice between realism and fantasy is always illusory.

> In Marcuse's terms, the radical imagination is not overthrown but defeated by being shown to never have been at all that radical in the first place. Far from being revolutionary, the imagination never breaks free from the prevailing status quo but merely shores up the symbols and images that sustain it. (*Angela Carter*, 131)

Carter shows that permanent chaos is as undesirable as deadening stability. One is made to ask whether it is possible to subvert an order without reinstating another equally totalitarian one. Ever since the beginning of the twentieth century writers like Yeats and Eliot are found lamenting the loss of a "centre" which can "hold" ("The Second Coming"). This loss of essence or Real is accepted in a playful manner by the postmodern writers who have abandoned the search for true self and could be found celebrating the superficial surface. As elucidated by Sarah Gamble, Carter talks of the "negotiations" that we have to make to discover any kind of "reality" (*Angela Carter,* 10). Carter believes that what we take to be the real world is a result of the most powerful stories. Peach considers Carter as "one who engages with the core of realism, questioning the limitations of what is normally taken as constituting reality" (164). She represents not only the transience of human life but even the replacement of signs, which once stood for real presence, by surfaces and simulacra. *IDH* also critiques the effect of media on society. Baudrillard says in *Simulacra and Simulations* that the images that newspapers, magazines and television broadcast are nothing but simulacra. In the postmodern era instead of the sign representing the real, the real imitates these simulacra. Hoffman's transmitters are also like satellite dishes and send dreamlike mirages to the city. Thus the desire machines could be read as simulacra producing factories which distance the real life by means of representation. The disruption of desire machines is Carter's dig at the contemporary cult of consumerism where desire is dominated by media images.

Sarah Gamble explicates how the master narratives of time, truth, identity and historical causation are deliberately mangled in *IDH*, and although the ending apparently sees them restored, it is not to their former state (*The Fiction of Angela Carter*, 73). The linear concept of time is subverted by the reign of Nebulous Time in the novel which reinstates multiplicity and parallel worlds. The magic samples that control the emission of erotoenergy from Hoffman's castle are models of all that can exist in the world. They also power the fantastical images and random mirages in the city. The destruction of these magic samples makes the secret desires of individuals create reality during Nebulous Time. This power of creation given to the minds of individuals by Carter overthrows the eighteenth century conception of mind as a passive recipient of the external world. Mind is rather perceived as the creator of the universe it apprehends. The concept of Nebulous Time in the novel makes it possible for Desiderio, the Count and Albertina to conjure real people and events from their imagination into the real world. All that Albertina and Desiderio encounter in Nebulous Time is derived from "their desires, their unconscious" (*IDH* 186). Truth in a classic realist novel, as Steven Connor (1996) argues, is "a matter not of correspondence to facts but of perspective" (53). According to Peach, what is important in the realist novel is the establishment of a vantage point from which disparate issues and widely separated experiences can be grasped. In *IDH*, Carter focuses not so much on the experiences of the protagonist as on the difficulty of establishing vantage points (Peach 102).

Carter destabilises the notion of a stable and unitary self by showing mutations in Desiderio's identity during his stay in different communities. The narrative is picaresque in nature and is often seen by the critics as an Oedipal quest of Desiderio for his identity. Desiderio experiences various cultural systems varying from the prelapsarian to the futuristic, like that of the Amerindian River people, cannibals on the African coast, the Centaurs, the Doctor's community etcetera. Each culture impacts a different part of Desiderio's personality, and finally, in his old age he confesses that he has lost the stability of his mind. According to Punter, the text dramatises the free play of the unconscious and shows subjectivity as constructed and not natural (76).

IDH also provides a critique of the cultural and political unrest of the 1960s. The "Sixties" or "Counterculture" was marked by new and subversive trends, but Carter knows that the sexual liberation of the sixties was not liberating for women. The portrayal of Albertina is deliberately made unrealistic by Carter which makes it impossible for the readers to identify with her. Robinson comments on her portrayal as a manifestation of a "language of signs", which utterly bemused her, because she "could not read them" (*Engendering the Subject* 25). Albertina is created by Desiderio's desire as the perpetually mysterious woman that slips all attempts to capture her. Robinson notes that "like Derrida's woman-figure, Albertina is nearly impossible to pin down; she assumes numerous different identities, experiences gender fluidity, and takes any form that Desiderio's desire imposes on her" (*The Anti-Hero as Oedipus*, 118). Carter explores various fictions about womanhood and creates a counter narrative which implodes them from inside. Reading Desiderio's story as a reworking of Oedipal narrative, Robinson in "The Anti-Hero as Oedipus" reads the figure of Albertina as a fetish, a foil, the exotic/erotic object awaiting the hero at the end of his quest, but never the subject (112).

Maggie Tonkin interprets *IDH* as a parody of Marcel Proust's novel *A La Recherche du Temps Perdu* which is a master text of sexual and gender ambiguity. The character of Albertina according to her is based on Proust's Albertine. Like Proust's Albertine, the otherness of Albertina as a Muse is so emphasised that it becomes her defining attribute. Tonkin also interprets Carter's text as performing the theme of dead beloved as Muse, with the heroine functioning as a free floating signifier, absent in any actual sense from the text she inspires. The Muse in popular imagination is always female. She herself is never a creator but only inspires men for creation. As Muses do not exist on their own but are a product of men's desire for an ideal femininity, so Albertina is also a product of Desiderio's memory and desire rather than being a real woman. She appears to Desiderio as a swan, a woman with a heart of flame and an androgynous ambassador. She travels with the Count as Lafleur and is the helpless victim of the Centaurs. By giving exaggerated archetypal identities to Albertina, Carter brings into force what Linda Hutcheon calls the ambidexterity of postmodernism. According to Hutcheon a postmodern feminist text "parodically inscribes... provokes our conditioned response and then subverts that response" (qtd. in Robinson *The Anti Hero as Oedipus*, 114).

The text shows that the portrayal of Albertina is a product of Desiderio's masculine desires, and all the African figures in the novel are also reifications of the European colonisers' desires. The description of the community of Centaurs represents the way in which the colonizers view the colonized. Moreover, the Centaurs' preference for the European myths like the Genesis story and the resurrection of Christ mimics the enslaved imagination of the colonized people. Carter parodies Christian beliefs like the Passion of Christ, the concept of the Original Sin, the cycle of sin, suffering and redemption, the Eucharist etc. Christian practices like creating stigmata, flagellation, mortification of flesh and the Inquisition are also mimicked by Carter.

The violently misogynistic attitude of the Centaurs towards women also represents their blind imitation of the imperialist attitude. The Centaurs believe that women are born only to suffer. Desiderio also applauds the Centaurs' exaltation of the "virile principle" which shows his compliant participation in the continuation of patriarchy. He watches the gang rape of Albertina and later on observes that "rape hurts the giver more than the receiver" (*IDH* 181). Linden Peach also studies the novel from the feminist perspective and points out that "in most of the societies which Desiderio visits, women are in a subordinate social position, but this is something of which he is insufficiently critical" (107). Throughout his memoirs, women are castrating Amazons, mutilated bodies or erotic toys, and his "otherising" of Albertina inhibits the development of a fully reciprocal relationship (Peach 108). According to Peach, Desiderio's growth as a character lies in his giving up of his misogynistic attitude and reconciliation with his own feminine side.

Though Carter does not openly support any of the sides, in terms of narrative and grammar she follows the dimorphism, openness and ambiguity prescribed by the feminist linguists. Liminality rules the text and many liminal beings like the bearded lady, Mamie Buckskin and the Alligator man populate it. The text is postmodern and does not have a clear theme or meaning. As Desiderio is attracted by the ever elusive Albertina, the reader also keeps making unsuccessful attempts at reaching a singular meaning. The critique of the principle of dominance, the interrogation of the status quo and the open endedness of the text make the novel feminist in nature. The celebration of the margins through the portrayal of the River People has a postcolonial appeal too.

The community of the River People is matriarchal, and Carter creates it in accordance with the descriptions given by Cixous about women's language. Cixous refers to the subversive aspects of female biology and discusses the relationship between maternity and language in *The Laugh of the Medusa*. Following the feminine code, the River People don't think in straight lines but in "intricate interlocking circles" (*IDH* 101) which defies the linear logic. Their concepts are relational not absolute and the opposites are maintained in a state of tension. Their writing is beautiful but lacks signification. They use sounds and music for communication. They sing their language in which intonation is more important and their speech poses "philosophical as well as linguistic problems" (*IDH* 90).

According to Robinson's reading of the novel in *The Anti-Hero as Oedipus*, Desiderio follows the trajectory of the Oedipal family romance when he makes love to his foster mother and faces the threat of castration by the father Nao Kurai, who intends to kill and eat him in order to acquire his intellectual abilities. This is intended as mimicry of the Freudian theory of castration where the son fears castration by his father for his incestuous feelings for the mother. Through her exaggerated portrayals, Carter mocks at Freud for having mythologized the unconscious by binding it to myths like Oedipus.

Desire is shown as elusive by Carter, and so it could never be fulfilled. Once let completely free, it gets perverted and destructive as in the case of the sadistic Lithunian Count. According to Gamble, "*IDH* constitutes a journey into the realms of perversion and subversion" (*Angela Carter,* 119). Albertina appears to Desiderio as a black swan who represents the destructive nature of desire. While the House of Anonymity designed for the satisfaction of perverse male desire is a satire on masculine imagination, the Count and the black Chieftain are comic caricatures of de Sade himself. Gamble observes that:

> Carter found a striking and disturbing way of showcasing female victimisation, for instead of turning away from de Sade's vicious treatment of his sexual partners, she confronts him head-on. In this way, she denies him what he most desires—the disgusted opposition that would confirm him in his sacrilege—and instead allows the extremity of his perversion to render him ridiculous. (*Angela Carter,* 128)

The Count is deliberately made comic rather than horrifying to mimic the Sadeian thought. He is an insanely egotistic pervert who "lives only to negate the world" (*IDH* 123). The Count is boiled up for soup by his double and his own imaginative creation, the black Chieftan, during the Nebulous Time. While in intense pain he laughs with joy. His laughter depicts the insatiability of his desire which in a symbolic fashion consumes itself (Gamble *Angela Carter*, 130).

Carter is a postmodern novelist and avoids all centralising tendencies in her works. As soon as *IDH* start veering excessively in favour of one ideology, she presents the opposite viewpoint to contradict the first. Carter believes that there is no essential truth and one must demythologise one's consciousness and learn to think in ways free of myths. Myths when put on a pedestal create a false and dictatorial centre, become a fetish. So Carter has devised ways of using patriarchal mythology fabricated by men "in the service of woman" (*The Sadeian Woman*). Carter says:

> All the mythic versions of women, from the myth of the redeeming purity of the virgin to that of the healing, reconciling mother are consolatory nonsense, and consolatory nonsense seems to me a fair definition of myth, anyway. Mother goddesses are just as silly a notion as father gods.... Myth deals in false universals, to dull the pain of particular circumstances. In no area is it truer than in the relation between the sexes... The savage denial of the complexity of human relation is also a consolatory nonsense. (*The Sadeian Woman*, 5)

Carter tries to deconstruct all the archetypes as they deny the complexity and uniqueness of an individual in the favour of a collective sexed being. In *The Passion of New Eve*, which was first called *The Great Hermaphrodite*, Carter blasts the myths about femme fatales, the great Mother and the essential femininity.

PNE is a speculative novel set in America. The novel is in the form of a dystopian romance like *IDH* in which the male protagonist Evelyn forcibly undergoes a sex reassignment surgery and becomes the New Eve. Wearing this new identity as a garment, (s)he experiences physical and psychological violence by various groups including the Mother who is the leader of a group of radical feminist guerrillas, Zero who is a sadistic patriarch running his harem and a group of juvenile delinquents considering themselves the holy crusaders. Amidst chaos and the American civil war, Eve learns the pain of survival as a woman in a world ruled by several totalitarian mythmakers. Carter parodies the Passion of Christ and shatters the Christian belief that there is virtue is suffering. She also uses the word "passion" in the title to show that the suffering of women is no less than that of Christ. The pain that the new Eve undergoes is not an outcome of the Original Sin but is a result of gender discrimination in society. Thus, Carter puts all patriarchal institutions like the Church, Courts and schools to task.

America serves as a metaphor for the postmodern chaos, decay and confusion which precedes complete revival. The book is replete with images of dead bodies, extra sized rats, revolts by marginalised groups, acid rain, excrement, vomit, fear and references to the judgement day. The world is shown as crumbling due to the ideological incompatibilities of the various factions. The protagonist, Evelyn, himself is a sexist and is brought to the masculine land of infertility and death for improvement.

Carter had a problematic relationship with her mother due to which mothers are absent or criticised throughout her novels. "Sexual hostility is the inevitable relationship between mother and daughter" (Carter *The Sadeian Woman*, 123). Irigaray suggests in *Je Tu Nous* that if mothers become women, the possibility of dialogue between them and their daughters could open up. Carter, like Irigaray, prefers a woman to the falsely idealized Mother (Meaney 97). She deflates the mysticism associated with the Great Mother through her grotesque portrayal in *PNE.*

The great Mother Goddess was the first object of human worship and dates back to around 35,000 BCE. She was treated as a symbol of earth's fertility and was worshipped in the Middle East, Rome, Greece and Asia as Cybele, Ishtar, Astarte, Isis, Gaea, Hera, Rhea, Aphrodite, Demeter, Maia, Ops, Tellus and Ceres ("Adam and Lilith"). The Mother Goddess was worshipped till the twelfth century, when the Catholic Church began the tortures of the Inquisition and radically removed the cult of the Mother Goddess. The ecofeminist thinkers in the 19th and the 20th centuries have re-imagined the Great Goddess and have placed the figure at the centre of their imaginary utopias. Feminists like Adrienne Rich and Mary Daly envision the Mother Goddess as a female charged with intrinsic importance. They hold patriarchy responsible for appropriating all myths and symbols to murder the goddess. Rich finds liberating properties for women in the figure of the Goddess and discusses it in her work called *Of Woman Born.* Mary Daly's *Gyn/Ecology* shares the same attitude and considers "goddess murder" as patriarchal. Carter makes her goddess an embodiment of the same principles as talked of by Rich and Daly but exaggerates them to a ludicrous extent.

Carter resurrects this archetypal goddess in a hilarious way, and the caricature she produces subverts the fetishization of the mother goddess. She also demystifies the maternal archetype by making the Mother exaggeratedly eroticised. Through undermining the idealization of motherhood, Carter tries to liberate female sexuality from the mothering function. The French feminists try to resurrect the womb as a nourishing space and assert that dissociation from the womb causes trauma. Carter's aim is to demystify the womb as motherhood does not have any innate glory for her. Thus, she subverts both the resurrection of the mother goddess by the ecofeminists and the valorising of the mothering function by the French feminists.

Mother in *PNE* is the goddess of Beulah, an artificial underground city constructed by her on the basis of the radical feminist mythology. She is a huge black female surgeon representing the radical feminists who in the wake of the1960s feminist revolt masterminded societies like SCUM (Society for Cutting up Men). At the entrance of Beulah is "a stone cock... in a state of massive tumescence" but "broken off clean in the middle" (*PNE* 47). According to Sarah Gamble, the analogies of castration are taken from radical feminism and are treated in a mock fashion. Gamble comments on the figure of the Mother created by Carter as a mockery of Adrienne Rich and Mary Daly's theory:

> Mother is unencumbered by taste or restraint, relying on the sheer potency of her manufactured symbolism to maintain her power: a power she underlines in her castration of the male subject. This is, again, in line with the discourses of the kind of radical feminism typified by Rich and Daly. (*Angela Carter,* 148)

Mother poses as a goddess with two rows of breasts to exaggerate her mythic essence as the goddess of fertility. She also sports a false beard which speaks of her masculine aggression and repeatedly chants radical feminist dictums like: "I am the Great Parricide, I am the Castratix of the phallocentric universe, I am Mama, Mama, Mama!" (*PNE* 67) The fear of castration by a dominating woman as expressed in the *vagina dentate* myth is actualised when Evelyn is both raped and castrated by Mother. Through Evelyn's castration Carter mocks at both patriarchy and the assumptions of radical feminism. Without getting into the debate about Goddess worship versus patriarchal religious practices, Carter takes within the circle of criticism every kind of mythologizing tendencies and fanaticism.

Sexism, lack of tolerance and fanaticism are for Carter masculine traits and even women could have them. The rigid ideological structure of Mother's totalitarian regime makes it masculine irrespective of the sexual identity of the individuals running it. Hence Mother, though being a woman biologically, is phallic and wears a false beard. Tristessa on the other hand is essentially femininc despite his/her male anatomy. Carter postulates a de-essentialized subjectivity that is the main topic of debate among the feminists. Men and women, according to her, do not form mutually exclusive and exhaustive categories. For Carter, to become a woman means to become naturalised into a subordinate position, regardless of one's "official gender". Thus she disrupts an essentialist equation between biological sex and social gender (Robinson *The Anti-Hero as Oedipus*, 107).

Towards the end of the novel, Evelyn/Eve having undergone the sex transformation surgery in Beulah is shown passing through a cave which serves as a metaphor for Eve's efforts to re-enter the womb in order to reach the essential site of femininity, that is, motherhood. Journeying back to the Mother's womb Eve finds that there is no essential femininity. Hence Carter proves that the myth of Mother is just another construction as the myth of a gendered or sexed body. In *The Sadeian Woman* too, Carter criticises the romanticization and poeticization of the womb. "If women allow themselves to be consoled for their culturally determined lack of access to the modes of intellectual debate by the invocation of hypothetical great goddesses, they are simply flattering themselves into submission." (*SW* 110)

Eventually Mother goes mad in an effort to make time stand still and realizes that the manipulation of myths is meaningless. Leilah tells Evelyn: "Mother tried to take history into her own hands but it was too slippery for her to hold" (*PNE* 173) and "when Mother realised that she could not make time stand still she suffered a kind of nervous breakdown. Became gentle and introspective" (*PNE* 174). Carter wishes to remove the "semi-religious coating" from the archetypal figure of the Great Mother through humour so that her readers can question the authenticity of such portrayals freely. Peach elucidates Carter's attitude thus:

> "That the mother at the end of *PNE* has now become a figure of speech is ambiguous and might suggest Carter's scepticism about the reclamation of the mother in contemporary French theory." (129)

In creating the Mother, Carter also borrows from the Bakhtinian notion of the post-Romantic grotesque, as illustrated in *Rabelais and his World,* which is a transgressive body meeting hostility and alienation. According to Bakhtin, grotesque bodies disrupt the limits set by power structures through their monstrosity, excessiveness and the feeling of revulsion they create. Carter's fiction is inhabited by bodily grotesques in the form of she-wolves (*The Bloody Chamber*), bird-women (*Nights at the Circus*) and drag queens (*PNE*) that represent body in a state of becoming. Mother with her two rows of breasts and her excessively large body is like a Rabelaisian grotesque. She is a Carnivalesque figure that disrupts patriarchal conventions about the female body and sexuality. Evelyn is disgusted by the Mother because her body transgressively emphasises pleasure in its functions. According to the feminist theorist Mary J. Russo, the female body is always already grotesque as it is marginalized in patriarchy (*The Female Grotesque*). Johnson observes that in creating Mother, Carter adds the Kristevan category of the abject as given in *Powers of Horror* and Bakhtin's model of the bodily grotesque to Russo's idea of the Female Grotesque. Abjection is defined by Kristeva as the horror evoked during the cognizance of things that disturb order. It is related to the bodily functions and abnormalities. In Carter's novels, the abject occurs when a body transgresses the socially defined boundaries of gender. Thus Eve is horrified at her physical transformation and finds herself as "mythic and monstrous" as Mother.

Foucault, a major influence on Carter, believes that what we call normality in gender relations is not objective, but is defined by those who are given the power to police sexuality in society. He notes in *The History of Sexuality* that right from the Middle Ages any person whose sexual status was not clearly marked was made to choose one sexual identity permanently on the basis of their anatomical status, generally decided by the doctor. Homosexuality and transgenderism were treated as gross misconduct and were severely punished. It was after the 1960s that many gender identity clinics were established and many researches were done on the gender dysphoria syndrome (Johnson 172). This anti-essentialist wave of the latter half of the twentieth century could be studied through the characters of Eve and Tristessa.

Androgyny is one of the key themes in *PNE*. The protagonist, Evelyn, too is given an androgynous name and is transformed into a female surgically. Androgyny is treated by some feminist critics as an expression of support for gender equality and as a corrective measure for the masculinisation of discourse. The modern novelist Virginia Woolf also prescribes androgyny of mind for the creative writers in *A Room of One's Own*. Some critics like Toril Moi are against such prescriptions and call Woolf's suggestion her "greatest sin against feminism" (*Sexual/ Textual Politics*). Carter adopts a Woolfian approach when she describes the androgynous traits in Tristessa as desirable. Tristessa, despite the "awfully ineradicable quality of his maleness" (*PNE* 173), represents the perfect woman. Tristessa is a Hollywood actress and a transgendered individual who considers herself a female trapped in a male body. She is viewed as an irresistible icon of femininity by the protagonist. Her feminine charm lies in being masochistic, tragic and mysterious. Tristessa wants to be a female because she is seduced by the femininity she represents, and her transgendered identity acts as the novel's central trope connoting the constructed nature of gender. Tristessa says:

> Passivity. Inaction. That time should not act upon me, that I should not die. So I was seduced by the notion of a woman's being, which is negativity. Passivity, the absence of being.

To be everything and nothing. To be a pane the sun shines through. (*PNE* 137)

By projecting Eve as a castrated man, Carter is mocking at the assumptions of many philosophical schools including Aristotle's which treat women as inferior men. The pre eighteenth century anatomical science used to view woman's body as an inferior version of man's. Thus women were treated as naturally inferior to men, and in this subordinate position they were considered desirable. According to the feminist psychoanalysts like Beauvoir woman is a man's other, and men prefer women to be a definitive other in front of whom they can appear complete and manly (*The Second Sex*). Tristessa's attractiveness lies in her "wonderful lack of being" and "her allure had lain in the tragic and absurd heroism with which she had denied real life" (*PNE* 4). Tristessa also mimics the "lack" in woman as conceptualised by Freud in a metaphorical way, and through her Carter mocks at the sexism and biological determinism at the base of Freudian psychoanalysis which was later modified and adopted by Lacan. Eisentein remarks: "It is as 'emptiness', 'void', 'negation' that 'Woman' exists, as the negative sign—'minus phallus, minus power'—that establishes the man as the standard of positive value" (89).

Tristessa is a perfect woman because she has modelled herself on the basis of male fantasies about a perfect woman and takes her masquerade with utmost sincerity. Tristessa is called the "greatest female impersonator" (*PNE* 144), and men find her irresistible because of her everlasting pain that she maintains by constantly remembering fake memories of sad events. She also has a coffin reserved for herself in her mansion where she sleeps like the Sleeping Beauty waiting for the kiss of a knight. Carter creates confusion of gender identities when Eve, a man turned woman, comes as a knight to wake Tristessa up who is a man masquerading as a woman.

Leilah, later on revealed as Lilith, is described as all flesh and Sophia all mind, which ridicules the polarity in popular imagination. Evelyn realises that Leilah never objectively existed and that she was mostly a "projection of the lusts and greed and self-loathing of a young man called Evelyn" (*PNE* 175). Dissatisfied with the canonical representations of her sex, Eve keeps looking for an authentic and complete experience of femininity, but her quest remains incomplete. Carter takes an anti-essentialist stance when Eve could not find, despite her picaresque journey through various cultures, the core of femininity. Carter being a third wave feminist critiques the essentialist thinking that influenced the second wave feminism in the seventies as well as the debates about the extent to which gender identity is based on biological difference.

Judith Butler says in *Gender Trouble* (1990) that femininity is not essential but performative. At times it is like a mask which needs to be taken off. Carter states in *The Sadeian Woman* that the social fiction of femininity is created by means outside ones control and is palmed off as the real thing. Like Butler, Carter explores how gender roles are performed through stylization of the body which undermines the stability of the "natural" sexual identity and challenges what she calls the "spurious charade of maleness and femaleness" (*SW* 8). According to Childs, Carter depicts that "as more gender-or race-based myths of human nature proliferate it becomes more urgent, if not more difficult, to reason away the stereotypes that serve to circumscribe identities" (117). Therefore, the narrative of *PNE* leaves behind the old fashioned discourses that restrict gender identities, and the questions about Eve's acceptance of the absence of essential femininity remain unanswered in the text.

PNE, its title redolent of both the Old and New Testaments, reassesses the construction of gender and replaces coherent identities with plural selves, echoing the French philosopher Jean Baudrillard's argument given in *Screened Out* that in a world where gender is a consumer commodity, we are all transvestites. Childs examines that "the novel's portrayal of identity parallels theories of the cyborg-self presented in Donna Haraway's work" (Childs 115). Reading through the theoretical lens given by Donna Haraway, Mother and Eve could also be viewed as Cyborgs due to their artificial duality as a fleshly female and a cerebral male. Haraway states in "The Promises of Monsters", technology has made natural identities malleable enough to be redesigned on the basis of strategic decisions. She asserts that organisms are not born; they are made: "In the belly of the local/global monster...often called the postmodern world, global technology appears to denature everything, to make everything a malleable matter of strategic decisions and mobile production and reproductive processes" (Haraway 297). Mother is a Cyborg double because she takes pleasure in having a mixed identity both as a male and a female, secular and sacred, spirit and flesh. In Beulah, body is as malleable as spirit and so the classic mind/ body dualism is subverted.

PNE also attacks the discourses like movies, myths and religion that strengthen and support the myths about gender. According to Sarah Gamble, "Carter in *PNE* forsook much of her humour in order to mount an openly polemical attack on socially sanctioned fictions of all kinds, from mythic matriarchs to cinematic femme fatales" (*Angela Carter,* 145). *PNE* suggests that the great communal myths are increasingly Hollywood projections and they expose the "ego ideals of the past" as grand illusions. (Peach 123)

Another predominant theme in the works of Angela Carter is female sexuality and the balance of power in man woman relationship:

> Since it was primarily through my sexual and emotional life that I was radicalised—that I first became truly aware of the difference between how I was and how I was expected to be —I found myself, as I grew older, increasingly writing about sexuality and its manifestations in human practice. (Carter "Notes from the Front Line", 72)

For the purpose of unveiling the social fictions that govern our lives she re-writes the mythical base of the folktales about women's sexuality, their role in marriage, their coming of age and their corruption. She shows the physical abuse of women in phallogocentric cultures and the objectification of women through the male gaze. Her treatise *The Sadeian Woman* is a satire on the sexual roles men create for women, and it boldly subverts the subject/object, spectator/spectacle, tiger/lamb dichotomy.

Being a professed feminist, belonging to the third wave of feminist thought, Carter is always on the side of the powerless. That is why she writes in a manner which blends the old wives tales, fairy tales, folklores and the mainstream novelistic form in a non-hierarchical fashion in her collection of short stories called *The Bloody Chamber*.

BC was published by Vintage in 1979 and won the Cheltenham Festival Literary Prize. Carter associates the traditional tales with the sub-literary forms like pornography, ballad and dream. Jack Zipes also observes in *Breaking the Magic Spell: Radical theories of Folk and Fairy Tales* that the folktales or folklores emerged from the oral culture and were anonymous. These stories were fluid and could be remade. In the 17th and the 18th centuries these tales were fixed by writing, and moral tags were added to them as means of instruction for children. He further states that the literary fairy tales were a product of the transformation of oral folklores into middle class commodities. Brothers Grimm and a few others converted the oral tales into literary tales which then became the bourgeois art form. Linden Peach notes that the "traditional fairy tales rewritten by male writers become vehicles for the socialisation of young women producing a subgenre of 'warning tales'" (Peach 74).

Jack Zipes (1988) points out:

> Almost all critics who have studied the emergence of the literary fairy tale in Europe agree that educated writers purposely appropriated the oral folk tale and converted it into a literary discourse about mores, values and manners so that children would become civilized according to the social code of that time. (3)

The contemporary writers were attracted by the latent magic and darkness of the written fairy tales, and found that subverting the tales can serve the feminist purpose. Writers like Suniti Namjoshi, Githa Hariharan and Angela Carter treat the tales as repositories of outmoded lies and rewrite their ideological structures. They do it with the reformist's zeal to transform the status quo and add modern psychoanalytic insights to them.

Carter sees fairy-tales as literature that "encoded the dark and mysterious elements of the psyche" (Makinen 22). Carter makes her fairy tales black and inverted in order to foreground the inherent sexual content of the tales by Grimm brothers and Charles Perrault. She also tries to maintain the feminine element in her literary tales by giving them the texture of the old wives' oral tales in the manner of narration. One finds that the values of the rural culture are replaced by the gender politics which highlights the sexual economy and power plays of the modern civilization.

The main intertexts for *BC* are the collection of fairy tales by Charles Perrault's called *The Tales of Mother Goose*, folktales collected by Brothers Grimm called *Grimm's Fairy Tales* and de Sade's novels *Justine* and *Juliette*. Carter produced her study of Sade's work called *The Sadeian Woman* just a year before *BC*, and one can find reflections of her study of de Sade in her retelling of the fairy tales clearly. The key premise of *The Sadeian Woman* is that passivity is not a virtue and the essay interrogates why the object of desire is always presented in a passive case?

Carter rewrites femininity in *BC* by critiquing male fetishism in the literary canon. Women in "Erl King", "Snow Child" and "The Lady of the House of Love" appear to be products of male fetishist's gothic imagination. She blasts the notion of the essential femininity encoded in the roles assigned to woman as a mother, a sacrificial victim or a dumb virgin while also interrogating the semantic linkage between men with culture and women with nature. Female desire and sexuality are shown in relation to their objective role as property. The stories are written from the point of view of women in order to show the way they feel and perceive the world.

Carter maintains in *The Sadeian Woman* that the subjection of women has resulted from "a process by which culturally defined variables, only partially derived from the fact of sexual differentiation, have been individually translated to the status of universals". So she translates the mythic timelessness of the oral fairy tales into specific historical and cultural moments which proves that gender roles and sexual behaviour are forms of culturally determined social interactions. Carter takes "sexual relations out of the domain of nature and restore their historically changing social and economic contexts" (Easton 9). Carter rewrites the tales of "Beauty and the Beast" and "Little Red Riding Hood" twice and thrice respectively placing them in different cultural contexts thus generating different narratives depending on the zeitgeist of the time.

Women are given subversive roles in *BC* to help them struggle out of the straitjackets of history, ideology and biology. *BC* is also packed with symbols and signs through which Carter challenges the middle class belief systems. She makes explicit the subtext of male sexuality and dominance. The tools used for foregrounding the latent sexual content of the fairytales are exaggerating the archetypes to make them appear unreal and the blurring of boundaries between opposites which destabilizes the subject's identity.

Her tales deconstruct the classical notion of an essential character in favour of a subject dependent on the contingencies of life and the cultural, political and economic positions inhabited. Like Rhys, Carter also uses the feminist strategies of doubling and reversal to achieve this end. She demythologises and denaturalises the socially determined essence of female experience. Carter uses Sade's portrayal of Juliette, his new woman, for imploding the stereotype of pure, angelic and innocent woman. According to Alexander, the shifting structure of the oral folktales is used by Carter to communicate to the readers the shifting structures of reality and sexuality (68).

According to Sheets, Carter in *BC* protests against the repression of women's sexual desire while also breaking the ideological link between sex and romance. To deal with the theme of female sexuality, Carter analyses and interrogates the male pornographic artistic tradition. In *Subversive Intent* Suleiman examines the beginning of pornographic writing with Sade and marks its growth through Lautreamont, Dada, the Surrealists and Bataille. She also explores how contemporary feminist writers like Carter have used the tradition of pornographic writing to revision female sexuality. The feminist debates about pornography started in the mid 1970s. On one hand there are the sex positive feminists and third wave feminists who see pornography, sex work, transgenderism and free love as matters of individual choice with no inherent harm for women, and on the other hand the anti pornography feminists believe that pornography and the practice of sadomasochism lead to misogyny and violence against women. While pornography remains a contentious issue among the anti pornography feminists like Andrea Dworkin, Catharine MacKinnon, Dorchen Leidholdt etcetera and the sex positive feminists like Ellen Willis, Kathy Acker, Susie Bright, Patrick Califia, Gayle Rubin etctera, Carter uses an egalitarian approach to view the issue. She rejects the idea propagated by Duncker and Palmer that the acceptance of pornography is the acceptance of the humiliation and objectification of women and therefore, represents the erotic in her work without inhibitions. Due to this Carter is also called the "high priestess of post graduate porn" (qtd. in Sheets 641). Carter in her works depicts the counterculture and free love, counteracts romantic love and dissociates women's sexuality from the mothering function. She views sexuality as a political reality and calls de Sade a moral pornographer for being able to get to the heart of contempt for women, and who offers a critique of the relationship between the sexes (*The Sadeian Woman*).

Carter's attitude towards pornography as a means of liberation for women resists easy categorization. On the one hand she states that pornographic practices give women the freedom to be as violent as men, and on the other, she realises that sexual liberation promotes violence against women as proved by the zeitgeist of the 1960s. "Indeed, in *The Sadeian Woman*, Carter appears to be one of the new Juliettes, a "bad girl" promoting an aggressive, power oriented sexuality" (Sheets 641). One such work in which Carter both uses and abuses pornography is *BC*. The stories in the collection anticipate many of the arguments made in support of pornography during the 1980s. The stories maintain sexual freedom for women and portray sexually liberated women in "Puss in Boots", "The Tiger's Bride" and

"The Company of Wolves". In *BC* Carter aligns with the anti-pornography feminists as she represents the negative impact of pornography in stories like "The Bloody Chamber" where the Marquis's desire for total control, sadism and misogyny gets a boost through pornographic pictures and literature of the counterculture.

The basic outline of the first story called "The Bloody Chamber" is taken from Charles Perrault's "Blue Beard". Peter Childs notes that Bluebeard is historically identified with Gilles de Rais, a fifteenth century French nobleman executed for murdering children. The fictional Bluebeard murders six wives for disobeying his command not to enter a locked room but was killed before he could murder the seventh (Childs 118). Carter selects the tale of Bluebeard to focus on the interplay of love, sex and violence in marital relationships.

Perrault includes two moralities in his version. In one he cautions women against the dangers of curiosity, and in the other he warns husbands against making excessive demands on wives and being unduly jealous. The two moralities are:

Ladies, you should never pry,—
You'll repent it by and by!
'Tis the silliest of sins;
Trouble in a trice begins.
There are, surely—more's the woe
Lots of things you need not know.
Come, forswear it now and here—
Joy so brief that costs so dear!

You can tell this tale is old
By the very way it's told.
Those were days of derring-do;
Man was lord, and master too.
Then the husband ruled as king.
Now it's quite a different thing;

Be his beard what hue it may—

Madam has a word to say!

(Perrault *The Tales of Mother Goose*, "Blue Beard")

Surprisingly, most of the 19th century versions of the tale treat the heroine's curiosity and disobedience as a more serious issue than the husband's violence. Carter shifts the focus in "The Bloody Chamber" back to the sadistic sexuality of Bluebeard. The castle described as a phallic tower floating upon the "amniotic salinity of the ocean" becomes a metaphor for the Marquis's sexuality. The Bluebeard of the story is called the Marquis in order to draw a parallel with Marquis de Sade. Carter also gives a description of the Marquis's collection of the 18th and 19th century pornographic paintings portraying young, passive and victimised women, for example, Moreau's "famous sacrificial victim with the imprint of the lacelike chains on her pellucid skin". The heavy influence of pornography on the Marquis's behaviour could be seen by his use of the mirrored bedroom where he could enact the matrimonial rituals in the most voyeuristic fashion. The gift of "a choker of rubies, two inches wide, like an extraordinarily precious slit throat" (*The Bloody Chamber*, 11) which he gives to the protagonist expresses his perception of the bride as a naive and vulnerable victim. The Marquis is an aesthete obsessed with such pornographic images and is attracted by the poor virginal girl because she can act as a perfect object for practising his fantasies. By linking the sadistic tendencies of the Marquis with pornography, Carter becomes a "moral pornographer" (*The Sadeian Woman*) who exposes the misogyny that distorts our culture and uses pornography as a critique of the current relations between the sexes.

She places her tale in the decadent French culture. References to the performance of Tristan at the Paris opera, the bridal dress designed by Paul Poiret and the placing of Marquis's castle on the coast of Brittany refer to the fin de siècle French era. Thus the fate of the protagonist and Marquis's other wives is influenced by the historical moment, the decadent culture which creates a feminine ideal of dangerous passivity and persecution. The capitalist culture to which the Marquis belongs is held responsible for the commodification of the girl. Ironically, the girl participates in her objectification mesmerised by the wealth of her future husband, and probes no further before fixing the match, though the mother remains suspicious. The economic basis of the girl's dependence on her husband is made manifest, and she has not been given a name to underscore her passive object position. According to Carter, pornography along with the economic, social and psychological forces leads to the victimization of women. In *The Sadeian Woman* Carter writes:

> To be the object of desire is to be defined in the passive case. To exist in the passive case is to die in the passive case—that is, to be killed. This is the moral of the fairy tale about the perfect woman. (76-77)

Carter's *The Bloody Chamber* is an explicitly feminist version of the Bluebeard tale. She tells the tale from the point of view of the wife, giving prominence to the experiences of a woman. Carter introduces the figure of the New Woman in the form of the bride's mother who is a strong, loving and courageous lady. She is the avenger, "eagle-featured, indomitable" who "had outfaced a junkful of Chinese pirates, nursed a village through a visitation of the plague, shot a man-eating tiger with her own hand and all before she was as old as I" (*The Bloody Chamber* 7). In Carter's version, the mother shoots the Marquis as she once shot the man-eating tiger and saves the protagonist from her husband. Flora Alexander notes that the replacement of the brothers by the Mother stresses the possibility of female power in the story. Childs illustrates that the mother saves the daughter not only from her murderous husband but also from patriarchy. Childs also comments that Carter complicates the stereotypical stock characters of the realist novels like a widow and her only daughter by making the narrator's mother "a kind of adventure hero" (118). The mother-daughter bonding is also brought to the centre and is shown as instrumental in fighting with patriarchy. Carter otherwise inimical to mothers shows tolerance for the figure of mother in this tale.

The anti-patriarchal nature of the text is repeatedly made explicit through various intertexts. The Bible is one such intertext, and the episode of Eve's transgression is being reread with reference to the order given by the Marquis to the new bride about not opening the secret chamber. The question raised is that if God really wanted Eve not to eat the fruit of knowledge, what was His intention behind placing the tree within her reach? Similarly why does the Marquis give the key to his wife? Carter suspects that the patriarchs tempt innocent women to transgress so that they can punish them.

Carter envisions a new world through the character of Jean Yves. The character of the blind piano tuner is introduced to envision an alternate masculinity which is sensitive, democratic and not voyeuristic. Yves is blind which frees his wife from his visual assessment and saves her from being trapped once again within the male gaze.

"The Snow Child" is another tale with a young, powerless female protagonist under the domination of an older powerful male. In the common version of the Snow White tale, except that collected by Brothers Grimm, the birth of Snow White is a result of her mother's desire. According to Kaiser "The Snow Child" is a stark, two page version of "Snow White", reducing the fairy tale to its skeletal outlines as a "fable of incest". Carter subverts the plot of the Snow White tale to show that the girl child takes birth as a result of her father's desire rather than her mother's, in order to delineate the themes of incest and patriarchal power. The small story crisply tells an allegorical tale of women's dependence on men for social and monetary power and their use of sexuality for barter. The Countess could also be read as a copy of Sade's Juliette, whereas the child is a creature of nature. Both the women though opposite in nature are dependent on the man for power and are shown as naked without his support. The rivalry between the mother and daughter for patriarchal support is made manifest as the struggle for power and survival. The Count is a tyrant who has the right to have both the girl and the wife, unlike in the traditional tale where he has to choose between the wife and the child. The Snow Child melts before the Count can possess her which shows according to Makinen "the unattainability and constant deferral of desire" (Makinen 30).

The "Erl King" is based on a German legend where an evil spirit haunts the Black Forest and tempts the travellers to their doom. Carter's version of the legend is a critique of romantic fetishizing. The Erl King has the traits of a hermaphrodite and is almost feminine in his romantic lure. Like the Pied Piper of Hamelin and Orpheus he lures the narrator to her golden cage through musical enchantment. He is also a hunter, lover and vampire. Like Bluebeard he collects birds and keeps them in cages as trophies. The tale metaphorically represents love hate relationship, trap of idealised domesticity and the commodifying male gaze. Makinen says: "'Erl-King' is a complex rendition of a subjective collusion with objectivity and entrapment within the male gaze" (30). The story is also a critique of romantic love in which women suffer a complete loss of identity while aspiring for a complete unification with the lover. The text clearly depicts the protagonist's insatiable desire for consumption by the Erl King which leads both to unity and annihilation.

Carter's tales blast the stereotype of pure and innocent woman by giving subversive roles to women. The portrayals are unconventional and shocking which make the reader uncomfortable about easy assumptions regarding women. Her women are active, not passive; they are the subject, not the object of passion. Carter explains her strategy thus:

> Beauty, youth and innocence in women give them an artificial ascendancy over a world that allots them love and admiration to precisely the extent a beautiful, young and innocent woman is deprived of the ability to act in the world. She is compensated for her defencelessness by a convention of respect which is largely false. Herself mystified by herself as Blessed Virgin, she has no notion at all of who she is except in fantasy. (*The Sadeian Woman* 73)

In her version of fairy tales the Red Riding Hood, Sleeping Beauties and Snow Whites are as sexual as their mothers and witches. The Red Riding Hood in "The Company of Wolves" is neither little nor naive, and she also knows well that she is nobody's meat. Carter's protagonist is on the verge of womanhood and has a strong survival instinct. The red cloak is read by Carter as "red as the blood she must spill" ("The Company of Wolves" 117). The red hood also connotes the sacrificial role given to her. Therefore Carter's Red Riding Hood throws it in fire along with her mental inhibitions before bedding the wolf. She refuses to feel fear and joins the wolf in her own defloration, and the wolf ends up being tamed by the girl. The legends about wolves in the beginning of the tale tell us that wolf is nothing but the personification of human fear. The girl overpowers her fear and thus overpowers the wolf. She is a wise child: "Since fear did her no good. She ceased to be afraid". Jack Zipes points out in "The Trials and Tribulations of Little Red Riding Hood" that the popular forms of Red Riding Hood tale reflect men's fear of women's sexuality by blaming the girl for befriending the wolf and being responsible for her own death or symbolic rape. Zipes notes that Carter by contrast, shows a strong-minded girl who can fend for herself and tames the wolf through a positive use of her sexuality (56-7).

In "The Company of Wolves" Carter transforms a tale which dramatizes the brutal subjugation of women by the patriarchal order into a story of the, "sexual maturation and potency of a woman who rejects male domination" (Francis 93). Carter subverts the moralities about prohibiting girls from talking to strange men and being unwisely late as given in the tale by Perrault:

> Little girls, this seems to say,
> Never stop upon your way.
> Never trust a stranger-friend;
> No one knows how it will end.
> As you're pretty, so be wise;
> Wolves may lurk in every guise.
> Handsome they may be, and kind,
> Gay, or charming never mind!
> Now, as then, 'tis simple truth—
> Sweetest tongue has sharpest tooth!
> (Perrault *The Tales of Mother Goose* "Red Riding Hood")

Carter shifts the moral from fearing men to fearing being dominated by men. "The Company of Wolves" and "The Tigers Bride" explicate the flexibility and strength of girls who adapt to the otherness of their animal lovers. These are tales of 'becoming' where the female protagonists become animal as a result of self-exploration. David Punter observes in "Postcolonial Imaginings" that the werewolf itself is a symbol of becoming and the malleability of flesh. The girls in "The Company of Wolves" and "The Tiger's Bride" stretch themselves to meet the other consciousness, the self of the wolf and tiger, non-human and ferocious. Wendy Swyt says:

> These narrative transformations, or 'becomings' as Deleuze and Guattari term them, suggest a (dis)ordering that explodes the 'natural' sublimation of civilised glances and table manners that hold the binaries of purity/evil, subject/object, and beast/girl... The werewolf serves as a challenge to the fixed traits and social definitions that establish boundaries between self and Other, the stable community and the depths of the forest. The becoming-wolf exists in the ruptures of social order, implying illegal alliances, strange couplings and pacts that threaten the very category of body. (Swyt 1-2)

The Beauties deny being a part of the male economy and refuse to gain love through either stooping or pretending to be foolish. They are powerful and strong women who win over men by being equally sexual and ambitious. "The Tiger's Bride" is a subversive take on the Beauty and the Beast tale. In Carter's version the Beast does not transform into a handsome prince through Beauty's love, instead Beauty becomes the tiger's bride by becoming an animal, a tigress. The Beast is also not majestic or ferocious. Rather he is a shy tiger, ashamed of his identity. Due to his inferior status as an animal among humans, he tries to masquerade as a man by wearing nicely tailored suits, masks and gloves to hide his hairy face and body. He avoids speaking and walks on hind legs as a homo-erectus. The reader automatically apprehends him as a being waiting for freedom from inhibitions, waiting for the kiss of acceptance.

Beauty, on the other hand, is proud and confident. Subverting the idea of Oedipal bonding between the father and daughter, Carter makes Beauty reject her father for being undeserving of her love and chooses the Beast instead. Once lost by her father at a game of cards, she starts living with the beast at her own terms. She also denies being commodified as a passive object of desire both by her father and the beast. When a view of her body is desired by the Beast she demands that her face remains covered which would successfully dissociate her from the process of her objectification. She does not fail even to hurt the Beast in order to awaken in him a sense of human dignity and respect for her autonomy. Beauty's character is reconceptualised as a thing wild and untamed right since her childhood. She has always rejected compliance and preferred freedom. Not being intimidated by the Beast's desire, she laughs out loud and selects the moment of her rendezvous with the tiger. She allows her skin to be ripped off by the rough tongue of the tiger and stands clad in a "patina of shining hair". Carter deconstructs the notion of a stable identity and biological determinism by using sartorial metaphors.

Carter problematizes the presence of a strict boundary between animals and humans and makes it permeable by transforming Beauty into a tigress, through the rejection of her false skin which she wore like all the other artificial appendages of civilization. The Beast is not a beast as a result of some curse. On the contrary, the girl is a girl due to the superficially imposed culture and her clothes. The text of "The Tiger's Bride" is also full of examples from the old wives tales about other liminal beings who inhabit the border spaces between humans and animals, for example, the bear man and tiger man.

Using the "ambidexterity of postcolonialism", Carter excessively exaggerates the innocence and purity of Beauty in "The Courtship of Mr Lyon". She is shown as an unscarred child of nature who can get soiled by a mere whiff of human civilization. She is almost mythical in her virtues and appears as a repository of the wish fulfilling fantasies of men about women. The Beast is also kind and gentle. His generosity to Beauty's father as well as his unconditional love for Beauty, subvert the mythical otherness of creatures like him. He also feels reciprocal awe and fear of Beauty which inscribes his similarity with human beings. Though initially Beauty is not able to overcome her fear and scepticism about the feline otherness of the Beast, she is slowly able to cross the superficial barrier. Carter's aim here is to fracture the stability of the unitary subject and open up the possibilities of new modes of being for the marginalised individuals. A comparative analysis of this story could be done with "The Tiger's Bride". In the former the humanity of the beast is revealed while in the latter the beastliness of the girl is made manifest.

"The Werewolf" presents the grandmother of Red Riding Hood as the werewolf, which foregrounds mother-daughter rivalry for power and autonomy. The girl is again a brave and unintimidated young lady. She chops off the paw of the wolf threatening her, and Carter tells us that the wolf "let out a gulp, almost a sob...wolves are less brave than they seem" (*The Bloody Chamber*, 109). Sarah Gamble interprets that making the grandmother the wolf suggests that to be a mature woman means to be sexual and animal. This horrifies the young girl. She calls the neighbours who drive the werewolf grandmother out of the house and stone her to death. In the end, she is shown as living in the grandmother's house and prospering. Gamble comments that: "Little Red Riding Hood may have been initially repulsed by the knowledge that becoming an adult woman will involve acknowledging the animal in herself" but her decision to remain in her grandmother's house declares "her readiness to grow up" (Gamble *The Fiction of Angela Carter*, 127).

Carter rewrites the ideological structures of the original tales and rewards her women for curiosity and sexual adventures instead of punishing them. Peter Childs observes that the value of *BC* is because it explores "the possibility of alternative gender roles across a spectrum of different stories that in their original written forms offered only stereotypes of female passivity" (Childs 121). *BC* therefore exemplifies Carter's enduring refusal to allow women the consolatory role of victim. These heroines do not "fantastically lie back and think of England, but instead join in, often enthusiastically, the process of their own defloration" (Gamble *Angela Carter*, 159).

Carter was also interested in the gothic and cruel tales of horror dealing with the imagery of the unconscious. Grotesque is her favourite motif, and through it she explores new realms of alterneity. She subverts the convention of fiction writing by introducing the grotesque as a part of the mainstream literature. She also presents the marginalised individuals like the vampire, the werewolf and the tiger in new ways, at times more vulnerable than human beings, in order to deconstruct the structures of power. "The Lady of the House of Love" deconstructs the "Sleeping Beauty" tale and the Transylvanian vampire tales.

Generally the wolves and vampires represent sadistic domination and therefore are envisioned as males, but Carter makes her vampire a female which subverts the stereotypical active male and passive female sexuality. In "The Lady of the House of Love" the woman is the aggressor and the male a virgin victim. Carter makes the portrayal of the Lady unreal to showcase her identity as a product of the popular imagination. She is a concretisation of people's fantasies, a manifestation of collective projections about the dangerous femininity. According to Merja Makinen "these are late twentieth-century adult fairy-tales conscious of their own fictive status and so questioning the very constructions of roles while asserting them" (24).

In the tale, Carter also interrogates issues like compulsive behaviour, the duality of victim/victimiser roles and the fixity of character. Talking of the compulsive behaviour of the sadists, Carter questions: "Can a bird sing only the song it knows or can it learn a new song?" (Carter, *The Lady of the House of Love*, 93). The possibility of learning a new song opens up the possibility of change within the perceived essential character. In the end, the lady vampire defeats the "ancestral desire" and spares the young British army officer. She is the arch femme fatale, but she is herself vulnerable and dies in the end. According to Makinen, Carter is "constructing a complex vision of female psychosexuality, through her invoking of violence as well as the erotic" (28).

"Puss in Boots" has a cynical tom cat as the protagonist who helps his master in various notorious adventures from stealing food to finding love. Puss views human love and desire with cynicism. Puss's narration, which is in a light hearted commedia del' arte manner, celebrates sexuality and separates it from romanticism. The story itself is a satire on the idea of platonic love which appears impossible from the point of view of a cat. Through the story Carter aims at freeing women from unreal idealizations. Chastity and purity are being mocked at through the portrayal of the heroine who assists in the murder of her miser and impotent husband and marries her lecherous lover. The woman acknowledges her desire and behaves against the dictates of wifely virtues while being both kind and generous. She is not immoral yet she does not let the opportunity to be free slip through her hands. The lover's licentiousness and rakishness get approval by the fun loving animal narrator. According to Margaret Atwood (1994):

> "Puss in Boots" is above all a hymn to here-and-now common sensual pleasure, to ordinary human love, to slap-and-tickle delight—not as an object to be won, achieved or stolen, nor to be reserved by the rich and privileged for themselves, as in de Sade, but available to all, tabby cats as well as young lads and lasses. (qtd. in Peach 132)

Though being a self-professed feminist, Carter's alliance with feminism is considered ambiguous by the critics. Some critics align her views with the post-feminist ideology. She opposes the misogynistic assumptions of the anatomical lack in Freudian psychoanalysis, but she also criticises the radical feminist movement through the portrayal of Mother in *PNE*. She subverts the French feminists' association of the feminine with the unconscious by creating male characters like Dr Hoffman who figure female desire and mocks at the feminist idea about the pre-Oedipal as a wonderful maternal space outside the symbolic order. Carter's imagination is not inspired by any ideology or critical approach, so the feminists find it hard to put her work in any political or cultural orthodoxy. The most important contribution of Carter's to feminism is her assertion that "there is no single female voice for portraying an authentic female experience" (Nicol 141). According to Meaney, "Carter's fiction and theory stress the danger of enclosure more often than they celebrate marginality" (86).

Though Carter alludes to Adorno, Barthes, Bataille, Fanon, Foucault, Klein, Lacan, Freud, Marx, Bakhtin, Levi-Strauss, Gramsci and Benjamin in her works, she does not owe her allegiance to any and her fiction remains disconcertingly elusive. While commenting on Carter's fiction, Alison Easton warns the readers that "Carter declared war on the myths of Western culture, and we need to be careful not to create new grand narratives out of favoured theorists."

WORKS CITED

Alexander, Flora. *Contemporary Women Novelists: Modern Fiction*. New York: Edward Arnold, 1989. Print.

Aristotle. *On the Generation of Animals*. Trans. Arthur Platt. eBooks@ Adelaide. The University of Adelaide library. 25 Aug 2010. Web. 10 May 2012.

Bakhtin, M.M. *Rabelais and his World*. Trans. Hélène Iswolsky. Bloomington: Indiana University Press, 1993. Print.

Baudrillard, Jean. *Screened Out*. Trans. Chris Turner. London: Verso, 2002. Print.

Beauvoir, Simone de. *The Second Sex*. Trans. and ed. H.M. Parshley. Harmondsworth: Penguin 1982. Print.

Butler, Judith. *Gender Trouble: Feminism and the Subversion of Identity*. London: Routledge, 1990. *Questia*. Web. 18 Dec 2010.

Carter, Angela. Interviewed by Les Bedford. "Angela Carter: An Interview". Sheffield: Sheffield University Television, 1977.

——. "Notes from the Frontline": *On Gender and Writing*. Ed. Micheline Wandor. Pandora, 1983. Web. 10 July 2011.

——. *The Bloody Chamber*. London: Vintage, 1995. Print.

——. *The Infernal Desire Machines of Doctor Hoffman*. London: Penguin, 1982. Print.

——. *The Passion of the New Eve*. London: Virago, 1982. Print.

——. *The Sadeian Woman*. New York: Penguin. 2001. Print.

Childs, Peter. *Contemporary Novelists: British Fiction since 1970*. New York: Palgrave Macmillan, 2005. Print.

Cixous, Helene. *The Laugh of the Medusa*. Trans. Keith Cohen and Paula Cohen. *Signs*. 1(4), 1976. Web. 10 Feb 2012.

Connor, Steven. *The English Novel in History 1950-1995*. London: Routledge, 1996. Print.

Daly, Mary. *Gyn/Ecology: The Metaethics of Radical Feminism*. Beacon Press, 1978. Web. 12 Mar 2012.

Deleuze, Gilles and Felix Guattari. *Anti-Oedipus: Capitalism and Schizophrenia*. Trans. Robert Hurley, Mark Seem and Helen R. Lane. London and New York: Continuum, 2004. Web. 18 Jan 2012.

Dworkin, Andrea. *Our Blood: Prophecies and Discourses on Sexual Politics*. The Women's Press (1982). Print.

Easton, Alison. "Introduction: Reading Angela Carter". *New Casebooks: Angela Carter*. London: Macmillan Press Ltd., 2000. Print.

Eisentein, Hester. *Contemporary Feminist Thought*. London: Unwin Paperbacks, 1984. Print.

Filmer, Kath ed. *Twentieth Century Fantasies*. London: Macmillan, 1992. Print.

Foucault, Michel. *The History of Sexuality*. Vol 1. London: Penguin, 1990. Print.

Francis, Anne Cranny. *Feminist Fiction: Feminist Uses of Generic Fiction*. Oxford: Polity Press, 1990. Print.

Gamble, Sarah. *Angela Carter: A Literary Life*. New York: Palgrave Macmillan, 2006. Print.

——. Ed. *The Fiction of Angela Carter: A Reader's Guide to Essential Criticism*. New York: Palgrave Macmillan, 2001. Print.

Haffenden, John. "Magical Mannerist: John Haffenden Talks to Angela Carter". *The Literary Review* (November, 1984). Web.

Haraway, Donna J. "The Promises of Monsters: A Regenerative Poetics for Inappropriate/d Others". Grossberg et al, eds. *Cultural Studies*. New York: Routledge, 1992. Print.

Head, Dominic. *The Cambridge Introduction to Modern British Fiction 1950-2000*. UK: Cambridge University Press, 2002. Print.

Irigaray, Luce. *Je Tu Nous: Towards a Culture of Difference*. NY: Routledge, 1993. Print.

Johnson, Heather. "Textualising the Double-gendered Body: Forms of the Grotesque in *The Passion of New Eve*". Ed. Alison Easton. *New Casebooks: Angela Carter*. London: Macmillan Press Ltd., 2000. Print.

Hunt, Anna. "The Margins of the Imaginative Life': The Abject and the Grotesque in Angela Carter and Jonathan Swift". Ed Rebecca Munford. *Re-Visiting Angela Carter. Texts, Contexts, Intertexts*. New York: Palgrave Macmillan, 2006. Print.

Kaiser, Mary. "Fairy Tale as Sexual Allegory: Intertextuality in Angela Carter's The Bloody Chamber". *The Review of Contemporary Fiction* 14.3 (1994). *Questia*. Web. 21 May 2011.

Keenan, Sally. "Angela Carter's *The Sadeian Woman*: Feminism as Treason". Ed. Alison Easton. *New Casebooks: Angela Carter*. London: Macmillan Press Ltd., 2000. Print.

Kristeva, Julia. *Revolution in Poetic Language*. New York: Columbia University Press, 1984. Print.

——. *Powers of Horror: An Essay on Abjection*. New York: Columbia University Press, 1982. Print.

Grimm, Jacob and Wilhelm Grimm. *Grimm's Fairy Tales*. Trans. Edgar Taylor and Marian Edwardes. *PublicLiterature.org*. Web. 18 May 2012.

Lacan, Jacques. *The Seminars of Jacques Lacan*. Web. 18 May 2012.

Makinen, Merja. "Angela Carter's *The Bloody Chamber* and the Decolonisation of Feminine Sexuality". Ed. Alison Easton. *New Casebooks: Angela Carter*. London: Macmillan Press Ltd., 2000. Print.

Matus, Jill. "Blonde, Black and Hottentot Venus: Context and Critique in Angela Carter's 'Black Venus'". *New Casebooks: Angela Carter*. London: Macmillan Press Ltd., 2000. Print.

Meaney, Gerardine. "History and Women's Time: *Heroes and Villains*". Ed. Alison Easton. *New Casebooks: Angela Carter*. London: Macmillan Press Ltd., 2000. Print.

Moi, Toril. *Sexual/Texual Politics*. Routledge, 2002. Web. 12 Dec 2011.

Monday, Ralph. "Adam and Lilith: Thanatos and the Resurrection of the Archetype." *The Mystica*. 7 May 2012. Web. 18 May 2012.

Neu, Jerome. Ed. *The Cambridge Companion to Freud*. Cambridge: Cambridge University Press, 1991. Print.

Nicol, Bran. *The Cambridge Introduction to Postmodern Fiction*. UK: Cambridge University Press, 2009. Print.

Palmer, Paulina. "From Coded Mannequin to Bird Woman: Angela Carter's Magic Flight". *Women Reading Women's Writing*. New York: 1987. Print.

Peach, Linden. *Modern Novelists: Angela Carter*. London: Macmillan, 1998. Print.

Perrault, Charles. *The Tales of Mother Goose*. *Ciff Ciaff: Old Tales*. Web. 18 May 2012.

Plato. "Phaedrus". Trans. Alexander Nehamas and Paul Woodruff. *Plato: Complete Works*. Ed. John M. Cooper. Web. 14 Feb 2010.

——. *The Republic*. Trans. Benjamin Jowett. *ebooks @adelaide*. 29 Aug 2010 Web. 26 Nov 2011.

Punter, David ed. *A Companion to the Gothic*. Oxford: Blackwell Publishers, 2000. Print.

——. *Postcolonial Imaginings: Fictions of a New World Order*. New Delhi: Atlantic Publishers and Distributors, 2000. Print.

Rich, Adrienne. *Of Woman Born: Motherhood as Experience and Institution*. 1977. *History is a Weapon*. Web. 17 May 2012.

Robinson, Sally. *Engendering the Subject: Gender and Self-Representation in Contemporary Women's Fiction*. New York: State University of New York Press, 1991. Print.

Robinson, Sally. "The Anti-Hero as Oedipus: Gender and the Postmodern Narrative in The Infernal Desire of Doctor Hoffman". Ed. Alison Easton. *Angela Carter: New Casebooks. London:* Macmillan Press Ltd., 2000. Print.

Russo, Mary. *The Female Grotesque: Risk, Excess and Modernity.* London: Routledge, 1994. Print.

Sade, Marquis de. *Juliette*. Trans. Austryn Wainhouse. New York: Grove Press, 1968. Print.

——. *Justine or Good Conduct Well Chastised. Scribd*. Web. 18 May 2012.

Sage, Lorna. *Angela Carter*. Plymouth: Northcote House, 1994. Print.

Sage, Lorna. "A Savage Sideshadow". *New Review* 4 (July 1977). Web. 3 March 2012. Print.

Sanders, Julie. "Bubblegum and Revolution: Angela Carter's Hybrid Shakespeare". Ed Rebecca Munford. *Re-Visiting Angela Carter. Texts, Contexts, Intertexts*. New York: Palgrave Macmillan, 2006. Print.

Suleiman, Susan Rubin. *Subversive Intent: Gender, Politics and the Avant-Garde*. US: Harvard University Press, 1990. Print.

Sheets, Robin Ann. "Pornography, Fairy Tales and Feminism: Angela Carter's *The Bloody Chamber*". *Journal of the History of Sexuality* 1.4 (1991). *Questia*. Web. 21 May 2011.

Swyt, Wendy. ""Wolfings": Angela Carter's Becoming-Narrative". *Studies in Short Fiction* 33.3 (1996): 315+. *Questia*. Web. 18 Dec. 2010.

Woolf Virginia. *A Room of One's Own*. London: Penguin, 1945. Print.

Tonkin, Maggie. "Albertine/a the Ambiguous: Angela Carter's Reconfiguration of Marcel Proust's Modernist Muse". Ed. Rebecca Munford. *Re-Visiting Angela Carter. Texts, Contexts, Intertexts*. New York: Palgrave Macmillan, 2006. Print.

Zipes, Jack. *Breaking the Magic Spell: Radical Theories of Folk and Fairy Tales*. Kentucky: The University Press of Kentucky, 2002. Print.

——. *Fairy Tales and the Art of Subversion*. London: Routledge, 1988. Print.

——. *The Trials and Tribulations of Little Red Riding Hood: Versions of the Tale in Sociocultural Context*. Heinemann, 1983. Print.

4

Re-Writing Religion and Patriarchy: Michele Roberts's Novels

> As a young writer in the 1970s, entering a literary world that was still dominated by masculine precepts and models, I sought for a tradition of fiction-writing that suggested possibilities of writing riskily, authentically, differently. (Roberts "The Novels of Colette")

Roberts's works are largely shaped by the consciousness of her gender. Being brought up and educated as a Catholic she feels that women have to overcome their annoyance for being blamed for the Fall of Man so that they "can start to enjoy the bizarre ways in which women are represented in religious culture and what it suggests about women's perceived relationship to God" (*Food, Sex and God* 39).

Catholicism has always been the subject of research by historians and feminists who study the presence of misogyny in various religions of the world. According to Jeana Del Rosso, "Women cannot dispense the holy sacraments" in Catholicism and may "receive only six of the seven sacraments" (2). Early Church fathers, like Augustine, Jerome and Aquinas (4th, 5th and 13th century), considered humans dualistic in nature, formed of body and spirit with body to be rejected as inferior and bestial. This was connected with gender dualism where women were associated with the body and the reproductive processes, and men to the intellect or spirit. Thus women were considered subordinate to men and also a danger to male salvation. In the late medieval period woman's body was regarded with disgust as something which was always dirty. Jeana Del Rosso notes that knowledge was denied to women in Catholicism and men became the only proprietors of religion, morality and truth. The convent was the only place where women could aspire to understand and practice religion, but unfortunately the convents were also heavily under papal authority and became another vehicle for repression. Reflecting on the effect of Catholic education on her early childhood Roberts says:

> What a start in life, to grow up believing, as I did, that you are responsible for Christ's agonising death. A double burden of guilt if you are female, since we all know the gender of the one lusting after food and the knowledge in the garden of Eden and so setting the whole caravan of blame and self-hate in motion. (*Food, Sex and God* 33)

The Church is read by the critics of Christianity as a place where passivity and submissiveness are instilled in women. It represents the imperial power which abuses the weak, supports the rich and acts as a lunatic or political asylum. Feminist theologians like Mary Daly in *The Church and the Second Sex (*1968*)*, Rosemary Radford Ruether in *Sexism and God-Talk: Towards a Feminist Theology* (1993), Elizabeth Schussler-Fiorenza in *In Memory of Her: A Feminist Theological Reconstruction of Christian Origins* (1983) have researched extensively on sexism in Christianity. While a few critics have proved that the true basis of Christianity was a pro-female ideology kept hidden by Catholicism, others consider Christianity as innately patriarchal. According to the latter, Old Testament has inverted the natural order of procreation in the form of the Creation myth where man is created first and woman is shown as being created out of his rib. Christianity also instructs that all the pains borne by mortals are a result of Woman's sinful nature. Thus a great body of literature from the advent of Christianity is found to be phallo-centric and phallo-cratic.

Contemporary women writers consider the religious texts like the Bible as patriarchal because they enforce the rule of the male in society, and they rewrite the stories of the female counterparts of the male heroes in order to subvert their phallocentricity. Contemporary Catholic women writers like Sara Maitland, Mary Gordon, Mary Mc Carthy and Michele Roberts have also interrogated the maligning of female sexuality in Catholicism which is seen as a sign of madness or evil by both clergy and medical practitioners. They rewrite both sexuality and madness in larger terms and look at the influence of the virgin/whore dichotomy in Catholicism on women's identity formation. Mary Daly states in *The Church and the Second Sex* that women in Christianity are considered solely in terms of virgin, bride and mother. Thus they are defined only through their sexual relation to men.

Michele Roberts dislikes Catholicism for being a religion which gets its power by instilling guilt in its followers. She once said to Newman Jenny in an interview that she was "made" a writer because women were seen as the source of evil in her religion, that they "had to be forgiven for being women" and "had to get over having the bodies we had". She further states that "This really pushed me to wanting to write as a way of opposing what was very constricting and actually painful in my life".

A look at the New Testament of the Bible and the Gospels brings out a very negative depiction of women. The characterization of women in these texts is limited and they are given almost a zero narrative role. Right from the depiction of the female figures in the Bible in terms of virgin/whore dichotomy to the imposition of the Original Sin on women, a lot of harm has been done to the process of identity formation in women. The female figures in the Bible are either passive or asexual like The Virgin, an impossible ideal, or obedient to a fault like Mrs Noah who follows every command of her husband blindly and against reason. Some like Mary Magdalene, who by the force of their personalities appear to break the binary structures of patriarchy, are deliberately defiled as profligate women or prostitutes.

The Secret Gospel of Mary Magdalene deconstructs the biased portrayal of Mary Magdalene in the Gospels and re-visions the character of Jesus and Mary in order to claim sexual and spiritual freedom for women. The book deals with the issues of religious tolerance, freedom for women and gender discrimination. It cross-examines the relevance of Christian beliefs and practices while valorizing women as visionaries and philosophers.

SG primarily subverts the images of women in the Bible, the Gospels, the modern Christ literature and films based on Catholic assumptions. *SG* was first published as *The Wild Girl* in 1984. It was translated in German in 1986 and then reissued in 2007 with the current title. Roberts mentions in the preface of the book that the inspiration to write this came from her intense desire to find solutions to the questions like "why traditional Catholic theology asserted that single women could not be both sexy and holy", "why the male-dominated church split women into holy sexless mothers and bad sexy whores" and "why priests and theologians seemed so frightened of women and so determined to keep women in a narrow corner, firmly under control".

In *SG* Roberts takes up one woman for re-assessment whose image Christianity has harmed the most, Mary Magdalene. The figure of Mary Magdalene is surrounded by many debates about her identity and relation to nature. A number of legends and the preaching of the early Church portray her as a prostitute who was purified of her sins by Christ's grace. According to Luke 8:2 and Mark 16:9, Jesus cleansed Mary Magdalene of "seven demons". Some major Christian saints, including Saint Bede and Saint Gregory, interpret the seven devils to signify that she was full of vices. Contemporary scholars and especially feminists believe that she was a holy lady and Christ's consort who suffered defamation by the power thirsty male followers of Christ. They believe that her identification with the sinful woman who wipes Jesus's feet with her hair is unjust. According to John Mac Arthur, Mary was a devout follower of Christ and was present during his Crucifixion. He further elucidates that according to the four Gospels in the Christian New Testament, she was the first person to see the resurrected Christ. According to Karen L. King:

> In the early Christian writings she is also called "the apostles to the apostles". In apocryphal and Gnostic texts she is

also portrayed as a visionary and the leader of the early movement, and as the one who was loved by Jesus more than the other disciples. She was also considered to have a deeper understanding of the teachings of Christ.

Other important modern scholars who have studied the feminist interpretation of the gospels and Gnostic works are Kevin Brown and William R. Telford. Brown believes that "feminist interpretation has debunked the image of the fallen and repentant Magdalene, substituting the figure of Mary Magdalene as the intrepid and faithful disciple of Jesus". He also notes that "apart from the other Mary, Mary the mother of Jesus, no other woman character in the Christian Scriptures has received as much attention" and that "Mary Magdalene is a character found in all of the canonical gospels", features in "11 gnostic/apocryphal works, where sometimes she is a major character"(291).

William R. Telford remarks that later Christian tradition describes Mary Magdalene in paradoxical ways as "the great sinner" (her seven demons as the seven deadly sins); the sensual woman (her demonic possession due supremely to sexual obsession); the fallen maiden rescued from moral depravity; the apostle to the apostles; the first missionary preacher sent to France, and so on (371), but Gnostics texts portray her in more radical ways as "the lover, companion, and friend of Jesus; the rival to the male disciples and especially Peter, and the receiver of divine revelations" (371).

Michele Roberts portrays Mary as a composite character, as a blend of three Marys found in the Gospels and the Bible: Mary Magdalene, Mary of Bethany and the sinful Mary who anointed Christ. William R. Telford explains Roberts take on the issue thus: "Roberts' Mary Magdalene combines the canonical Mary Magdalene (cf. Mark 15:40, 47; 16:1–8 parr; Luke 8:2; John 20:1–18) with Mary of Bethany, the sister of Lazarus and Martha (John 11:1–46; 12:1–8; cf. Luke 10:38–42)" (371) and that "at a number of points, Roberts has exercised her literary prerogative in adding to or altering the biblical or apocryphal texts in developing the characterization" (371).

Roberts conceives Mary Magdalene as the composer of the only gospel by a woman. She writes in the preface to *SG*: “The figure of Mary Magdalene presented herself through dreams” and “I imagined the gospel that she might have written, which would have been suppressed as a heretical document”. This fifth gospel written by a female is contrary in theme and style to the gospels by Matthew, Mark, Luke and John. In her memoir called *Paper Houses* Roberts talks of the damage done to women by Catholicism which she explores in *SG* while also thinking of ways to recover from it. Quite subversive in its nature the book makes use of symbols and metaphors to deconstruct the binaries and reclaim both sexual and spiritual powers for women.

Roberts has always been very sensitive to the importance of freedom for women which she explores in her work. To delineate this theme Roberts has given her novels the Bildungsroman form where women are shown experimenting with ‘becoming’ or ‘unbecoming’ what they are expected to be by the society in terms of gender. According to Du Plessis:

> Michele Roberts's first three novels, *A Piece of the Night* (1978), *The Visitation* (1983), and *The Wild Girl* (1984), interrogate established notions of history and identity through an unconventional form of Bildungsroman. These narratives are uncomfortable within their covers, wriggling within the confines of the novel as a place in which female characters traditionally have been written as wife, daughter, nun, and whore (qtd. in White).

Roberts re-establishes Mary Magdalene as a girl in need of freedom and acceptance. After the death of her mother, Mary runs away from home in order to escape the fate of womanhood which ailed her mother. She is raped on the highway, at the age of fifteen, by the merchants who treat her as “a wild beast in need of taming” (*SG* 15), but she never takes rape as humiliation, never finds herself responsible for it. She rather starts paying men for favours using her body which was “the only coin” she had and still remains holy and spiritual. Roberts deconstructs all the conventional modes of characterising an ideal woman and makes Mary simultaneously passionate, imaginative and spiritual. Jesus, who is shown as a champion of women's liberation, says to Mary that she is dear to him because she is not an ideal woman, which suggests the hypocrisy underlying the ideal.

SG is at once an elucidation of feminist and post- feminist creative thought. The challenge thrown to narrow-minded certainties encompasses all assumptions of self-righteousness, even those of feminists. Mary finds herself very angry with her brother for his extravagance and irresponsibility, but slowly she masters her anger which gets replaced by forgiveness. Mary finds herself improving with each day as she is filled with love not only for Jesus but for the whole universe. She finds her meanness and pride dissipating. Slowly she even learns to accept Peter, the arch misogynist, as a part of her own self and pardons him for his bias against women.

Mary's vivid dreams and visions form the foreground of the text. Her dream of the origin of the world subverts the traditional creation story of Adam and Eve. In her vision she sees that God is a female called Sophia-Wisdom and gives birth to a son called Ignorance and a daughter called Zoe-Eve. The latter is sent "as an instructor to raise up Adam, in whom there was no waking soul, and to inspire him". It is the children of Ignorance who spread the fiction that Eve was created out of Adam's rib. Thus the dream offers an alternate myth which deconstructs the masculine bias in Christianity.

Jesus is introduced in the book from Mary's point of view. She relates her first meeting with Jesus in which she realizes that he is the new Adam who has the "grace of a woman" (*SG* 79) and is in touch with his feminine side. The relationship of Jesus and Mary includes physical intimacy, and Mary's playful addresses to Jesus as "My dear ape. My monkey husband" (*SG* 95) foregrounds the earthy side of Jesus's character and subverts his flat characterization as the son of God. Jesus preaches egalitarian principles and talks a great deal, on themes such as justice, rights of the poor and the "love of the Most High whom he called our Father and Mother" (*SG* 37).

The stories in the Bible, both in the Old and the New Testaments are based on sets of mutually exclusive binaries like male and female, good and bad, virgin and whore which maintain the structural and thematic stability of the Bible. Jesus does not differentiate between men/women, father/mother, pagan/Christian, light/dark, animal/human, man/woman, life/death, conscious/unconscious, anima/animus, good/evil etc. He gives a speech on the need for men and women to realise the other within their own selves so that they can rise above the narrow limits of self and can be essentially bisexual:

> I myself, Jesus said: shall lead Mary in order to make her male, so that she may become a living spirit resembling you males. For every woman who makes herself male shall enter the Kingdom of Heaven. And I shall lead you, Peter, in order to make you female, so that you may become a living spirit resembling these women. For every man who makes himself female will enter the Kingdom of Heaven. (*SG* 60)

Roberts appears to be considerably influenced by the Jungian concept of anima/animus when she talks about the integration of female anima in male psyche and the male animus in the female psyche. It is a long discourse which could be read as an intertext to the Woolfian concept of androgyny where she opines that an artist should let go the limited gendered self in order to capture the universal spirit, but unlike Virginia Woolf Roberts prefers the word 'bisexual' to 'androgyny' as she makes clear in *Food, Sex and God*.

SG not only subverts the either/or logic but also asserts that the Bible is an insincere documentation of the Christian ideology dictated by Peter who betrayed Christ. Peter is presented as a staunch patriarch, one who calls women unworthy of life and who lays the foundation of present day Christianity after the death of Jesus. He is the one to suggest the division of roles that men and women were to play in the propagation of Christianity. The novel shows how instead of Saint Peter, the first Pope, Jesus entrusted the leadership of the Church to Mary, a woman, who was his closest disciple. The work opens up the possibility of challenging the very base of Christianity by questioning the authority of Peter. *SG* shows that Jesus entrusted his innermost ideas both before and after his crucifixion to Mary, not to Peter or to any of his male followers. Thus there is a suggestion that a woman, Mary, should have been the first Pope.

The influence of women in early Christianity has always been a topic of debate among scholars. Medieval and modern paintings like *Kreuzigung* (1465), *Noli me Tangere* (1524) by Hans Holbein the Younger and *Crucifixion* (1868) by Gabriel Wuger as well as painted glass windows in Cathedrals like *Mary of Magdala at the Empty Tomb Window* at St Matthew Lutheran Church at Charleston, South Carolina are also a testimony to the fact that women played a more influential role in Christianity than is commonly accepted.

The book not only deconstructs the male hierarchy but questions the very nature of Christ by rewriting the myth of Resurrection. Roberts claims that Christ did not resurrect in body, and the resurrection of Christ signifies a spiritual manifestation of Christ in the souls of those who loved him dearly and believed in his philosophy. In *SG*, Mary is the first one to find the tomb of Jesus empty. The first thought that comes to her mind is that "with the Lord's body gone, there would be plenty to believe him resurrected in the body and immortal, that error he had so often warned against" (*SG* 103). According to Roberts, the Resurrection also means the unification of the male and the female in a person's soul. Mary addresses the male disciples after the Resurrection and announces that "the man and the woman within us have become separated and exiled from each other" and "Christ came to repair the separation and to reunite the two" (*SG* 110).

Christianity supports the Eucharist as a symbol of Christ's sacrifice of his body for the sake of humankind. Roberts sees the ceremony as a way of supporting the idea of cannibalism. She also emphasises that the Eucharist should be understood as a metaphor instead of being taken literally:

> I told you: he or she who shall not eat my flesh and drink my blood has not life. What does that mean? It means that my flesh is the word and my blood is Sophia. Receive the spirit and the word and you shall have food and drink and clothing and shall not suffer want. And you souls shall know God

> and shall laugh and dance, free from the bondage of time and ignorance, released, *in this life*, into eternity. (*SG* 111)

Jesus celebrates joy and happiness. For him suffering is a sorry affair and people must avoid it if possible. Right action should be done even if it causes pain, but pain should not be celebrated per se. In this way The Passion of the Christ is also reconceptualised.

The description of the community of Christ's followers in the novel matches with the description of the socialist commune in which Roberts lived as described in *Paper Houses*. Roberts, by introducing the homoerotic relationship in her text, is deliberately undermining the narrative pattern of romance plots, in which the female protagonist represses her zeal to experiment and valorizes heterosexual ties.

While Roberts reconfigures the character of Mary Magdalene and Jesus in *SG* for the purpose of feminist remythologizing, she reworks the Biblical myth of Noah and his Ark in order to envisage a feminist utopia in *The Book of Mrs Noah*. *BMN* is a polyphonic narrative which, like Roberts's Ark, accomodates a number of voices debating with each other on issues about sexual and religious norms, the position of a girl child in the family, the role of women in marriage, the implications of motherhood, the problems faced by women writers, the causes of writer's block and the possibility of finding a new democratic language. Roberts also uses the stories by the Sibyls on the Ark to illustrate her ideas about the importance of food, bonding with the mother and a fruitful relationship between the sexes.

BMN won the W.H. Smith Literary Award in 1992. By bringing to the fore the fictionally sidelined character of Mrs Noah, Roberts delves into the reality of female existence and shows the alternate ways of doing things and decision making. She charts the forbidden emotions and projects the different facets of women's interpersonal relationships. The object of attack here is the Catholic faith which restricts morality and reality to a flat mono-dimensionality in favour of men.

The first person narrator of the book is Jack's wife who is accompanying him to Venice for his research in medicine. It opens with a dream in which the narrator dreams that she is Mrs Noah and sees Noah struck by lightning. This dream is a kind of catharsis of the forbidden desire for freedom from patriarchal subjugation. She also wishes to avenge Noah's betrayal as she feels that Noah has betrayed her by denying her the child she wants. Unlike Antoinette in *WSS* who burns the patriarchal mansion Roberts's protagonists target their husbands to express their ire. Though the women love their husbands, they still want their space and autonomy. Her novel called *Reader, I Married Him* also has a protagonist who murders all her three husbands. Through her, Roberts looks into and questions women's notion of identity before and after feminism.

In the second dream, Mrs Noah sees herself as the Arkivist of an Ark which is a library and a refuge for women. She ensures that her Ark is structured on the principles of equality and liberty. Roberts presents the Ark as a seed of new growth, a womb for rebirth and a bestiary where the phoenix, the bearded lady, the Siamese twins and all those who inhabit the borders are welcome to stay. It is a repository of all human knowledge, literature and experience. The Ark is Roberts's vision of providing a perfect haven for nurturing women's creativity. The companions invited on the Ark are female visionaries called Sibyls. All the Sibyls tell stories to each other one by one in a Chaucerian fashion, which is also a way of celebrating the age old oral tradition of storytelling.

The Sibyls in *BMN* write to find individuation, as a rebellious response to patriarchal oppression. Thus the process becomes an act of healing according to the Jungian theory which illustrates the formation of a coherent personality (*Psychological Types* 1962). The setting of the stories told by the Sibyls ranges from the Old Testament to the fourteenth century, Protestant England, modern time and finally to a dystopian future. Roberts's shows how though the time frame changes, the position of women does not.

The first story in *BMN* reshapes Noah's myth to offer a fresh mode of thinking about the Biblical Flood. Mrs Noah is presented as a shrewish, colourful and earthy woman. She critiques the Judaeo-Christian religion as monotheistic and hegemonic, and she conceptualizes a new religion which would not discriminate against women, would not prescribe the renunciation of bodily pleasures and would be based on happiness "like sweet fresh milk" (*BMN* 73) rather than fear. Mrs. Noah is a thinker who finds her religion through the daily chores:

> God is in my hands as they scrub, wring, knead, scour, caress, sew, carve. I act, I create, and God pours through me. At these times I am not-myself, I go into a strange country. Sometimes I come to with a shock, to find myself kneeling, my forehead bowed to the ground. (*BMN* 72)

Roberts redefines the Flood as the breaking of the waters of the mother earth and the Ark as "the seed of new life" (BMN 74). The destruction of all life on earth is not caused by the wrath of God but is perceived as the inevitable part of the natural cycle of birth and death. Instead of Noah it is Mrs Noah who dreams about the Flood and prescribes the building of an Ark which would become a womb to house the whole of Creation in safety. Noah, her husband, claims that the vision about the Flood and the Ark is a result of his communication with the Father God. When his wife resists he "goes as pale as sour milk" (BMN 77) and threatens: "Don't blaspheme or you'll be cursed and thrown off the Boat" (BMN 77). Prof. Sudha Rai notes that Roberts in BMN rewrites Genesis, accords the suppressed female voices "the power to contest knowledge and truth" and deflates the male characters "to unheroic dimensions" or exposes them "in their anxieties and weaknesses" (25).

Mrs. Noah is given a detailed portrayal as a new eco-feminist who is concerned about the natural balance of elements on Earth and "dreams of harmony between all created things" (*BMN* 87). She is also an animal rights activist who hates the slayers of animals and the tradition of making sacrifices to God: "I swear that I shall never kill an animal again, shall never shed blood again, shall never eat meat again. I am sick of killing and so would your God be if he had any sense" (*BMN* 85). When she witnesses Noah sacrificing a lamb to God, after the Flood, she leaves the family in order to live freely, to meditate and to communicate her desire for equality in a new language. Susan Sellers observes:

> In the new world that follows the Flood, it is her husband's religion that predominates, instituting a regime of mastery and sacrifice. Significantly, Mrs Noah's response is to invent words that will communicate her experience of God as connection, a language she incorporates in her new invention of writing. (75)

Instead of being a blindly devoted wife as depicted in The Old Testament, she becomes a feminist who creates a new language for her daughter-in-law, Sara: "Sara will need to break the circle I drew in two, and find a new world... I've given my words to Sara, to do as she likes with" (*BMN* 89). She wants Sarah to break all the patriarchal closure, deconstruct logocentrism and create a new world.

Among the Sibyls on the Ark one male who represents male pride and chauvinism is also present. He is called the Gaffer which means one who gaffes. The Gaffer keeps gaffing and his statements like "I am truth incarnate. I am incapable of lying" (*BMN* 55), women are "empty to start with" (*BMN* 55), "It's the male who represents humanity, creativity" (*BMN* 56), "It's only frustrated neurotic women who write, women who can't have children" (*BMN* 56), and androgynous means being "more like me" (*BMN* 56), reflect the patriarchal attitude to women's creativity which if not restricted to giving birth, in their opinion, is a folly. By calling such statements gaffes Roberts is deconstructing the relation between pen and phallus according to which writing is a male prerogative. The Sibyls take up the job of opening up such patriarchal stories, like the one about Apollo and Daphne, to new possibilities and making them secular.

Roberts has always inspired her students in creative writing classes to indulge in collective or collaborative writing as a means for young people to learn from each other. She also collaborated in the writing of *Tales I Tell My Mother* in 1978 and *More Tales I Tell My Mother* in 1987. The Sibyls start off with writer's block but slowly become productive through the means of their joint creative effort. Their stories include themes related to the pleasures of eating, the virtues of a clean and healthy body, the fake religious ecstasy achieved through pain, psychological aberrations in religious zealots, healing power of love, position of the girl child in the family, the status of women in marriage before the introduction of the contraceptive pill, denigration of female sexuality, and subverting the romance plots by giving voice to homosexual desire. The last story lends out hope of a generous and loving relation between the sexes when Turtle, a young man, rescues Mouse, his childhood protégé, from a legalized prostitution centre.

The novel is structured in such a way that their storytelling is interrupted by arguments; they contradict and agree with each other on issues related to female identity which is ever changing and indefinable. One of the main topics raised by Roberts is women's zeal for conformity to religious, social and sexual norms which dries up their creativity and leads to writer's block. She wants women to be liberated enough to be able to choose between conformity and non-conformity to these norms. So, on one hand the Babble-on-sibyl cuts down her waist long hair and on the other the Forsaken Sibyl maintains her stack of lip colours and powder.

> The selves that chose to slap on makeup, the selves she feared she was, the selves she feared she might become, that she longed to escape into and towards, all these clamoured for attention and wanted to stop being secret. (*Food, Sex and God* 175)

While visiting the nearby islands, Mrs Noah also meditates on issues related to the unconscious, memory and motherhood. She thinks of reinventing the meaning of "feminine" through restructuring language, contemplates about female sexuality, its repression and the sustenance of patriarchy and misogyny by women who pass on these attitudes to their daughters:

> I could saw off my daughter's clitoris with a razor, my friends holding her down when she screams. To cleanse her, to make her pure, to make her grateful enough to do it herself in turn to her own daughter when the time comes. (*BMN* 134)

Mrs Noah's dream ends with a vision of the sibyls as better adjusted individuals. They are shown as being at complete peace with themselves and their surroundings as they have learnt to let go the false ideals of womanhood and embrace their real selves. In order to do justice to their vocation and interests they take time out for themselves and do what they love. The Deftly Sibyl finds a garden shed as her retreat. The Forsaken Sibyl gets herself a month long job in Italy, on the seventh day decides to break free, hires a motorcycle and roars off up into the hills to see the countryside. The Correct Sibyl becomes less strict with herself. The Babble-on-sibyl and the Re-Vision Sibyl learn to exercise their right to love freely.

The stories and issues taken up in *BMN* aim at removing the film of familiarity from the commonly accepted beliefs and render them suspect. According to Sengupta, "writing and voicing of oppressions in the past are the subversive forces of the semiotic which find expression through Mrs. Noah's diary" (101). *BMN* and *SG* analyze the oppression of women and give expression to the autonomous feminine self. These two texts explore the role of the female artist and art and interrogate the notion of a complete identity for women. *Impossible Saints* (1997) on the other hand takes up the motif of "saint" in Catholic religion and demonstrates that the metaphor of woman as saint is as exploitative as the ideal of angel in the house. She tries to rescue women's biographies from historical inscriptions by men in sexist texts like *The Golden Legend,* and re-inscribes them to offer radically different accounts of the saints' lives. The stories of the eleven women saints along with the life of Roberts's fictional character Josephine, inspired by Saint Teresa of Avila, reveal the patriarchal abuse of women hidden behind the veil of sainthood. *IS* also unravels the secret methods used by women to resist patriarchy and their ways of subverting the restrictive structure from within. Roberts shows how historical women became heretics and found a means of survival in the tyrannical order through dissembling, hiding facts and leading double lives. The text proves that these intelligent women even managed to win accolades from the same institutes which they were demolishing from within.

Roberts observes that historical records are subjective because the historians are also subjects conditioned by their unconscious, their personal past and their desires. She says to Sanchez that an examination of the "Church history will reveal the interest of priests and Popes. And probably, the history written by abbesses will be subjective in another way". Roberts aims at undoing the polarity between novel, history and biography by highlighting the quasi fictional character of both history and biography which rely on personal fears, biases, desires and memory of the writers.

IS revises eleven female saints' lives based on a thirteenth-century text called *The Golden Legend* by Jacobus de Voragine alongside a fictionalized life of Josephine. Roberts subverts and fictionalizes the lives of these women who have been canonised as saints by the church in order to question the concept of the female saint. The title suggests that saints are impossible ideals imposed upon women. Roberts's saints are "impossible saints" because of their transgressions, their sexuality and their independence. Roberts says that she envisions in *IS* "what a modern female saint would be like" (*Food, Sex and God* 195).

Sevinc Ozer comments that Roberts "locates her novel within the borders of the Roman Empire during the period of the first Christians spreading the new religion" and captures how women's status and their conditions haven't changed since those days. Starting from individual cases, she is able to make generalisations about the problems faced by women. In rewriting the saints' lives and offering fictionalised alternatives to their historical counterparts, Roberts's novel is engaged in an interrogation of history and one can read *IS* through Adrienne Rich's definition of revision as "the act of looking back, of seeing with fresh eyes, of entering an old text from a new critical direction". Rich argues in her essay "When We Dead Awaken", named after a play by the feminist playwright Henrik Ibsen, that women have lead their lives sleepwalking and dreaming about ideal domesticity which has proved harmful for both the sexes. She uses the word "dead" to imply that not to speak, not to awaken into consciousness of one's true identity is to die. She says that the "drive to self-knowledge" in women is more than a search for identity as it is also a "refusal of the self-destructiveness of male-dominated society". Hence she drives home the point that re-visioning old stories means refusing to pass on tradition which would be "an act of survival". Thus by rewriting these stories Roberts not only denies being a carrier of "tradition" but to "break its hold over us" as suggested by Rich. Roberts says to Rodriguez: "Because women's autobiographies have been lost, because women have not been encouraged to tell their life stories, I want to tell them; I want to rescue women from history". She explores the limits of traditional historiography and demystifies the female prototype in patriarchal Christian discourse.

Josephine's story is partly inspired by the life of Saint Teresa of Avila, a Carmelite nun and a predecessor to Therese Martin. Saint Teresa of Avila is famous for the religious reforms she brought into effect. In an interview with Rodriguez Roberts says that Teresa of Avila was:

> Teresa of Avila...she was almost a heretic, all the way through. I read and read and read about her when I was writing *Impossible Saints*, and it was so interesting how she became very, very closed to being condemned by the Inquisition. So that fascinates me, because that's my image of the feminist actually, it's the heretic.

Josephine faces the same fate as a result of her independent thinking and free spirit. Josephine escapes the cruel investigation of the Catholic priests on the charge of heresy by lying in her first autobiography called *Life*. She hides facts, calls herself a sinner and falsely praises the male inspectors for their kindness.

> "She kept one step ahead of them in the game and did not let them suspect. The sentences she wrote knelt down. Her prose was modest, humble and grateful. It lowered its eyes and kissed the ground". (*IS* 33)

Ironically, the inspectors remain oblivious to the subtext of Josephine's *Life* which exists in silences.

> When you read Josephine's official *Life*, the one that saved her from being burned at the stake, if you read it very carefully, you start to get a smell, almost, of something awkward, something missing, a bulge under the graceful phrase here, a crack in the grammar there, one sentence that tails off and another that hastily starts, something left out, shouting from the margins, in the gaps between (*IS* 34).

The second autobiography of Josephine called *Life* is a true account of her beliefs and practices and so had to be kept hidden from the inspectors. To create this secret document she rolls each leaf of her autobiography into beads which she strings together in the form of a rosary and gifts it to her niece Isabel.

In an article called "The Little Flower" which speaks about the writings of another Carmelite nun called Therese Martin, a successor to Saint Teresa of Avila, Roberts explains how women know how to hide their true intent in a disguised prose style, the way Josephine does in *IS*. Therese Martin was named after Saint Teresa of Avila and later became known as "The Little Flower". She died of tuberculosis in a dingy convent in Lisieux, northern France at the age of twenty four. She was "swiftly canonized by a Pope eager to promote sexless and self-sacrificing ideals of womanhood" and became the third female doctor of the Church. Her autobiography called the *Story of a Soul*, some poems, short plays, notes and letters were published posthumously. Roberts comments that Therese Martin's "pious effusions are hopelessly saturated with the sentimental excesses of genteel bourgeois fervour... she concealed her toughness and willpower, in her writings at least, under a cloak of sugar-sweet childishness and repression." Roberts perceives "the gap between the carapace of goodness smothering the surface of her texts and the soft drumbeat of anger and desire pulsing underneath in images and slips". Roberts tells Sanchez:

> I'm telling stories about women who fight back, who might be crushed by the Church in some ways, but might find ways, even through the Church, to fight back. But it's not that the Church liberates women. The Church, I think, is misogynistic and oppressive and terrible. The Catholic Church is a force of dreadfulness in history, but women are very clever. They fight back. They become heretics. They involve themselves in alternative religions. They become poets.

Roberts once intended to be a nun but gave up the idea when she realised that the nuns are forbidden to indulge in intellectual debates. They have to suit themselves to the liking of the male ecclesiasts and do not have much independence in religious matters. One could find in Roberts's works a clear mockery of the nun's compliance to the Catholic order and their more than dull existence in the convent. She even effaces the falsely idealized characterization of the nuns as detached or asexual females and tries to free them from unreasonable expectations. Her portrayal of the nuns includes emotions of jealousy and rivalry. They chatter and gossip, seek attention and are sensual. "If you didn't join in they thought you were a snob forever in a huff despising them and they would bang past your chair in the library or the dining-room extra loudly, upsetting your book or your plate, just to show they didn't care" (*IS* 100).

The dependence of churches on relics, genuine or fake, for sustenance is the object of subversion in the novel. Long after Josephine's burial, her body is still found intact which makes the cardinals canonize her and declare her uncorrupt body to be an invaluable relic having the potential to bring about miracles. In reality the body is simply preserved due to the presence of salts and the absence of moisture in the cold earth. Peter and Lucian almost rape the dead body of Josephine under the disguise of testing its validity as a relic. They "tore away the shreds of golden cloth" to "reveal fully the naked body underneath" and "Lucian whispered in surprise at how full and firm the breasts seemed to be". Lucian and Peter put out their hands and touch "the flesh, the nipples" and say that they are fresh like "fresh beef suet" (*IS* 12-13).

Josephine is thus canonized on a false premise and her body is greedily hunted for by various churches and convents as a means of attracting visitors and profit making. Pilgrims arriving from far off places to see the body of Josephine stole pieces of her body as they all wanted a relic of their own. Roberts points out how psychological aberrations like sadism, cannibalism and necrophilia find expression in the devotees' love of the relics. The description of the faithful biting into Josephine's body is a criticism of the Eucharist based on the Last Supper where Christ asked his disciples to eat his flesh and drink his blood:

> It took the nuns several days to realise what was happening. Some of the kisses were greedier and less reverent than others. Some of the faithful were feasting on Josephine. Taking bites

> out of her. They scurried off with little chunks of her flesh concealed in their cheeks or under their tongues.... Someone had torn open the habit and bitten off the nipples. Someone else had nibbled the earlobes. The mouth was badly bruised. (*IS* 14)

After Josephine's death the way her body is cut, divided and merchandised by the cardinals for the relic market is a bitter satire on the whole concept of canonisation and relic worship. The last chapter "The Golden House" is a lampoon on the same. The Golden House houses bones of holy women and appears more to be a charnel house designed by a psychomaniac rather than a place for meditation constructed by religious people. For Roberts, the fractured and dismembered body of the martyr represents the fragmented nature of women's writing and the silencing of women throughout history.

Roberts once asserted that she always had a muse for her works. The muse could be her mother, father or lover but they were the person with whom she had problems with at that point in time. Roberts tells Rodriguez: "I've looked back at my novels and I've seen that there is a muse for every single novel: a person I've been very, very upset with". In the interview she further says that "I think my mother was the muse for at least the first three novels" and "I think my father was the muse for *Impossible Saints*". Roberts confesses that *IS* is a book about her relationship with her own father and that "he inspired that book; he hated it; he really found it very painful and uncomfortable". Writing *IS* thus become for Roberts a way of coping with her own conflicts with her father. One can find portrayals of bad and sexy fathers in *IS* who have erotic feelings for their daughters resulting in the girls' exploitation, imprisonment and destruction.

Saint Agnes, Saint Thais, Saint Dympna, Saint Uncumber and Saint Barbara die in their youth as a result of being abused by their father. Some of these young women find themselves irresistibly attracted towards their fathers who lead them to suffering and death. Saint Agnes who is considered a patron saint of young girls is the epitome of innocence. She has long yellow tresses, big eyes and carries a cage of finches and a lamb with her. Through revising the story of Saint Agnes Roberts not only tries to show the seduction of innocence by experience but also blurs the line which divides women into virgins and whores. Deflowered by her father in a moment of failure of recognition, Agnes is punished for her father's act by her father. Stripped and expelled from home she starts working as an assistant at a barber's shop, cuts her hair and slowly becomes well known as a "red petticoat". All women in town imitate Agnes and start wearing red satin petticoats and wear their hair short which are considered as signs of a tart. "Now all the women in the town were dressed alike. You could no longer distinguish a good woman from a bad one" (*IS* 148).

Thais is in love with her father and sleeps with men considering them her father. She is finally rejected by all and dies in a murky pit. Dympna's fate is similar. Her story is an illustration of daughters' love for their fathers ending in sexual abuse and disillusionment. Using the hunter hunted trope Roberts plays on the theme of deception and death. Uncumber's father is a psychomaniac, obsessed with himself and tries to rape his daughter. Uncumber is a survivor and retaliates with a castrating zeal. The mothers of these girls are either absent or passive which highlights women's compliance to male treachery.

The girls' desire for a father finds an expression in the stories through their dreams which serves to reveal that which is kept repressed. Roberts explains to Rodriguez in an interview that "the stories work through the idea of a bad father who oppresses the daughter and then we get the rebellion of the daughter in various ways: we get various ways in which the daughter fights her father, loves him, flirts with him, gets raped by him". However the last story offers a promise of fulfillment through heterosexual ties, as the father here is a good one. Here one finds not a biological father but a Christian priest who becomes a lover of his former house maid, Saint Mary of Egypt, and learns to accept the concept of free love as redeeming. He lives with Mary in Africa away from the society, shuns his book learned beliefs and enjoys for the first time the beauty and sensuousness of life. The story is all about similarities between the coloniser and colonised, England and Egypt, Catholicism and Heathen culture, the spiritual and sensuous modes of loving God, desert and island. Mary here is the housekeeper, the faithful lover and the prostitute.

Changing the time frame of the stories, Roberts presents Thecla who though being a modern, working and independent woman becomes a victim of patriarchal evaluation. Thecla leaves her lover Thamyris for a preacher who seduces her with his philosophical ideas. After a brief relationship with Thecla the priest leaves her in order to live with a female disciple of his whom he considers an ideal female because of her "very sweet, peaceful, feminine soul". Paul describes her as a desirable woman because "she needed a man to care for her and to protect her" and "she was so delicately made that it was easy to hurt her while making love" (*IS* 93). The attitude of the priest breaks Thecla's confidence and she is left doubting her femininity. When Paul leaves the café she sits on feeling like a "giantess ten foot tall" who must "not move or she might break". She sees for the first time how gross and huge she was, how aggressive and unlovable. Seeing herself through Paul's patriarchal "gaze" (Berger 47) she finds herself both "an insatiable monster that terrified men and threatened to devour them" as well as a tiny "flea squashed under Paul's foot". Paul's voice declared that "there was something terribly wrong with her but she didn't know what it was" (*IS* 94). Marita Sturken and Lisa Cartwright comment on how "gaze" could be used as a means of control as the object of gaze loses some sense of autonomy upon realizing that they are visible objects (94). Roberts takes up the issue of women's self objectification in her essay "Seeing Differently: What Self-Portraits Might Be" and asks:

> When she looked at herself in the mirror what did she see? With whose eyes was she looking? When she screwed up her eyes and stared at herself was it really she who was doing the looking? How could she know?...She looked with the eyes of the others, the eyes of judges, the eyes of potential lovers weighing her up before rejecting her. (*Food, Sex and God* 173)

Thecla freezes to death inside a cave and becomes a saint as a result of self mortification. The story is also a satire on men's insecurity and lack of confidence which makes them fear strong women.

"Christina the Astonishing" takes up issues of psychological difficulties faced by girls with their entry into pubescence. Christina's bracing of grotesque and her desire to be othered by family and society results from the inability of her parents to cope up and empathise with her teenage maladjustments. Roberts explores the themes of freedom, commodification of body, perversion, rebellion and patriarchy through the images of chains and birds, mermaids, snakes, phallic pillars and self-mutilation.

The stories of saints are examples of forceful construction of gender by society. Saint Paula's is a case of blind obedience to a male spiritual guide who works for the preservation of the status quo. Saint Agnes, Saint Thais, Saint Dympna and Saint Uncumber are cases of patriarchal abuse. They are kept secluded in towers in exile and suffer from the lack of sympathetic female figures. Saint Petronilla, Saint Thecla and Saint Christine rebel against their allotted destiny and use the medium of dancing and flying for expression. As a result, they are forced to live in exile as freaks of nature. Saint Marine uses the strategy of masquerade and transvestism because of her need to integrate in the man's world. Saint Barbara and Saint Mary of Egypt challenge the official views about religion. According to Sania Villegas Lopez, Saint Barbara re-interprets the Holy Trinity when she calls the spirit of her dead mother as the Holy Ghost.

It is made easily noticeable that along with Saint Josephine all the other women saints in the book are born into favourable conditions. However, all of them end up in despair after becoming exposed to public humiliation either by their fathers or by men they fall in love with. Christina finds herself morally ruined because of loss of honour and is forced to adapt to whatever identity is offered to her, even grotesque and abject. After having suffered profound pains, these women are left to die either in a cold room of a monastery or in a deep well they are thrown into. As for the men, they do not get punished in any sense in return for the crimes they commit against women.

One of the major concerns of Roberts is the mind/body split propagated by philosophers like Rene Descartes which led to the maligning of body in favour of the spirit. In her collection of essays called *Food, Sex and God* Roberts repeatedly talks of the evaluation of the body as unruly and having a corrupting influence on those who are spiritually inclined. Female body in this regard is considered more rebellious, hence considered more malignant. The fear of the female body and misogyny are read by Roberts as both the cause and effect of patriarchy. She comments on how the Church has always found the female body a problem and how it tries to cage it within moral laws. Using the image of a perfect baby recommended by the Victorian experts on childcare she examines the guidelines of the Church for the female body. The ideal body should be:

> ...tidy, clean, smiling and controlled. There are bodily processes the Christian religious tradition would find it impossible to let us think of as sacred: bodies that retch, leak, menstruate, piss and shit, vomit, come ecstatically, are not supposed to exist inside a church and are generally not welcome. (*Food, Sex and God* 37)

Valorizing the body and especially the female body is a key theme in all of Roberts's works. In *Food, Sex and God* Roberts sets out her own views on religion, many of which echo Irigaray's argument that men have been viewed as guardians of the spirit and women as keepers of the flesh. This makes it impossible to believe that women are created in God's image. Women being the daughters of Eve inherit her guilt and her flesh, and the only way left for them to gain redemption is by denying their bodies and their sex. Roberts resurrects the figure of Mary Magdalene to undo the either/or split between spirituality and sensuality and to show that the desires of the body can be a source of religious joy.

Roberts tries to bring body to the centre of discourse by giving glorified portrayals of the prostitutes and hetaeras. Sibylla, though being a prostitute, is very intellectual and kind. She belongs to the most elite group in the town and represents human grace and dignity. Roberts portrays Mary as a sensual woman who confesses that sex work suits her well as an occupation. The assertion is that sex work does not close the gates of heaven on a woman. Jesus himself is also not a celibate and had known many women before meeting Mary. Mary says "Jesus forgave me nothing, because he said there was nothing to forgive" (*SG* 45).

In his last days Jesus talks of the importance of raising the body from its denigrated position. Jesus's speeches are aimed at valorizing the otherwise marginalised body in religious discourse "all the human bodies that have suffered and been degraded shall win back their dignity" (*SG* 71) and he includes the bodies of the menial labourers, women's bodies abused by their husbands, prisoner's bodies, criminals' bodies, bodies of the prostitutes and the poor, diseased and the raped, bodies of those dying of privation and neglect. He further says that "the body is the mirror of the soul, and through the body, not by denying it; we enter the other world, the world of eternity which co-exists with this temporal, fleshly one" (*SG* 108).

Mortification of flesh is practiced in many religions of the world. Mortification of flesh at times involves not only fasting and asceticism but serious bodily harm like piercing, cutting, whipping, flagellation, circumcision, clitoridectomy, infibulations etcetera. Roberts satirizes these practices and also the medieval fest of Corpus Christi which is based on the notion that burning the heretics would cleanse them of sin:

> The lures and wiles of the world and the Devil, from which Christ rescued us with his own body. Over and over he rescues us with his body, in Holy Communion at Mass. Corpus Christi. The body of Christ. Also it was a celebration of the fact that the souls of the heretic were going to heaven after their bodies had been burned. (*IS* 135)

BMN has many stories about women who practice mortification of flesh blindly because right from childhood they are fed on stories about the vileness of female sexuality. A little girl narrates that "our parish priest, a holy man...explains to me that a woman's beauty evokes men's lust, and drags them down to vileness, away from their search for God". Hearing the words of the holy man the young girl believes that the agony of women in childbirth is a result of their physical beauty which makes them sin against men's chastity. When her father tells her "every Sunday for sixteen years" "how pretty" she is, she develops a fear of her own sexuality (*BMN* 105). The female protagonist imbibes from the Catholic tradition a sense of guilt for being a woman and chooses the order of the flagellants instead of matrimony on getting young. Roberts implodes the religious ritual of flagellation by describing it a product of the protagonist's sado-masochistic sexual fantasy rather than being her zeal for spirituality:

> They hurt me and hurt me, and I sing and sob along with the pain until the tide of pleasures rises in my running blood, in the urine I cannot stop myself form passing, and overwhelms me, and I drop to the cold floor, panting and crying out.... this goes on for five years. God slips away from me. (*BMN* 113)

The close and clear description of the physical aspects of flagellation shows how the ensuing ecstasy is a result of the endorphins generated by the excess of pain rather than by any divine visions. The course of the narrator's life changes when her sister Joanna introduces the concepts propagated by Christian liberals like the Brethrens of the Free Spirit and the Beguines to her. Joanna and Master John represent domestic felicity and show to the narrator:

> How humans can attain a sinless state, in which the sensuality is so guided by the soul that the body can be allowed any gratification it likes...How carnal act is not a sin, but, on the contrary, a route to God. How the perfect have no need of the Eucharist and the Mass, nor of the Passion of Christ. (*BMN* 120)

"The Life of Saint Paula" in *IS* also deconstructs the practices of mortification of flesh by showing how if not moderately practised it can become a disease hard to cure. Paula is a disciple of Jerome, a priest, whose estimation of women rests on their ability to denigrate their bodies. Under the influence of Jerome Paula develops somatophobic beliefs. The opening of the story is quite satiric:

> Once she had born her husband a son she was able to stop having children. She had four daughters already and that was quite enough. She learned to regret that she had ever got married and enjoyed sex. She learned to mortify her flesh, to give away most of her wealth to the poor, to eat and dress badly, and to rejoice when her husband suddenly died and left her a widow. (*IS* 20)

Saint Jerome, whose aim is to make women believe that sexual intercourse introduced the original sin in to the world, convinces Blesilla, Paula's daughter, after her husband's untimely death that she has worn out her husband by seducing him too often. The priest fetishizes virginity in women as a source of vitality and women's sensuality as a cause of death. Blessila develops disgust for food. The writer shows how excess of religious zeal in Blesilla is nothing but perversion of the passion she once had for her husband. The love she had for her husband turns into hatred for her body which she fought with all her might. She discovered that "there was no end to self-mortification. You could never do enough. There was always another step you could take. Another privation you could embrace. Once you were in, you could not stop but had to go on. It was exactly like a seduction" (*IS* 24).

Reducing her sleep, living only on mouldy bread and a few drops of water a day, revelling in ugliness Blessila dies. Paula follows Jerome to found a monastery for both men and women, and dies leaving her young daughter Eustochium pennyless "as a lesson in holy poverty" (*IS* 30). The story implodes the religious fanaticism as propelled by the holy fathers who beguile women and lead them to their destruction only to run away in the end scared of the mess they create.

Being brought up in a restrictive Catholic culture, Roberts always longed for equal status of women in society and freedom of expression. Thus in Roberts's works one could also find a longing for an ideal world for women, a feminist utopia. The motif of water is used by her to signify womb and new birth. She deploys the myth of Flood from the Old Testament to create an opportunity for the construction of new world order after the annihilation of the first. Her Ark is utopian in the sense that it not only is a nuclear shelter and an independent city fighting against the ills of poverty, unemployment, racism, superstition and all forms of marginalisation but is also a creative haven for women writers.

Jerusalem in *SG*, the Ark in *BMN* and the new convent conceptualised by Josephine are blissful havens created by Roberts where women can be free and creative. They are perfect places of equal standing and opportunities. Her utopias are based on a subverted social order where the opposites are reconciled and the differences between powerful and powerless, the saved and the lost souls are done away with. Roberts shows how along with the sexual exploitation of a woman's body, numerous responsibilities of motherhood and housekeeping such as cleaning, cooking, and childcare also serve in the maintenance of "inequality" between man and woman. The Ark is a floating house which provides refuge to women who need a temporary escape from the stress of real lives, their family responsibilities and social expectations. It's an ideal place for nurturing talent, a land of opportunities, the Promised Land for women.

The Deftly Sibyl is sick of living in her husband's space at his rhythm. She is tired of the chores, the children and the circle of domestic existence. The Re-Vision Sibyl is separated from her husband and is afraid to acknowledge her lesbian affair as her daughter Kitty might be lawfully taken away from her. The Babble-On Sibyl is called an "authoress" by her in-laws and is trying too hard to be a "real woman" by cooking for the family at the cost of her writing. The Foresaken Sibyl is scared of her passion for Julia and is struggling with her own emotions. The Correct Sibyl is suffering from writer's block. These Sibyls take up the journey on the Ark to find out how the other women survive. On the Ark, the Deftly Sibyl gets a chance to enjoy all that which was unthinkable at home like being ill, remaining in bed, having a room of her own, daydreaming, being a child again and refusing the demands of others.

The Ark of Women has been founded by an international committee of Sibyls "in order to guard and encourage women's creativity". Women come on the Ark for peace, to think about their lives and question them. On the Ark, women have the freedom to express their mixed feelings, doubts and different attitudes towards feminism. Feminists who are lesbians, feminists who are feminine, feminists who are androgynous, feminists who are misandrists, feminists who like men, feminists who are confused, all find their voice on the Ark. They can think, discuss, shout, fight and be a recluse there. Women who "hate the very idea of writers workshops" come here to "get away from other women, to live in cells of silence and isolation, to be as selfish and unsisterly as they like" and "women come here to free their imaginations, to learn to play again, to destroy" (*BMN* 20-21).

According to Lucy Sargisson, the description of the Ark as a refuge for those women who are fitted in only as monsters like "the gorgons, the basilisks, the sirens, the harpies, the furies, the viragos, the amazons, the medusas, the sphinxes" expresses a desire for "non-possessive and non-acquisitive relations to the other; relations in which difference is not feared or viewed with arrogant perception" which is similar to the embracing of the other as "theorized by Irigaray, Cixous and Young" (200). Sargisson also calls this approach towards the other as "transgressive utopianism which disrupts the opposition of self to other" (200).

Another criterion for utopia given by Roberts is the freedom to do what they want without being restricted in narrow definitions. She believes that women should not be straitjacketed in a fixed definition of "Woman" but should be able to bring into play the multiple aspects of their personalities. Mary Magdalene in *SG* is shown as a woman who embraces the various aspects of her identity is simultaneously shown as a singer of songs, a prostitute and the lover of God:

> I am a daughter and a mother, and tread more or less happily in that circle. I have been a singer of songs and a prostitute and the lover of the Lord, a traveller and an outcast and an exile. I have been proclaimed as both demon and goddess, as pagan and disciple and Jew. Now, at last, I have become an ordinary woman, settled in my home and in my work, peace dwelling in me. (*SG* 153)

Calling Mary Magdalene a "figure of glorious contradictions", one who unifies the maternal and the sexual, Roberts further states in *Food, Sex and God*: "It's difficult to be a Catholic saint who is both holy and actively sexual". Roberts further says that "Mary Magdalene is the missing half—the sexual half—of the Virgin Mary, the mother of God". Putting them together, back to back, would create a "whole saint: passionate, maternal, sexy, visionary. (*Food, Sex and God* 38) In *SG* Mary dreams that the whore of Babylon and the Virgin called themselves sisters and she took it as a good omen of reaching Jerusalem, the Promised Land. By allowing sexual license to women, Roberts tries to free them from bodily assessment and relocate them in the spiritual sphere as much as men. Talking of Michele Roberts's fiction Rosie White observes:

> The paradox evident in all these novels parallels that found in contemporary feminist theory: that of the desire for and distrust of a static and unitary identity. Contemporary feminist fiction and theory frequently appear to be in dialogue in their attempts to describe a position within the social and cultural order which does not impose untenable restraints on the feminine gendered subject, but frees her up to a productive and creative existence in relation to herself and others.

In *SG* Roberts contests the preference for virgins in the Church firstly by presenting the figure of the virgin as an oppressive patriarchal motif and secondly by rewriting the virgin holiness as virgin (w)holiness in which the female becomes whole by reclaiming the other which could be the mother, the male or the whore. In *On Gender and Writing* she gives four archetypes which make up the female psyche, namely, the mother, who creates babies and art signifying physical and spiritual pregnancies; the lesbian, who loves women and may be a mother as well; the companion to men, who is men's lover and comrade; and the Sibyl, who periodically needs to withdraw into what can be seen as madness but who is in touch with the ancient memories, inspiration and gives birth to poetry and art. Susan Rowland comments that these are personality types and can co-exist within a person in different proportions. Treated separately they are mere fictions of identity. The five Sibyls when introduced in *BMN* represent one of these personality types. The Deftly Sibyl is a mother, the Re-Vision Sibyl is a mix of mother and lesbian, the Babble On Sibyl is a companion to men, the Foresaken Sibyl is a lesbian and the Correct Sibyl is a full time writer. All the Sibyls are blocked as they are trapped in narrow roles, but towards the end their identities become more heterogeneous. In the end the Sibyls commingle as the different aspects of Mrs Noah's self. Jayita Sengupta asserts:

> Her (Mrs. Noah's) fellow voyagers are creatures of her fantasy or several selves of her own personality or the 'otherness' of the Jungian 'other'...she is the Re-vision Sibyl, the Deftly Sibyl, the Correct Sibyl, the Forsaken Sibyl, the Babble-On Sibyl-the split personalities of the same 'I'. (100-101)

Magdalena's House and the new convent that Josephine establishes in *IS* are very much like the utopian Ark. Magdalena throws parties; enjoys music, jokes, conversations, games and also promotes endless courtships among the members of the party. Conversation, freely done without any inhibitions was the cure for dullness and grief in her house. Humour, fun and stories are highly valued just as dance, song and plays. "Almost anything was possible in the quest for amusement and pleasure" (*IS* 160). In Magdalena's house the virgin and mother, whore and hetaera coalesce into the figure of Josephine and set her free.

Inspired by Magdalena's house Josephine conceives a new convent which would be both religious and profane. It would be based on the freedom to choose thus making the women living in it complete. It would be a spacious house, a place of visionary bliss, where God would become manifest in sensual joy, where women would be both nuns and courtesans simultaneously. Josephine envisions that "each house would be a double house, looking two ways, with one entrance on one side and one on the other" and "nobody except the inhabitants, on entering the double house from either side, would know that the other half existed" (*IS* 192). She takes a drawing of some Siamese twins seen in childhood as a model for the new convent. "Two houses together, back to back; two bodies joined by a single skin". "The existence of the other side would be kept secret. Each woman who lived here would be able to live two lives: a double life; it was that simple". (*IS* 192)

The mother-daughter relationship and the position of the girl child in family and society are recurring concerns in Roberts's construction of female utopias. Roberts expresses her concern about the role of women as the most powerful agents of patriarchy through her novels. She shows that if the equality of the sexes is to be created then the change must come from women. In *IS* it is Paula who leads her daughter to excessive privation and instils faith in her for Jerome's somatophobic preaching. Though Mrs Noah is a champion of the feminist principle she is also criticised by Sarah for her apathy towards her daughters-in-law. Sarah also accuses Mrs Noah for her failure in instilling tenderness in her sons. It is Sarah who fills the gap in Mrs Noah's philosophy by teaching her to value a girl: "I want a daughter, she says: I'll love her properly. The way no one loves me".

Roberts tells Jenny Newman that:

> I don't think my childhood was terribly happy—no-one's fault, one knows that now—but I felt very separate from my mother, much too separate: she was the paradise from which I had been 'expelled untimely'. The image of the maternal body as paradise became very important to me. Obviously it's there in psychoanalytical literature, but it was a journey to discover it.

Roberts often mentions that the muse for most of her works had been her mother. The search for reconciliation with a mother figure is a motif in her works. The protagonists in her works keep searching for a reunion with the lost mother. "A story about a mother" in *BMN* is in the form of a confessional letter written by the narrator in the Protestant Queen's prison to her infant daughter. The letter written by a mother for her daughter telling her about her "beginnings", setting her as "my judge" and asking for forgiveness speaks of the inevitability of mother-daughter interdependence for identity formation. She writes here as a friend, a mother and a sinner. She writes: "I want you to inherit me. A daughter needs a mother. A daughter should know who her mother is. In order to accept her, or to reject her" (*BMN* 170-71).

Mother-daughter continuum in Roberts could also be studied through the relationship between Mrs Noah and Sarah, Josephine and Isabel, Mary Magdalene and Deborah. Josephine wants to share her learning with Isabel and bequeaths her autobiography to her. Mrs Noah gives Sarah her word and Mary Magdalene gives her religious experiences to Deborah. Mothers also express their love by practising the generous and unselfish arts like cooking and sewing which fills their daughters with contentment and confidence:

> Oh the pleasure of this receiving; of this being given to; of being loved by her. Do nothing to break the beautiful cords of this love, this definition of yourself; for without it you are outcast, dying, monster, bad daughter. Done for. (*BMN* 129)

Mrs Noah also feels that her grandmother "Nana" guides her to dive into the sea, which symbolizes her unconscious, and spend some time on the Ark for recreation with other Sybils. The jump symbolises an adventurous escape from all the patriarchal structures into the Kristevan "chora". Mother's absence is replaced by the Ark which seems like a womb.

In *SG,* after Jesus's death Mary embarks on a journey to find the Promised Land Jerusalem, which also becomes the search for her lost mother. "Then I came to a great city, and I thought: perhaps this is Jerusalem, and perhaps my mother is here" (167). The mystic experience of Mary is guided by a midwife Salome, a mother figure, who prepares Mary to take the journey to the womb of the earth to meet Jesus after his crucifixion. Throughout the journey to the centre of the earth which is symbolic of her entry into the womb, Mary keeps having thoughts about Martha, her mother and sees the midwife as the queen of heaven who becomes all ancient goddesses, Ishtar, Astarte, Athar, Artemis, Aphrodite, Isis, Inanna, Dumuzi, Hecate, Demeter and Persephone. The midwife initiates Mary in the sacred drama of sexuality and death. She forms the holy trinity; she's the mother, housewife and the prostitute.

Rewriting the Holy Communion Roberts says that the true Holy Communion happens in between a mother and a child when a child gets nourishment in the womb from the mother's blood and body.

Roberts also uses her works to convey her ideas about the virtues of female friendships. Roberts does not prescribe homosexuality like the radical feminists and takes sexuality as strictly a matter of personal choice. Roberts's notion of desire in interpersonal relationships including erotic desire contradicts the Freudian and Lacanian concept of "lack" (*The Ego in Freud's Theory and in the Techniques of Psychoanalysis*) and is more in confirmation with Irigaray's dialogical feminine desire as conceptualised in "When our Lips Speak together".

Roberts is also a champion of secularism. In *SG*, Roberts sets Mary apart as a gifted girl who denies being introduced to God through men and has her own intuitive way of communicating with God. Roberts tries to bring the body to the plane of spirituality and shows the entry of Mary's body into femaleness as holy and also brings pagan form of nature worship to the centre. In her four year long stay with Sibylla, Mary learns from the household slaves about pagan culture, its medicines and gods. When her brother Lazarus almost dies, it is by using the herbal science that Mary preserves his body till Jesus's return.

Jesus and Mary become spokespersons for Roberts's plea for tolerance of difference. One of the motifs in *SG* is criticising the use of religion to perpetuate injustice against women, minority groups and weak nations. Roberts writes in the Preface of the novel:

> These days, when fundamentalist versions of Christianity are once more on the rise, when political leaders use biblical imagery to excuse their crusades against other countries, Mary Magdalene remains, for me, a figure who challenges their narrow-minded certainties.

The inordinate desire to bring all people under common rule and religion is subverted by the desire of Christ to convert people not to Christianity but to a new concept of unity. Mary preaches pantheism to her daughter Deborah saying that "all of us, men and women alike, are the ovens and wine-skins of God...and we are God's wells, in which God kicks and swims like a fish" and that "there is no clear name for God, I tell her, since God is expressed in the movement and change of every tiny seed of being in the world" (*SG*158). This is very similar to Roberts's personal opinion about the nature of God who she defines as "the force that grows us and wants us to flourish. God is our eating and drinking and gardening and love-making. God is the energy in our bodies, their knowledge and suffering and love" (Roberts *Food, Sex and God*, 44).

Roberts also emphasises the need for writing as a means of bringing social change and call writers "new saints" in an interview with Sanchez:

> ...the point about being interested in characters who are writers is that, there is that quality of invention, that writing could stand as a metaphor for people who try to invent themselves and invent their lives, and invent a world they want to live in, which I think is probably quite fundamental to human being.

She believes that writing is fun too because through it one can play with and rearrange the world. As told to Rodriguez, writing for her is also like creating a baby and her ten books are her ten children from different people who inspired them. She declares that "it's fun, it's a very sexy image. It's about being unfaithful, I think, and having a career as a very promiscuous woman, going about the world, falling in love and making novels". Adrienne Rich believes that writing which includes confessional writing, autobiography, storytelling and re-writing the old stories is a basic need for women as it is one of the ways in which they can assert themselves, make a place in history and survive ("When We Dead Awaken: Writing as Re-Vision"). The realization that social transformation can come only through speech instils in women the will to speak about their selves which remain inscribed by androcentric ideologies.

All of Roberts's female protagonists find a pressing need and compulsion to write about their experiences and life. Their experiences are valuable and need to be passed on to posterity for the understanding of injustice done to women by religion and patriarchy. The "word" of Mrs Noah, the "gospel" of Mary Magdalene and the "diary" of Josephine are gifts that they give to their daughters. Their writing becomes the means by which they survive both historically and bodily.

The physical details of preparing pen and parchment for writing by Mary reveal the sensuous aspect of writing as well its urgency. She strips the layers of bark, softens them in water and then presses them flat under the weight of a rock. She cuts herself pens from the feathers of the birds and uses wood ash moistened from the juice of a blue berry for ink. She decides that "when I have written the last page I shall sew them together with a strong seam down one side, and then I shall wrap the whole in a sheepskin coat" (*SG* 154).

Mary keeps struggling with expression in the form of words. The failure to communicate accurately makes Mary realise the need for a new, more vivacious language. One could see that Mary's theory about the limitations of communicating epiphanic moments through words is very similar to the endless deferral of meaning theorized by Derrida:

> I keep on remembering that day, long ago, when the world and language dissolved, and I along with it. That is just as much a part of the truth, but one which I cannot set down in sentences. How much I wish that this book could be a window into that world, a transparency. How much I wish that these leaves were of glass. It is impossible. With every mark of ink on the page, I obscure what lies behind it. What my language reveals, it also hides. (*SG* 162)

Mrs Noah invents her word in the form of pictures and signs. She opens up the fixity of language and makes it more intuitive and visual: "I draw pictures on the mud slabs, one by one, of all the new words I've made up. I keep the pictures as simple as possible...God is a circle...So belief-in-God comes out as a circle holding a bee and a leaf" (*BMN* 87). She gives her "writing" to Sarah with a wish that "Sarah will need to break the circle in two, and find a new word" (*BMN* 89). The breaking of circle suggests the breaking of structuralist and logocentric paradigms.

Roberts believes that for writing well the writers should be in touch with their unconscious, and it is exemplified through Mrs Noah's journey down to that dark windowless place in the Ark which represents the dangers of the unconscious. Like the Kristevan category of abject "it's dangerous. And it's filthy" (*BMN* 267). This is the place where one can delve into the unconscious realms, be seduced by it and be free.

In *BMN* Roberts also deals in detail with the common problems faced by women writers. While studying Library Science, Roberts once made an important observation about the status granted to women:

> All public libraries in Britain used the Dewey decimal system, which categorised human knowledge as a pyramidal structure. Subjects were arranged one to 10, and under them came sub-divisions, and then sub-divisions of sub-divisions. The system locked subjects into fixed places. Under category seven, Sociology, you could find Women, alongside Lunatics and Gypsies. (Roberts *The Guardian)*

Using a computer-based theory Roberts once designed a revolutionary new library classification model that puts women at the centre of the world, as thinking subjects. In a similar fashion she deconstructs the hierarchical structure of Ark and makes her floating library a democratic one.

BMN also explores the common problem with modern women writers that causes the writer's block most of the times. There is a gap between what these women are and what they are expected to be. Tied up by the desire to please everybody they constantly try to fit into the mould offered to them and fail in creating honest and inspired work. One of the Sibyls wonders: "Will her mother still love her once she reads what she writes?" (*BMN* 130) The fear of criticism by other writers also makes the Sibyls unable to write. They fear that the male writers would criticise them if their work lacks political bite, avant garde experimentation and true artistry and the feminists would criticise them for unsisterly behaviour if they show their liking for men. Pleasing everybody thus becomes impossible. While talking about the problems faced by women writers Roberts also takes up issues related to creative writing like the intrusion of theoretical jargon in creative endeavours. Roberts also points out that the overemphasis on theory is shifting creativity to the margins.

Resisting the impulse to please everyone a Sibyl tears away her false clothing and begins "to hunt for her own words" (*BMN* 179). Roberts notes in "Novels of Colette" that a woman writer is made to feel that she is some sort of monster for not writing pretty verses to be recited in drawing rooms. She confesses that she admires Jean Rhys, Nathalie Barney, H D, Katherine Mansfield, Dorothy Richardson and Virginia Woolf and Colette for "bursting out of the misogyny of the belle époque" and redefining what it is to be a woman.

At times women writers are also compelled by the dictates of intellectualism and secularism which deny them the freedom to be religious. The Foresaken Sybil feels the sudden urge to pray on her knees but knows that "The only taboo subject is spirituality" (208).

Another problem is that of a woman writer's place in marriage and her over-definition as a wife. The Re-Vision Sibyl remembers how "her neglected marriage starts to break down" because "Jim wants to lie with a woman between ironed cotton sheets not ruled paper ones. He wants a woman with powder not ink on her nose. He wants a woman who looks at him more often than she looks at a book" (*BMN* 130).

Ark provides women the freedom to write honestly and here they feel that they can use their pens to oppose any kind of subjugation. The book ends with the narrator promising herself to write daily.

Roberts belongs to the second wave of feminism and does not believe that men and women can be similar. Hers is a different but equal feminist ideology. She says in *Food, Sex and God:* "If different means worse, we are all going to rush towards the norm, which remains masculine, though it pretends not to be, but to be bodiless, gender-free" (11).

Reading the works of Michele Roberts one can observe her progression from the use of an intensely sentimental and prescriptive tone as in *SG* to an increasingly relaxed and detached perspective in her later works like *BMN*. In an interview with Jenny Newman Roberts tells her that her earlier novels had always been about homeless women but she stopped writing about it as a result of falling in love with a male artist that provided her with "an imaginary space of warmth" which she calls home. Her obsession with the libidinous exchange between father and daughter got resolved after writing *IS*. She confesses to Newman that by writing *IS* she had "laid a ghost, which was my terrible fear that my father and I had loved each other too much". She says that the childhood fantasy of having a sexual relationship with her father "really damaged me". Discussing the same issue she says to Rodriguez: "But I think with *Impossible Saints* I really grabbed something. I sorted out some big conflict in myself about sexuality and spirituality, religion, fathers and, in a sense, I think that I've done with the religious issue in a way" and so "there are less nuns in my books now".

Patriarchy and religion are always interlinked in Roberts's works. One finds that after coming to terms with her childhood conflict about her father Roberts's strong dislike for her Catholic education has also mellowed down. Though she dislikes the inherent misogyny and hierarchy in the religion which "stumps out freedom of thought" and "takes over your emotional life" she tells to Sanchez that she cherishes "the old bloody Church" because "it gave me language, it gave me stories, it gave me folklore".

Reporting the shift in her perspective, Roberts tells Sanchez that while *SG*, *The Visitation* and to some extent *BMN* are saturated with Jungian thought she would probably not write the novels in the same way now. Roberts discusses her disenchantment with the Jungian thought with Rodriguez too: "I read some very good feminist critiques and developments of Jungian thought that I found very exciting, and I think now they don't speak to me in the same way". She reasons that with growing age and confidence she does not worry that much about being a "complete woman". She has learned to accept imperfections as natural and calls the earlier attitude a "confidence thing". She also does not use the language of archetypes anymore for the same reason "I think, because I took in all the archetypes when I was that young woman, that I'm now tired of them in a way and I don't think about being a complete woman anymore".

It could be concluded that Roberts in her fiction re-evaluates Catholicism from women's perspectives. She foregrounds the unfair misogynistic and somatophobic practices in Catholicism which make it a religion of fear rather than a religion of love. With the aim of subverting the religious ideology governing Catholic customs Roberts rewrites the myths about both idealised and demonized women like Mrs Noah and Mary Magdalene. She also exposes the abuse of women, wives and daughters, in patriarchal families while also discussing the themes of incest and homosexuality.

Roberts's fiction aims at conceptualizing a new utopia for women which would nurture their individuality and talents. Undoing mind body dualism which forms the basis of misogyny as well as the mortification of flesh in religious doctrines, Roberts aims at valorizing the body through a celebration of its materiality and by bringing to spotlight the joys of cooking, eating and being loved. Michele Roberts's oeuvre offers a critique of the virgin preferring Church and tries to free women from being over-determined as virgin, mother, hetaerae or Sibyl. She brings to the fore the importance of mother-daughter bonding and female friendships as a means of undermining the heterosexist assumptions of patriarchy. The ultimate goal of Roberts's works is to rearrange the world which could be done in various ways but the most important means remains the pen, traditionally equated with the phallus, which must be used to re-write women's identity and their place in society.

WORKS CITED

Aristotle. *On the Generation of Animals*. Trans. Arthur Platt. eBooks@ Adelaide. The University of Adelaide library. 25 Aug 2010. Web. 10 May 2012.

Arthur, John Mac. "The Resurrection of Jesus Christ—Part 2". Web. 26 March 2010.

Berger, John. *Ways of Seeing*. Penguin Group, 1972. Web. 7 Jan 2012.

Brown, Kevin. "'Tis Pity She's a Whore: The Revision of Mary Magdalene in Contemporary Fiction". *Papers on Language and Literature* 42.3 (2006). *Questia*. Web. 18 Feb 2011.

Cixous, Helene. "The Laugh of the Medusa". Trans. Keith Cohen and Paula Cohen. *Signs*. 1(4), 1976. Web. 10 Feb 2012.

Daly, Mary. *The Church and the Second Sex*. Harper and Row, 1968. Web. 16 Oct 2009.

Fiorenza, Elizabeth Schussler. *In Memory of Her: A Feminist Theological Reconstruction of Christian Origins*. New York: Crossroad, 1983. Web. 30 April, 2009.

Howard-Laity, Elizabeth. "Rewriting the Body in Michele Roberts' *Impossible Saints*". Web. 10 Feb 2012.

Irigaray, Luce. "When Our Lips Speak Together". Trans. Carolyn Burke. Signs 6.1, 1980. JSTOR. Web. 2 Jan 2011.

Jung, Carl Gustav. *Psychological Types*. Pantheon Books, 1962. Web. 12 May 2012.

King, Karen L. "Women in Ancient Christianity". *The New Discoveries. Frontline: The First Christians*. Web. 2 Nov 2009.

Lopez, Sania Villegas. "Telling Women's Lives: Vision as Historical Revision in the Work of Michele Roberts". *Atlantis*. Vol xxiii. 1 (June 2001). Web. 10 Dec 2011.

Ozer, Sevinc. "Women's Body as Colony: Impossible Saints". *Gale: Cengage Learning* (2008). Web. 3 Jan 2012.

Rai, Sudha. "*The Book of Mrs Noah*: Theory and Practice in Feminist Rewriting". Eds Santosh Gupta and Preeti Bhatt. Contemporary British Fiction: History and the Present. Jaipur: Rawat Publications, 2007. Print.

Rich, Adrienne. "When We Dead Awaken: Writing as Re-Vision". *College English: Women, Writing and Teaching. National Council of Teachers of English* 34 (1), 1972. 11 Sep 2008. Web. 12 May 2012.

Roberts, Michele. *Food, Sex and God: On Inspiration and Writing*. London: Virago, 1998. Print.

——. *Impossible Saints*. New York: Harcourt Brace and Company, 1999. Print.

——. *Paper Houses: A Memoir of the '70s and Beyond*. London: Virago, 2007. Print.

——. Interviewed by Maria Soraya Garcia Sanchez. *Talking about Women, History and Writing with Michele Roberts. Atlantis*. 27.2 (Dec 2005). Web. 26 Oct 2011.

——. Interviewed by Jenny Newman. *An Interview with Michele Roberts*. Web. 12 Dec 2011.

——. Interviewed by Patricia Bastida Rodriguez. *On Women, Christianity and History: An Interview with Michele Roberts*. Atlantis 25.1 (June 2003). Web. 13 Nov 2010.

——. "Questions and Answers". Ed. M Wandor. On Gender and Writing. London, Boston, Melbourne and Henley: Pandora Press, 1983. Print.

——. *The Book of Mrs. Noah*. London: Metheun, 1987. Print.

——. "The Little Flower". *New Statesman*. 12 Jan 2004. Questia. Web. 3 Mar 2011.

——. "The Novels of Colette". *New Statesman*. 27 Nov 2000. *Questia*. Web. 7 Mar 2011.

——. *The Secret Gospel of Mary Magdalene*. London: Vintage, 2007. Print.

Rosso, Jeana Del. *Writing Catholic Women*. New York: Palgrave Macmillan, 2005. Print.

Ruether, Rosemary Radford. *Sexism and God-Talk: Towards a Feminist Theology*. Beacon Press, 1993. Web. 17 May 2010.

Sargisson, Lucy. *Contemporary Feminist Utopianism*. New York: Routledge, 1996. *Questia*. Web, 7 Mar 2011.

Sellers, Susan. "Becoming Gods and Umblical Wordbows: The New Hagiography of Michele Roberts". *Myth and Fairy Tale in Contemporary Women's Fiction*. New York: Palgrave, 2002.

Sengupta, Jayita. *Refractions of Desire: Feminist Perspectives in the Novels of Toni Morrison, Michele Roberts and Anita Desai*. New Delhi: Atlantic Publishers and Distributors, 2006. Print.

Sturken, Marita and Lisa Cartwright. *Practices of Looking: An Introduction ot Visual Culture*. Oxford University Press, 2009. Web. 3 May 2012.

Telford, William R. "Jesus and Women in Fiction and Film". Ed. Ingrid Rosa Kitzberger. *Transformative Encounters: Jesus and Women Re-Viewed*. Boston: Brill, 2000. *Questia*. Web. 19 Feb 2011.

Voragine, Jacobus de. *The Golden Legend or Lives of the Saints*. Trans. William Caxton. Ed. F.S. Ellis. Temple Classics, 1900. Web. 12 May 2012.

Warner, Marina. *Alone of All Her Sex: The Myth and the Cult of the Virgin Mary*. London: Picador, 1976. Print.

Waugh, Patricia. *Metafiction: The Theory and Practice of Self-Conscious Fiction*. London: Routledge, 1984. Print.

White, Rosie. "Permeable Borders, Possible Worlds: History and Identity in the Novels of Michele Roberts". *Studies in the Literary Imagination* 36.2 (2003) *Questia*. Web. 18 Dec. 2010.

5

The Narrative Journey of Subversion: Rhys, Carter and Roberts

> If we continue to speak the same language to each other, we will produce the same story. Begin the same stories all over again. If we continue to speak this sameness, if we speak to each other as men have spoken for centuries, as they taught us to speak, we will fail each other. (Irigaray "When Our Lips Speak Together")

Feminist critics continuously discuss the inadequacy of the phallocentric language and keep trying to seek ways of making it more flexible and accommodating. The French feminists like Julia Kristeva, Helene Cixous and Luce Irigaray play an important role in the reconceptualization of a new women's language or the *ecriture feminine* using an approach which takes psychoanalysis and linguistics together. Irigaray states in *The Sex Which is Not One* that women's writing should reflect the female body and should be fluid, nebulous and uninhibited by the rules of the phallocentric language.

Helene Cixous suggests in *The Laugh of the Medusa* that writing can serve as a springboard for the subversion of social and cultural structures. She heralds the return of the repressed and proposes a style that would embody abundance, extravagance and playful excess. According to Cixous, aesthetic creation should flow like desire without being restricted by the ego. Cixous's laughing Medusa in the 1970s and the 1980s became exemplary for the women writers, full of revolutionary potential and bisexuality. Cixous also sees the possibility of creating a feminist utopia through linguistic experimentations.

Julia Kristeva believes that subversive writing has the potential for reorganizing the psychic space (*Revolution in Poetic Language*). Therefore, she tries to form a theory of a new signifying practice that would emphasise the descriptive and revolutionary force of the repressed aspects of language, and aims at overhauling the socio-political setting by altering the representational system. Julia Kristeva brings *ecriture feminine* closer to the pre-Oedipal consciousness or "chora" which she defines as an unstructured space similar to Mary Daly's "wild zone" (Gyn/Ecology). Kristeva prescribes the "chora" as the point of genesis of *ecriture feminine*, the anti-phallic literary style which would bring body back to discourse. The aim of this new language would be to create unfamiliarity and newness, even at the cost of comprehensibility and consistency. She suggests that disruptions in a static, linear form could be brought about by the use of similes, silences, puns, rhythms and novel images.

Apart from the French feminists, feminist scholars all over the world also realize the need for a new women's language. Dale Spender in her book *Man Made Language* (1980) and Tillie Olson in *Silences* (1976) draw attention to gender biases in language such as the use of generic pronoun "he" to refer to both men and women that make women invisible. The naming of the world has also been done by men to reflect the male perspective so that the objects and feelings related to women have remained unnamed. Moreover, the words which denote the females have negative connotations, for example, "poetess" and "spinster". This strengthens the view that a separate language for women is needed. Norwegian feminist Toril Moi in *Sexual/Textual Politics* (1985) analyses the role of language in creating sexual dichotomy. These feminist critics want to open the fixity of words and their connotations by pluralising meanings.

These feminist critics, especially the French feminists, establish the primacy of the women's body in the identification of the women's self and emphasize the need to recast language itself as a women's language. Therefore, a close scrutiny of the language, structure and form in the works of Rhys, Carter and

Roberts would be relevant to the study of the ideological and narrative art of subversion in their fictional works. These three women writers are well known for the effective use of narrative voice, tone, images, symbols, motifs, punctuation, offline narration and intertextuality for subverting the false patriarchal assumptions about gender, race and religion.

Foregrounding the power of language and searching for new ways of communication are important motifs in Rhys's *WSS*. The impact of language on Antoinette could be seen when as a result of being called a "white cockroach" (*WSS* 101) by the natives she creeps away to hide against the wall. Antoinette knows that concepts like justice are just a play of words. Therefore, justice for her is a "cold word" (*WSS* 146) without meaning. Helene Carr remarks that "Rhys's protagonists are acutely aware that the social machine is kept in place by a use of language which ignores nuances, complexity, deviance, ambivalence, a language which reiterates the fetishistic phrases and preserves the status quo" (80). Mona Fayad considers that Antoinette's real loss of innocence comes at the moment of her "insertion into language" when she calls Tia "cheating nigger" (*WSS* 24) and sets up the barrier of racial hatred between them.

Carter also depicts the interconnectedness of a subject's mind and language. In *IDH* the fragmentation of Desiderio's language, the blending of cold logic and emotional amorphousness, show that he is a typical postmodern schizoid subject who is caught between the ideology of the reason freak Minister and the poetic Hoffman. Carter also invents some subversive linguistic features based on the principles of feminism while describing the language of the matriarchal Amerindian River People. Their language does not contain words for "yes" and "no", only a word for "maybe" (*IDH* 88) signifying their openness to possibilities. "The meaning of their words depends not so much on pronunciation as intonation", (*IDH* 89) and their language consists of "neither grammar nor vocabulary" but is only "a play of sounds" (*IDH* 222).

While Rhys draws a picture of how her protagonists are trapped in linguistic structures, and Carter theorises about the likelihood of a feminine mode of communication, Michele

Roberts portrays her female protagonists as continuously striving to embrace the physicality of their bodies in their writing. Roberts endeavours to unshackle language from patriarchy and constructs her words out of flesh and blood. Roberts also uses language to talk about those experiences of women which remain unexplored in the male narratives. Through the use of unruly structures and forms she encodes the semiotic and the subversive drives of the body in the subtext of her stories. Roberts also challenges the representational politics of gender in history and reconfigures the characters of Mary Magdalene, Mrs Noah and many others through the use of fresh and subversive images.

The protagonist of *IS*, Josephine, invents a language which celebrates the earthiness of the female body and the biological processes of the womb:

> What was going on was this *earth language*, with Josephine now a part of its grammar, *earth sentences*, the *earth* was the speech she could hear, that spoke her and spoke to her, that attracted her into its structure and dissolved her into a part of speech, a part of *earth*. How terrifying at first, the fall, into *the chasm that opened its brown lips* and *drew her in*, and then what a *flood of bliss*, the rains pouring in torrents through the valleys into the parched fields. *She belonged here. The earth was a great body and she belonged with it and was part of it*. She and the *earth* were the same body. The one body was both of them. (*IS* 190)

The repetitive use "earth" and the use of phrases like "the chasm", "brown lips", "drew her in", "flood of bliss", "a great body" suggests the wish of the protagonist to re-enter the womb of mother earth. This wish for re-entry into the womb also signifies unification with the mother.

In the times of eating disorders like anorexia, Roberts valorises the joys of eating and cooking. Cooking is treated with a lot of respect as a mode of creation and a means of caring for the loved ones. Being a cookery book writer she "code switches" with extraordinary ease from the description of "making crème patissiere" to the invocation of "God the father and God the Son" (*BMN* 26). One finds detailed descriptions of food items and cooking processes as Josephine "conjures" "fish cakes" from the bits of sardines left on the serving dish; "gnocchi" from leftover egg and potato, "flavoured croquettes" from cold rice and "sausages" out of "bread crumbs, grated heels of cheese, minced sage" (*IS* 233). Cooking is also described as a highly sensuous activity: "We lick the juice of the fruit, sticky and red, off our fingers, then ladle the sweet pulp into the black iron pot hung over the fire" (*BMN* 145).

Roberts braces the feminist motto which treats cooking, sexual activity and religious rituals as different but equal ways of expressing oneself. The lumps of beaten eggs are equated with "lumpy female bodies" and "lumpy bellies and breasts" (27) in *BMN* through syntactic parallelism. For introducing the materiality of the body in discourse, Roberts equates the body with imagination and book through syntactic parallelism: "Ark. Imagination. Body. Home. Book" (*BMN* 274). The device is at times used for unveiling the hypocrisy of religion. For example, the religious order of monks is equated with the birds of prey: "A nest of eagles: a nest of monks" (*IS* 242). Syntactic parallelism is again used to counteract the patriarchal association of male with light and female with darkness: "Both express God: masculine and feminine, darkness and light" (*SG* 78).

Adverbs of time are repeatedly used to show that women are not copies of any timeless and static notion of "Woman" conceived by men. They feel and behave differently at times just like human beings do. The Deftly Sibyl who aspires to be the ideal "Woman" learns to acknowledge this and says: "I don't like my children *at the moment*" (*BMN* 139). To deconstruct the linearity of time and show the continuity of past, Roberts uses the present tense to recollect the past of the sibyls: "When I am seven, I'm given an Advent calendar for the first time" (*BMN* 63).

Transitivity patterns in sentences are largely studied by the linguists to analyse writers' idiosyncratic preferences as well as deliberate stylistic choices. The feminist linguists consider language as phallocentric due to the rigidity of its grammatical structures and their semantic associations. They criticise the linear syntactical structure in which the action travels from the subject to the object in one direction. Generally, the male is placed at the subject position and female at the passive object position which is also related to the viewing of their psychosexuality as "active" and "passive" respectively. As part of writing in the *ecriture feminine*, Roberts makes ingenious and subversive use of lexical items and syntax. For example, Nana exhorts her granddaughter, Mrs Noah, to create meaning in her life through the use of strong action verbs: "*Get on* with you, you storyteller. *Become* a journeywoman. *Build* your Ark. *Sail off* in it. *Get going*" (*BMN* 14). Another example which subverts the subject-object convention is "Venice loses me" (*BMN* 10). In order to subvert the "ridiculous grammar based on male subject and female object" (*BMN* 49), Roberts constructs verbless sentences which consist only of noun phrases:

- Daphne, fierce priestess of the women's mysteries. Daphne, with a knife in her hand and her face daubed with blood. Daphne, who leads her troop of maenads up to the hills outside the city, in the grey smoke of dawn. (*BMN* 52)
- Rattle at the latch as the door opens. Neil's footstep in the passage outside, his cheerful voice upraised. (*BMN* 28)
- Hot breath blowing in the ear. (*BMN* 34)

Roberts aspires to challenge the myths about women by deconstructing the regular tense and transitivity patterns. On the contrary, Carter heightens the use of the conventional patterns in an attempt to mimic and sabotage them. For example, Beauty's opening sentence in "The Tiger's Bride" suggests her objectification. She is treated as a commodity to be sold by the father and bought by the lover when she is held at stake during a game of cards: "My father lost me to The Beast at cards" (*BC* 51). Peter Childs observes that Carter "uses juxtaposition and pastiche to undermine the authority of traditional stories, re-working some of the conventions (even clichés) of romantic fiction" (120). In order to mimic the mystery associated with women Carter uses paradoxical statements like: "She was fully clothed in obscene nakedness" (*PNE* 59). Generally, Carter's style consists of long descriptive sentences but at times a cluster of one word sentences is deployed to create meaningful pauses and capture the reader's attention. For example: "Tristessa, Enigma. Illusion. Woman? Ah!" (*PNE* 6)

At the level of graphology Roberts and Carter make use of free direct speech which reduces the gap between speech and thought. The interior monologues and thoughts are brought at the same level as the utterances of the characters which remain unmarked and unframed by the signifiers of quotation. The young wife of the Marquis in "The Bloody Chamber" narrates:

> I telephoned my mother. And astonished myself by bursting into tears when I heard her voice.
>
> No, nothing was the matter. Mother, I have gold bath taps. (*BC* 24)

Roberts separates the narration and utterances by the use of just a hyphen:

> She pauses to draw a breath. True to ourselves as would-be sisters, we wait for her to finish.
>
> — Some of my best friends are men. Writers. They don't call themselves male writers. Why should they? (*BMN* 48)

Unlike Carter and Roberts, Rhys does not normally use free direct speech. When she does so, as in Grace Poole's narration in Part three of *WSS*, the unquoted sentences get foregrounded and are read by Simpson as instances of "irony, serving notice that the audience ought not to believe in what is written but rather look for implications in the spaces of the text" (129). The use of parenthesis which makes the readers peep into the mind of the characters are also instances of Rhys's experimentation with graphology. Antoinette says to Christophine: "Even if I got away (and how?) he would force me back" (*WSS* 113).

Decontructionists like Derrida have theorised the slippage of meaning between the signifier and signified which makes the verbal language an imperfect tool for communication. A study of ambiguity in language also supports the view that there is no stable relationship between the signifier and the signified. On the lines of Kristevan theory, Carter and Roberts use a language which is syntactically as well as semantically open to ambiguity and invite the reader to interpret the text subjectively. Claims to a singular meaning are defied through the use of double entendre as in the use of the noun "surfaces" which stands both for Tristessa's presence on the silver screen as well as the myth of woman that she maintains. Roberts wittily uses structural ambiguity to subvert the mortification of flesh while seemingly reinforcing it so that the "political ambidexterity of postcolonialism" is syntactically manifested: "They mortified their flesh which stopped them from rising up to meet God" (*IS* 242). "Which stopped them from rising up to meet God" could be read both as the object complement and an adverbial. To underscore the violence inherent in the Catholic practices, she uses the verb "pray" as a transitive verb suggesting to "prey". "I cannot pray; I let the force of the cloister pray me" (*BMN* 114).

Satire is frequently used by Carter and Roberts to unlock the subversive potential of language. It is successfully used by these writers to subvert the status quo while apparantly re-inscribing it at the surface level. Roberts uses a sarcastic narrative style to implode the assumptions behind the patriarchal Catholic ideology. The witty and ironical tone is quite pronounced in the following statement:

> Don't you know? That women are the gateway to evil and to death? It's written in the sacred texts: the creation of man followed that of the earth, and the woman followed the man, and marriage followed the woman, and reproduction followed marriage, and death followed reproduction. Therefore we should shun all intercourse with women and become virgin again, so that we may be resurrected and conquer death and have eternal life. Don't you see? *It's logical.* (*SG* 62)

The faulty "logic" used for interpreting the "sacred texts" unravels the obtuseness of the male generated knowledge systems.

In another example the use of "real" is a way of problematizing the role of an ideal woman and the fallacy of generalisation: "The Babble-On Sibyl very much wants to be loved by her mother-in-law, very much wants to be a *real* woman. So she will cook the lunch". (*BMN* 28) The unemotional and blunt tone in the following extract heightens the satirical impact.

> Daughters are a difficulty, a drain on family resources. Dowries to be found and argued over, jointures to be agreed. Luckily there are only two of us to be settled. Harder on my second younger brother, I think to myself, who has to make his own way in the world, no estate at his back. Everything goes to the heir. (*BMN* 150)

The use of transferred epithet in the phrase "faithless religion and science and poetry" in the following example speaks of the unreasonable laws of the ecclesiasts who mould language to justify their tyranny:

> At the heart of the wilderness was a neat patch of herbs, each one a plant that was now forbidden to be grown. *Faithless medicine* had been banned, along with *Faithless religion and science and poetry*. (*IS* 155-6)

The use of adverbs and noun phrases like "intimately", "promiscuously" and "glorious confusion" in the following example suggests mutiny by the dead virgins for breaking down the heterosexual norms:

> Sister Maria and her community of nuns renamed themselves the Little Sister-Keepers of the Bones. They worked day and night sorting and labelling the hills of remains. They prayed for guidance in classification and it came. Faced with mixed bones from eleven hundred virgins plus one, all *embracing* each other *intimately* and *promiscuously* in *glorious confusion*, they put them confidently into neat piles. (*IS* 307)

The implosion of patriarchal language could be studied through the following example:

- You're the *boss, old boy*, they cried to Saint Peter: you can work a miracle if you want to. Go on, heal her, the *little hussy*.
- I'll leave her to suffer, thanks, Saint Peter retorted: she doesn't deserve to be cured. Let her stew in *her own juice*!
- Oho, mocked his friends: so you are not too sure of your *powers*, eh? (*IS* 56)

The use of "juice" by the author satirically refers to the male discourse in which women are treated as leaking bodies and filthy objects of denigration. The repetition of words like "boss", "old boy", "little hussy" and "powers" are terms charged with various gender biases. The commodification of female body could be seen in the use of "damaged goods" for referring to a girl:

> You couldn't be too careful. For in those far-off days a girl had to be kept pure, for the sake of her future husband, who must not be sold *damaged goods*. He had to know that his sons were his, in order to pass his property on to them. (*IS* 138)

Satire could be found recurrently in Carter's texts too: "But she herself had known no pleasure at all. She was a perfect lady" (*IDH* 136). In the story "Wolf-Alice", as Childs observes, it appears to Wolf-Alice that the "congregation in the church was ineffectually attempting to imitate the wolves' chorus" (125). This is Carter's way of playing a joke on the treachery and greed of the Church authorities. At times ironical, tongue-in-cheek style and hyperbolic descriptions such as: "my mother herself had gladly, scandalously, defiantly beggared herself for love" ("The Bloody Chamber" 7-8) find way in Carter's works. Robert Clark comments on Carter's style as one which defamiliarizes the textual world to the reader for facilitating the working of satire:

> The brilliant and choice lexicon, the thematization of surfaces and odours, of beauty, youth, and power, the incantatory rhythms and tantalizing literariness, are strategies that bind the reader poetically, give the illusion of general significance, and put the reason to sleep, thereby inhibiting satire's necessary distancing of the reader from both the text and the satirized illusions. (158-9)

The techno feminist remake of the Great Mother in *PNE* is introduced through a long poetic invocation containing mythical allusions, given in an incantatory mode, which strengthen the poetic element in the novel. Using a burlesque style, Carter portrays her with two tiers of nipples and a beard (*PNE* 59). Peter Childs also points out Carter's "exaggerated use of rococo description and ornate language" (119) while discussing the artificiality of the narrative process in "The Bloody Chamber". Fin de Siecle decadent style of Baudelaire, the French symbolist style and the surrealist styles blend to give *BC* its colourful texture and make it a postmodern pastiche. For example "we lay in his great ancestral bed in the sea-girt, pinnacle domain that lay, still, beyond the grasp of my imagination...that magic place, the fairy castle whose walls were made of foam, that legendary habitation in which he had been born" ("The Bloody Chamber" 8).

Alison Easton also believes that reading Carter's books is especially delightful due to "the sensuousness and shocks of the experiences described", and their "exuberantly decorative linguistic surface" (1). Carter makes innovative use of semantically deviant imagery in *IDH* to depict the chaos imposed by the Doctor, for example, "roses emitted low but intolerably piercing pentatonic melodies which were the sound of their deep crimson colour and yet we heard them inside our nostrils" (35). Unusual metaphorical descriptions like the clocks having "innocent faces" and "water-melon munching, opaquely-eyed visages of slaves" (*IDH* 41) are also deployed by Carter for the purpose of subverting the norms of the animate and inanimate worlds. By treating the "roses" and "clocks" as human beings, Carter topples the hierarchical relationship between the inanimate and animate subjects.

PNE is a highly sensuous novel and the descriptions take the reader into a dream like trance. Munford observes that the steely "white room lit only by a fringe of pinkish luminescence at the foot of the wall" and the "technical marvels" (*PNE* 49), of the underground city Beulah which is "far from the light of the sun" (*PNE* 50) capture the senses of the reader like a psychedelic drug and serve the purpose of defamiliarization. Suggestiveness and sensuousness also fill the text with layers of meaning. The "poignant brightness of the hollyhocks still bravely blooming in the shaggy gardens, and the beauty of the flaming sunset" (98) in "The Lady of the House of Love" suggest the tragedy of the compulsive vampire. The "perfume of spiced leather" (8) used by the Marquis in *The Bloody Chamber* indicates his sadistic sexuality.

Roberts's style is also considered extremely sensuous and voluptuous. Unlike Carter, she uses a sensuous style not for distancing the reader but for celebrating the body in discourse as prescribed by the theorists like Kristeva. She makes it clear to Jules Smith in an interview: "I want to put the body back into language", "to touch it and smell it and make it into language" and "I'm voluptuous: I'm not thin and I never will be, so I want to celebrate voluptuousness in real life, too". Images of womb, rebirth, and water abound in the opening scenes of *BMN* set in Venice. The fluidity of style and metaphors related to the womb symbolize birth, growth, femaleness, chaos and the fluidity of the female identity. The use of vocative like "ugh", "tsk", "tsk", "yuk" in the dialogues takes one closer to the impulsive feelings, both mental and physical, of the characters. The intimate and fictionally unexplored spaces like the "bathroom" are described in detail as means of character portrayal and revealing the secret aspects of women's personalities. The Babble-On Sibyl keeps items like "packets of hair dye", "ladies' razors", "laxatives", "discreet bags in flowered cotton containing rubber domes and tubes of foul-smelling cream" secretly in her bathroom.

Rhys also uses sensuous images in *WSS* during Antoinette's narration for portraying the protagonist's Creole sensibility. A language rich in sensuous imagery is used to depict Antoinette's closeness to nature and her aversion to the artificiality of culture. The vivid details of the naturescapes are drawn which include visualization, ocularization, tactilization and olfactorization to prove that the "real" for Antoinette is the sensuous:

> ...something you can touch and hold like my red dress, that has a meaning...I saw it hanging, the colour of fire and sunset. The colour of flambouyant flowers...The scent that came from the dress...grew stronger. The smell of vertivert and frangipani, of cinnamon and dust and lime trees where they are flowering. The smell of the sun and the smell of the rain. (*WSS* 185)

The use of poetic imagery and the tone of uncertainty leads to ambivalence in the novel which is also a way of deconstructing patriarchal certainty.

Kristeva recommends the use of fresh metaphors for writing in the *ecriture feminine*. One can find in *WSS* an inventive use of spatial metaphors which add a psychological relevance to the geographical details. The Sargasso Sea of the title stands for the psychological barriers between the English and the Jamaicans. Actions like swimming in a pool, climbing down a staircase, walking in a forest etcetera have high symbolic significance. Mirrors according to Helene Carr are a leitmotif in Rhys's work and are used as privileged sites of power. "Her protagonists spend a good deal of time looking in mirrors, sometimes at photos, even at ghosts of themselves, descending into the unknown, searching for some understanding of their being which is other than the definitions thrust upon them" (Carr 58-9). Antoinette sees herself in a mirror and considers her mirror image as a "ghost" (*WSS* 188). The disowning of her image by Antoinette suggests her dissociated sense of identity. Gilbert and Gubar note in *The Mad Woman in the Attic* that Antoinette has internalized the patriarchal judgement of Edward Fairfax Rochester's gaze and thus sees herself as the "other", i.e. a ghost. Carter uses the mirror metaphor like Rhys for depicting women's subjection to the patriarchal gaze in *The Magic Toyshop* whereas, Roberts uses it to explicate her concept of bisexuality in *SG*.

Irigaray talks of the importance of the use of symbols and metaphors and advocates the use of "an allusive and suggestive style which reverberates with meaning and cancels out the possibility of the production of hard-and-fast explanations or fall into mourning over the impossibility of putting experience precisely into the form of words" (Simpson 2005, 15). Ground-breaking symbolism is a part of Carter's narrative strategy too. The names given by Carter to her characters are also emblematic. Evelyn has an androgynous name, Eve+lyn, Zero's name signifies the hollowness of his being, Mother does not have a name and is referred to as Mother due to the feminist role she plays, Lilith's name alludes to the rebellious first wife of Adam, and Tristessa's name has a phonetic hiss which connotes mystery and ambiguity. According to Gamble, Desiderio's name is anagrammatically ambivalent and contains "the desired I" and also the "desired O", that is, the desired self and other (*The Fiction of Angela*

Carter, 80). It symbolizes his picaresque and unfulfilled quest for the desired object which keeps eluding him. In "The Bloody Chamber" the Count is called the Marquis in order to draw a parallel with Marquis de Sade and the young wife's individuality remains unmarked due to the absence of a first name. The Beasts in the stories are called Beast and the Beauties are named Beauty for maintaining the simplicity of the folktales.

IDH and *PNE* are written in a highly figurative prose style which is deviant in its connotations. The Doctor whose character is based on Breton, the founder of the surrealist movement, stands for the anarchic forces of the imagination. The war symbolises the anti-realist movement as it intends to overthrow the bourgeois and the mundane. Albertina is visualized by Desiderio as a black swan in one of his dreams. Swan is a motif in Carter's novels and is also used in *Nights at the Circus* and *The Magic Toyshop* to explore the different aspects of male and female sexuality. The wings of Fevvers in *NC* emphasise her freedom and her identity as the new woman. Reading Carter's works from *TMT* and *BC* to *NC,* Paulina Palmer notes that her symbolism progresses from the "alienation of the femininity of the coded mannequin to the libratory prospects of the woman with wings" (qtd. in Mary Russo 153).

Through Tristessa, who is a "symbol of sadomasochistic spectacle of female tragedy", (*PNE* 145) Carter mocks at the cultural fascination with such symbols. Tristessa's glass mansion, according to Linden Peach, is the central symbol in the novel and signifies the postmodern cycle of self-replication. According to the critic, the lovemaking between Evelyn and Leilah is symbolic of male domination and female resistance. Castration is also a trope in *PNE* which explodes the myth of woman as "lack".

BC follows an evocative prose style which blurs the distinction between sexuality and violence through the use of motifs like blood, meat, flesh, fur, wolves and beasts etc. In *BC* the motif of skin and flesh are used to symbolize pleasure, as meat gets transformed to flesh through libido (Makinen 31). The stories are generally allegorical and the wolf tales use the figure of the werewolf to diminish the gap between the animals and the humans.

Roberts also draws on ingenious metaphors and similes which fracture the strictures with which faith in God is maintained and the religious rituals observed. "Belief in God was a problem" for Josephine "like a petticoat she was not sure whether or not to discard" (*IS* 111). In a subversive comparison between God and a petticoat she says: "If God were a petticoat, better to let go" (*IS* 111).

Mrs Noah compares words with clothes when she says: "Words can be given away, lost, put out with the rubbish" (*BMN* 181) like clothes. Body is metaphorically called a "house with many windows" (*BMN* 63) and women's language is considered "as changeable and delicious as food" (*BMN* 127). In one of the stories told by a Sibyl, Roberts describes delivery pain in terms of food: "A glass of wine. Hot wine, with spices in it" (*BMN* 159). At times she treats lexicon as a wardrobe filled with dresses e.g. "At a loss for words, she has invented this wardrobe in order to enrich her vocabulary" (*BMN* 172). In a similar parallelism one of the women on the Ark calls herself a "cloth cap, torn mackintosh" which "used to hang onto words like hooks" (*BMN* 140). Roberts shows in *BMN* how women can use make up and haircuts figuratively to express their diversity and multiplicity. The Forsaken Sibyl has her hair cut in two different lengths; "one side of her head bristles in a crew cut and the other sprouts with curly red tufts weighted with amber and turquoise beads" (*BMN* 46).

WSS is also a highly suggestive text where small actions speak a lot about the characters. According to Carl Plasa, Rochester's drawing of Antoinette, where he makes a dot for her face, a larger one for her body and a big triangle for her skirt, reveals not only his dehumanization of Antoinette but also the way he perceives her. Plasa comments on the symbolic drawing of Rochester thus: "Antoinette's identity has been erased by the politics of imperialism and of patriarchy. Only the skirt, the sexual marker, identifies her as a woman. Dehumanized, depersonalized, renamed, she is now a helpless puppet, a character under Rochester's control" (110).

WSS is a dialogic text and one finds in it a constant exchange of ideas among characters belonging to different socio-cultural-racial backgrounds. Rhys makes Bertha the narrative subject and delegitimizes the images of women disseminated by the nineteenth century sister text *Jane Eyre*. Antoinette's valorization happens through the process of "doubling" in which the differences between her and Edward get slowly diminished. On the one hand, Antoinette is given poignant but intelligent utterances unlike the animal grunts and moans of Bertha, and on the other hand, Rochester is depicted as fallible. Antoinette confesses the truth about her mother Annette to Edward in a way that shows her intelligent understanding of her mother's suffering:

> "And very poor. Don't forget that. For five years. Isn't it quick to say. And isn't it long to live. And lonely. She was so lonely that she grew away from other people. That happens." (*WSS* 130)

The repetition of the noun phrase "twenty thousand pounds" in Rochester's narration underlines Rochester's monetary concerns and the phoniness of his "sad heart" (*WSS* 79) speech with which he woos Antoinette. Rochester is both cunning and melancholic. Rochester's dejection becomes explicit when he considers himself wronged by his father who he thinks has sold his soul to Antoinette: "She has bought me" (*WSS* 70). The placing of himself as an object after the verb "bought" confirms his self pity and establishes his self image as a victim rather than as a ruthless plunderer. The "Dear Father" motif in his narration shows his deference to patriarchal authority as well as his uneasiness. According to Mary Lou Emery, the narrative elements in Rhys challenge the psychological essentialism and the evaluation of characters in terms like "helpless", "passive" and "masochistic".

Carl Plasa notes that the opening of the novel with "They say" (*WSS* 17) gestures towards the multiple utterances to come and the novel's disregard for monologism (Plasa 12). Deconstructing the possibility of a centre and margins the voices of Antoinette and Rochester; Daniel and Christophine; Christophine and Rochester; and in the end Grace Poole and Antoinette continuously reason and quarrel with each other without reaching a resolution. Rochester's narrative intermingles with Antoinette's and the patriarchal order is opened to the marginal voices. The English caretaker's voice which sympathizes with Rochester collides with Christophine's, whose opinions in turn are challenged by the spiteful Daniel. Anne B. Simpson reads in Grace Poole's narration the presence of "a medley of voices, suggesting the larger social world that cannot grasp Antoinette's complexity" (129). The text is also a polyglot in which English, French patois and Jamaican Creole co-exist. There is no authorial intervention as Rhys maintains a distance from the text so that the dialogue between the natives, the Creoles and the English is presented without partiality. All the voices, including those of Daniel's, Tia's and of the natives, are treated equally. No individual discourse stands over the other. According to Sue Spaull, Rochester's voice is deconstructed, but not marginalized, in order to "demonstrate the fallacy of a patriarchal mono-dimensional reality" (Gynocriticism 105). Ashcroft, Griffiths and Tiffin also note that subversion of a canon does not merely include the replacing of one set of texts with another but replacing a set of reading practices.

The style is a blend of modernist techniques and West Indian sensibilities. The oracular mode of Christophine's narration articulates Caribbean fatalism and the lack of faith in a moral superpower which leads to pessimism. West Indian folklore, tradition and omens find way in the narration. For example, the burning of the parrot Coco is seen as an ill omen by the natives because for them parrot represents the soul. Carl Plasa calls Rhys's description of the Caribbean atmosphere as "brooding, sinister, compounded of heat and rain and intensely coloured flowers, of racial antagonisms and all-pervasive superstition" (21).

Carter also experiments with voice in her novels. Her originality lies in using a male homodiegetic narrator, generally a male chauvinist and sometimes even a misogynist, to create feminist texts. This style of "ventriloquism" where Carter, being a female author, speaks through a male voice achieves remarkable results (Gamble, *The Fiction of Angela Carter*, 85). Through the excessive masculinisation of narrative, gory details of bodily mutilations and stylistic kitsch Carter first distances the readers from the text and then makes evident the hollowness of male chauvinism and the artificiality of gender norms. According to Peter Stockwell, the term "defamiliarization" was originally used by the Russian formalists to explain this type of processes. The use of a male voice for feminist purpose is called "male chauvinist drag" by Robert Clark.

According to Robinson, Carter mimics the oedipal narrative in *IDH* where a man who is the questing subject is supported by a father figure during the quest and attains social stability at the end of his journey through heterosexual relationship with a woman object. "Oedipal narrative is one of the master narratives based on Freudian psychoanalysis" (Robinson *Engendering the Subject*, 244) and is heavily masculinist. Through a postcolonial mimicry of Oedipal narratives, Carter shows the construction of woman as the "other". Both denigration and celebration of the exotic female "other" are revealed to be masculinist strategies for maintaining patriarchy. Robinson observes in *The Anti-Hero as Oedipus* that Carter inscribes the image of the Woman through a sexist narrative schema only to subvert it eventually. While reading *IDH* as a feminist postmodern narrative, Robinson further states that "like Irigaray's strategy of mimicry, Carter's parodies and masquerades point to an 'elsewhere' of discourse, what de Lauretis refers to as the 'chinks and cracks' in the dominant representational practices" (*The Anti-Hero as Oedipus*, 109).

In *IDH* and *PNE* the first person frame narratives are given in analepsis or flashback and contain the narrators' critique of their past actions. According to Herman, at times in homodiegetic texts the narrating "I" and the experiencing "I", though linked through a biographical identity relation, are separated in time and space. This creates an occasionally unstable union between the current, remembering self and what French critics term an "autre", an other. Desiderio says "It was I who killed her" (*IDH* 14). Here the narrator is treated as second person, so the young experiencing subject gets separated from the old narrating "I". David Herman borrows Dorrit Cohn's term "dissonant self narration" for depicting a form of flashback narration in which the narrating "I" disagrees with the experiencing "I", while the old narrator reflects upon his life as a young man. The old Desiderio too looks back at the young man that he once was who "could not surrender to the flux of mirages" (12) and by killing Albertina subjected himself to permanent defeat. Carter represents the dilemma of the old Desiderio in a telling way: "Old Desiderio asks young Desiderio: 'And when he offered you a night of perfect ecstasy in exchange for a lifetime's contentment, how could you possibly choose the latter?'" (*IDH* 267)

Homodiegetic narration by nature is open to multiple interpretations due to the absence of an omniscient voice. Carter uses the mode for showing the susceptibility of memory to gaps and slips. Introduction of *IDH* starts with "I remember everything. Yes. I remember everything perfectly" (*IDH* 11) whereas the first chapter begins with a contradictory statement "I cannot remember exactly how it began" (*IDH* 17). Both Desiderio and Evelyn try to impose order on the chaotic happenings of the past through their narration and confess that their descriptions might not be accurate as their memories have grown hazy. Sarah Gamble notes that heteroglossia and multiplicity make Carter's text "feminist in both its narrative structure and its story" (*The Fiction of Angela Carter,* 96).

Roberts's novels have a single homodiegetic narrator, yet they are dialogic too. The Sibyls as well as the characters in the Sibyls' stories debate and disagree so that their voices create polyphony in the style suggested by Bakhtin. Different stories, theoretical attitudes, viewpoints and belief systems coalesce in the textual fabric of *BMN*. The Sibyls together straddle different strands of feminism like Amazon feminism, ecofeminism, liberal feminism and lesbian feminism which in the end merge to form the egalitarian approach of Mrs Noah. The stories by the Sibyls in *BMN* and the histories in *IS* are arranged in a non-hierarchical style, which fractures phallogocentricism. Roberts makes fun of omniscient narration, which privileges the voice of the author God by introducing the Gaffer on the Ark who says: "I am the speaker of the Word of God" (*BMN* 51). The last chapter of *SG* also brings together the voices of patriarchs and feminists in a dialogic interlock. A conglomerate of female voices speaking of injustice and trauma is presented, and one voice is made distinct from the other only through the use of graphological devices like dashes and spacing.

Postmodernist thinkers believe that the past cannot be destroyed so it should be revisited with irony. Therefore, unlike the modern literary works by Yeats and Eliot, which are collages of previous literal, religious and theoretical texts, the postmodern writers use intertextuality as a means of parodying and mimicking the earlier "readerly" (Barthes, *S/Z*) or monologic texts. The theory of intertextuality given by Julia Kristeva in her essay "Nous Deux" and the intertextual view of literature offered by Roland Barthes facilitate multiple interpretations of texts. One finds that the works of Rhys, Carter and Roberts are also anti-monologic as they continuously refer to and re-inscribe the older works.

Jane Eyre could be called an intertext to *WSS* because the latter is composed of "allusions to, memories of, and characters, images and quotations" from the previous text (Lane 27). Helene Carr calls Rhysian narrative as "counter discourse" (77) which is:

> ...always a collage of texts, echoes of conversations, songs, advertisements, poetry, law reports, quotations from books, letters, even prayers: in short, postmodernist fictions, told by a narrative voice or voices which re-inscribe, re-invent, resist and transform the multiple stories into which, as Lyotard says, we are born. (86)

Carter places myths, fairytales, primitive gods and machines at the centre of her works like Joyce, Yeats, Lawrence and Ezra Pound respectively to study contradicting ideas about truth and unravel the social fictions about gender. Mimicry, parody and pastiche are Carter's ways of challenging the theoretical paradigms of the Enlightenment and the 1960s Britain. The agenda of "demythologizing" includes replacing the central grand narratives by multiple mini narratives mimicking and parodying the former. This deconstruction and rewriting of the master narratives of the Western world is described by Carter as "putting new wine in old bottles and, in some cases old wine in new bottles" (*Notes from the Front Line,* 76).

Sarah Gamble observes the use of intertextuality in Carter's fiction and comments that "Shakespeare, Milton, Poe, Ibsen, and Joyce are some of the writers to whom she alludes, with the effect of creating a polyphonic interplay of European cultural attitudes and moments" (*The Fiction of Angela Carter,* 140). The popularity of Carter's works among the critics and researchers is mainly a result of their dense intertextual nature.

> Carter's novels frequently, explicitly and implicitly, refer to mythology, the Bible, European and English literary works, Renaissance drama, fairy stories, European art, film, especially Godard and Bunuel, opera, ballet, music, and psychoanalytic and linguistic theory. It is an indication of the subversive nature of Carter's work that often she refers to two or three different frameworks for the same referent in the same paragraph! (Peach 18)

Carter uses contemporary theoretical jargon to create pastiches in *IDH* and *PNE* which destabilise the stereotyping and over-determination of women as the Woman. Her collection of subverted short stories, *BC,* tries to unshackle women from flat idealizations found in the traditional fairy tales by giving them alternate portrayals as active, uncompromising and at times even violent. Jack Zipes, in his book, *Fairy Tales and the Art of Subversion*, suggests that fairy tales have historically served as codes of social conduct that reinforce gender roles. Roland Barthes asserts in *Mythologies* that the very principle of myth transforms history into nature. He unveils the process through which the historical and cultural fictions are treated as natural and sacred. According to Lucy Sargisson, myths are stories of imagined or supernatural figures that embody popular ideas on natural or social phenomena and "if myth has (historically) embodied ideological values and aspirations, re/deconstructed myth perhaps can embody or at least inscribe different values" (217). Carter believes that myths are products of human mind designed to make people unfree.

Carter fulfils her aim of demythologizing by parodying the myth of a bird woman based on the figure of Helene of Troy in *NC*, the myth of a phallic mother in *PNE* and that of the mysterious femme fatale in *IDH*. The myth of Centaurs in

IDH is appropriated by Carter to subvert the assumptions behind Biblical imagery. *IDH* is a parody of Marquis de Sade's unfinished novel called *The One Twenty Days of Sodom* which he wrote in 1786 when he was a prisoner in Bastille. *PNE* is a dense pastiche of references to the myths of Europa, Antiope, Medusa, Leda and Erigone which are used only to subvert their latent content. The fertility myths of Osiris, Isis, Attis, Cybele, Adonais and Aphrodite, in which a male is loved by a fertility goddess, dies and is reborn, are playfully enacted when Evelyn is reborn as a girl.

Barthes suggests in *Mythologies* that the best weapon against myth is to create an artificial myth. Like Dorris Lessing, Michele Roberts creates new myths instead of just mimicking the old myths for deconstruction. Roberts uses history and myth as treasure troves of stories which could be reworked for creating new myths. *The Golden Legend* is used as a satirical intertext to the stories of the female saints in *IS*. Michele Roberts also creates dissimilar myths about the lives of Mrs Noah, Mary Magdalene, Jesus Christ and Peter. Roberts rewrites the story of Apollo and Daphne in *BMN* and calls her story as the original version which was later on appropriated by men:

> Hear me. This story has an earlier version. Rewritten, it has been almost erased. Its forgotten words, trampled in the dust of the male scholars' sentences, yelp in their elegant pauses, poke through the gaps between their graceful lines. (*BMN* 52)

BMN is full of intertextual references to the male literary canon and one can find subversive allusions to *Tess of the D'Urbervilles* (*BMN* 204), *Rape of the Lock* (*BMN* 162), *The psychoanalytic theories of Freud and Lacan* (*BMN* 152, 209), *The Old Testament* (*BMN* 154, 241) etcetera. A new reading of these old texts is offered to the readers. *SG* and *BMN* offer playful feminist rewritings of the Biblical themes like the myth of Creation, the fall of Adam from grace and the Flood.

According to David Herman, genre study helps the readers read and interpret texts. A study of the avant garde experimentation and subversion of the genre norms in the postmodern literature is also relevant because it represents the changing social and ideological atmosphere. The postmodern writers explore all possible interactions between perception, memory and identity and express it through experimentation with genre. According to Aristotle's theory of mimesis the "real" world can be captured in art through clear mimetic prose. In the postmodern times, however, life becomes a simulation of art rather than vice versa. Thus the notion of "real" has become open to interrogation and appropriation in the postmodern literature. Carter and Roberts show how "reality" of Woman is a result of powerful stories about bodies, pain and ethics. These contemporary British women writers reject the realist art as it does not present reality but "feeds the nostalgic desire for a world of moral certainties and experiential coherence, a world that can be grasped and known as a totality" (Morris 30). French literary critic Roland Barthes also criticizes realism for purging the world of the uncertainty of existence.

As social realism fails to explore certain areas of experience, the need for defamiliarization is felt by the postmodern writers who use the fantasy and gothic forms to suspend the illusion of reality and introduce the unreal. Carter also uses the Gothic style like the novelists Horace Walpole and Ann Radcliffe to dramatize the unconscious and parody the clichés by exaggerating them. *Heroes and Villains* is written in the gothic mode. *TMT* is a suburban gothic novel. Marianne, Melanie and the heroines in *BC* are post-feminist gothic heroines. "The Earl-King" in *BC* follows a gothic narrative style which shifts to mystery and pastoral romance with the shift in point of view between the third person and the first person. "The Lady of the House of Love" draws on a gothic vampire tale. The use of gothic by Carter as in *Shadow Dance*, *Several Perceptions* and *Love* also serves the purpose of undermining the authenticity of realism in narratives. As David Punter explains: "At all events, the gothic writer insists, realism is not the whole story: the world, at least in some aspects, is very much inexplicable-or mysterious, or terrifying, or violent-than that" (*The Literature of Terror*, 407-11).

Rosemary Jackson in her work called *Fantasy: The Literature of Subversion* (1981) observes the subversive traits of the fantasy genre. Jackson sees fantasy not as an escape from the realities of life rather as an expression of the unconscious drives. She also defines fantasy as a genre which aptly uses images of desire and disenchantment to express the cultural unease. Carter uses fantasy with contemporary gothic in *Love*, *Shadow Dance* and *Several Perceptions* to portray an alternate universe with a different set of rules and characteristics. Carter also believes in the importance of imaginative experience and frequently uses hallucinations, metaphors, fantastic happenings and dreams to comment upon the social and psychological realities. Gerardine Meaney believes that "fantasy, by its very ability to make non-sense its sense and impossibility its reality, radically undermines the referential claims of language" (86).

According to Meaney, in fantasy, reality is contravened only to be reinstituted. In contrast, speculative fiction guards against such a possibility by using the device of alienation and by providing a futuristic or quasi-scientific context in which the unexpected rules. *PNE* and *IDH* are called speculative fictions and annihilate all possibilities of the re-institution of reality. While a fantastic narrative follows a different set of rules than a realist narrative, a magic realist novel does not have any set of rules. Carter and Roberts also challenge the notion of "real" by writing in inherently subversive genres like magic realism, and use them to investigate the social fictions which regulate the lives of women.

The term magic realism was introduced in the 1950s by a German art critic called Franz Roh to refer to a painting style which crosses the genre boundary between fantasy and reality. In magic realist fiction magical events and happenings are depicted in a realist matter-of-fact narrative (Bowers 1-7). Magic realism defies the conventions of realistic fiction like fixity and close endings. Zamora and Faris note that "magical realist texts are subversive: their in-betweenness, their all at onceness encourage resistance to monological political and cultural structures" and so it is a mode suited to exploring and transgressing "ontological, political, geographical and generic boundaries" (qtd. in Bowers 67). In the postmodern era the grand narratives of French Enlightenment, German knowledge,

Marxist philosophy and Christian notion of salvation are replaced with a carnival of micro-narratives and language games. Magic realism could be called a postmodern genre because it also subverts the conventional hegemonic structure of the established ideologies and distorts the notions of linear time and history. It allows the narrative to be playful, anarchic and rhizomatic. Magic realism portrays the anarchic postmodern condition of the late capitalist world which is ruled by communication explosion, synthetic hyper-reality, transitory identities and chaos theory. The postcolonial critic Brenda Cooper notes: "Magical realism at its best opposes fundamentalism and purity; it is at odds with racism, ethnicity and the quest for tap roots, origins and homogeneity" (qtd. in Bowers 4). The avante garde style and underlying cognitive base of magic realism aptly supports the antirealism and antihumanism of the postmodern condition.

Carter's motive is to open up all certainties in favour of the liminal, the in-between and the marginal. Maggie Ann Bowers calls Angela Carter "the most celebrated English feminist writer of the 1980s and 1990s, who wrote carnivalesque, exuberant magical realist narratives influenced by the comedies of William Shakespeare and the literary theories of the Russian Mikhail Bakhtin" (48). It is because of Carter's skilful use of magic realism in her works that she earned titles like the "fairy godmother of magic realism" (Johnson) and "a very good wizard, perhaps the first wizard de-luxe" (Rushdie). Carter commingles realism and fantasy in a magic realist style in her works like *IDH*, *PNE*, *WC*, *NC* and the short stories in *BC*. Makinen notes that Carter's texts are "open-ended, written with a space for the reader's activity in mind...and says that Carter "disliked novels that were closed worlds and described most realist novels as etiquette manuals" (25).

Franz Roh gives a list of the defining characteristics of magic realism such as "sobriety and sharp focus; an unsentimental and unemotional vision; description of everyday, banal and insignificant subjects; the absence of timidity with regard to painting the unpleasant; a static, tightly unified structure; and a new spiritual relationship with the world of things" (qtd. in Bowers 116). Carter's works could be called magic realist narratives according to Roh's criteria. Carter's style foregrounds the "textuality of the text, the delightful sensual materiality of the words themselves" (Morris 30). The reader sees the textual world through the viewpoint and psychology of the first person narrators like Desiderio, Evelyn, Dora Chance and Fevvers in these works. The happenings during Nebulous Time in *IDH*, the disruption of linear time in *NC* and the challenging of the notion of history by mingling past and present in *WC* are all instances of magic realist moments in Carter's fiction. The monstrous, grotesque and uncanny portrayals of Mother, Fevvers and Albertina in *PNE, NC* and *IDH* respectively also form part of Carter's magic realistic style. In *BC* the short story form is blended with the oral forms like fairytales, folklores, old wives tales, nursery fables, myths and fantasy in a magic realist fashion. In "The Bloody Chamber" the new bride narrates: "I thought how the car would be rolling silently towards the closed courtyard gate; the more I scrubbed the key, the more vivid grew the stain." (33)

According to Morris, Fevvers in *NC* refuses "the conventional humanism type of life narrative of rational and moral development", and instead creates and performs her own "instantaneous little histories making a playful burlesque out of all the cultural fictions available to us" (31). As in *NC* which has a working class girl who grows wings, the protagonist of *WC* also "subverts the authority of the patriarchal upper class by emphasizing to excess the attributes of the female, illegitimate working class" (Bowers 69). The setting of *WC* is mid twentieth century Britain. While *NC* celebrates the liminality and in-betweenness of the female protagonist who straddles the animal and the human world, *WC* transgresses the boundaries of all the other categories like high class/low class, legitimate/illegitimate, sacred/profane, logic/imagination, superstition/rationalism. The festive exuberance of Nora and Dora Chance epitomizes Bakhtin's idea of "carnivalesque" (*Rabelais and his World*) in literature which relies upon the reversal of categories. Dora, the music hall actor, subverts the authority of patriarchal figures including Shakespeare through the use of rough slangs and camp exuberance. Magic realist episodes, like a girl coming out of a box, remove the film of familiarity thus making the topsy turvy and hybrid world of *WC* authentic. Multiple and conflicting voices from the exclusive North London and the dreary South populate the text creating polyphony. In the novel, uncertainty prevails and the rational, fabulous and serious is placed side by side with the irrational, commonplace, and the comic.

Magic realism is associated with fictions that tell the stories of those on the margins of political power (Bowers 33) and so does the British new wave science fiction. Science fiction of the 1970s was utopian, dystopian or complex and hybrid like heteropian or critical utopian. Carter had always admired the British new wave science fiction writers of the sixties like J. G. Ballard and Michael Moorcock who use the genre and avante garde experimentations to comment on society. Roz Kaveney maintains that "the new wave were guerrillas of interior landscapes, like the Surrealists, but not as obsessed with putting people in their proper place" (174). Women's science fiction holds a dialogue with the male oriented science fiction. Adam Roberts studies the growth of feminist science fiction which started in the 1960s and investigates gender and sexuality as social constructs. Carter uses science fiction to show the metamorphosis between man and woman, human and animal in *PNE* and *NC*.

Like Carter, Roberts too crosses the frontiers of genres and travels many genre territories at once. She says to Sanchez that "pastiche goes on interesting me" as it is "potentially subversive". In *Fair Exchange* she deliberately uses romance form to write about the eighteenth century revolutionary feminists. She blends picaresque narrative with history and romance in *SG*. Her magic realist works include historical revision as in *IS*. This makes clear the relationship between magic realism and postmodernism according to which history is created by those in power to justify and maintain their position (Bower 76-77). Roberts's use of magic realism could be viewed as interacting with historical postmodernism in order to reveal the constructed nature of historical and cultural realities. While exploring the psychological life of Saint Christina and the mysteries of life in the story of Saint Barbara, Roberts uses the technique of magic realism. Magic realism in *IS* detaches the reader from the patriarchal norms and defamiliarizes the world of Western intellectual domination:

> Each girl held out her left hand. Each one wore, on her wrist, the tight handcuff to which was attached the long chain whose other end was fixed to the pillar in the middle of the room. Christine cut off the others' left hand one by one, letting the severed and bleeding chunks drop to the floor, the cuff and chain with them. They left these in a gory heap for the doctor to find on his return from holiday.

The snakes knotted themselves together to make a ladder from the window down to the garden. One by one the girls slithered down. Girls and snakes leaped onto the back of the lorry. The driver roared them away into town. (*IS* 123)

For undermining the supremacy of realism, Roberts shifts the focus to the magical through the use of imagery in *BMN*. For example, the screams of Mrs Noah "withers the vines on the hillsides outside the city", "blackens the olive trees" and make "pregnant women miscarry" (*BMN* 134).

Roberts deconstructs the polarity between discourse on literary theory and creative writing by making the multi-voiced narrative of *BMN* both theoretical and fictional. Tatiana Teslenco notes that Roberts's fiction is "illustrative of fiction theory because it is more than fiction; it is also a piece of creative theory" (70).

Roberts believes that "the form and the content are absolutely integrated" (Rodriguez 104). Her contribution to the novel form, according to her, is blending short stories with novels. Rather than having the form of a single narrative, *BMN* and *IS* are fragmented into short and unconnected stories. Roberts tells Sanchez that the traditional form of storytelling had "entrapped and bruised women" so she keeps experimenting with form. Her first novel, *A Piece of the Night*, also structurally follows "the zigzag and the spiral of memory". The fragmentary narratives of Roberts refuse to accept the linearity and the authority of male time. Roberts's attitude towards the role of narrative is expressed through the voice of Mrs Noah while visiting the House of Memory thus:

> A narrative is simply a grid placed over chaos so that it can be read in descending lines from left to right, if that's what you want to do. Some writers prefer the chaos, prefer simply to record, rather than to interpret, the interlocking rooms and stairs and galleries of this palace, the web of dream images that shift and turn like the radiant bits of glass in a kaleidoscope. Others, like the Gaffer, make a clear design, slot incident into a discernible thread. (*BMN* 67-8)

Stylistically and structurally, Roberts's novels exemplify the theory of *ecriture feminine* conceived by the French feminists and linguists. Order in her works appears arbitrary and generally fails to structure chaos which prevails throughout. Order and chaos exist in a state of continuous tension, and the narrative does not collapse in favour of either. Nevertheless, Roberts allows the feminine "chora" at times to overshadow the narrative "topos".

The feminine psyche, otherwise repressed, finds release in Roberts's works through imagination, dreams, stories and fantasies. Interior monologues abound in the text and are used to portray the innermost action of the Sibyls' mind. The focus shifts from the external to the internal, from the mundane to the psycho-spiritual which is also a part of the feminist agenda. Language in Roberts's fiction erupts out of silence. Dreams are used to interfere with the flat two dimensionality of language which represses desire. Mrs Noah, the first person narrator of *BMN*, narrates her dream about the death of Noah, her vision of grandmother, "nana", who beckons her to the Grand Canal into which she jumps. The canal is a water body holding the Ark which becomes symbolic of the womb and gives a new birth to Mrs Noah. Mary's dreams in *SG* also help in disrupting the linear and rational order of language. The Freudian slips and dreams become Roberts' tools to reconstruct the personal feminine space and unravelling the unconscious.

BMN is one long dream seen by Mrs Noah during her slumber after being saved from the canal. In the end Mrs Noah wakes up from her dream, and *BMN* closes in Venice again giving the narrative a circular structure: "My story, I write: begins in Venice" (*BMN* 288). The frame narrative set in Venice moves on to the smaller frame of a long dream which has independent stories containing more dreams and other forms of sub conscious experiences like visions and hallucinations. The complete structure seems like two concentric circles having many sub circles within, small bubbles of narrative freely popping up in the main plot of the novel. To emphasise women's intuitive powers prophetic dreams populate the text, and telepathic communication scores over technical means of transporting messages.

In *SG* Mary sees several epiphanic dreams about a woman being the creator of the world and the source of all knowledge (*SG* 77), about hell as a place of the lost connection with mother (*SG* 115) and about the reunion of the male and female aspects of God (*SG* 165). The narrative of *SG* itself moves like a dream as internal actions rather than external events overpower the text. There is a series of four dreams in the last chapter of the book. Through these prophetic dreams and visions Roberts achieve for her female protagonists like Mary Magdalene, Josephine and Mrs Noah a claim to spiritual powers which are traditionally ascribed to men by the Greek philosophers.

In narration, Roberts stylistically breaks the boundaries between space and time by using space between paragraphs to show the passage of time or narrative ellipses as in the "story about a mother" (*BMN* 162). The time in the Ark is non linear. The psychological aspect of time is underscored through the intermittent use of stream of consciousness narration where the past becomes the present in the Sibyls' psyche as they recall it. The use of present tense while recollecting the past could be seen throughout the text:

> The home of her childhood *is* all bustle and movement. She share*s* a bedroom with her two sisters. Inside her rounded bedroom cabinet live*s* her doll, the curved cupboard her room where she sit*s* peacefully alone. From time to time she open*s* the white door and peep*s* in at her, then close*s* the door again quickly, not wanting to disturb her solitude for too long. What doe*s* the doll do behind the closed door when she can't see her. (*BMN* 60)

The narration in *BMN* is both mimetic and deigetic. It includes long narrative discourse by the first person narrator and also dialogues between the characters. The direct speech is made free by omitting the quotation marks which blurs the boundaries between thought, emotion and utterance to a great extent:

> She turns scarlet.
>
> – I didn't think it showed yet.
>
> Then she looks at me in her old way.
>
> – How do you know it won't be a daughter? That's what I want. A daughter. If it's a boy I'll throw it over the side. (*BMN* 80)

Like Roberts, Rhys also writes in a fragmented and non-linear narrative style. Maren Linett says that "Rhys was certainly influenced by Joyce and other experimental novelists; she participated in the general dismayed reaction to linear narrative that Woolf articulates in her essays" (439). Linett disagrees with the assumption that the fragmented style of Rhys is an inevitable product of her own traumatized psyche, and reads her style as a deliberate attempt to make trauma "legible". "Her fragmentary style is, in my view, strategic and mimetic rather than symptomatic" (Linett 439).

Form is important for Carter too, and she makes the form of her stories in *BC* very suggestive. For example, the shortness of some of the tales like "The Snow Child" speaks of its allegorical character as it encodes pure experience within the short narrative trajectory. Ahearn says about the narrative strategy in *PNE* that "it refutes linear narration, reversing conclusions and starts, ending with birth" (7-8). In *IDH* Nebulous Time collapses the linear order in narration. Desiderio's adventures with the River People, freaks of the fair, the Count and the Centaurs are all unconnected and non-linear. Moreover they do not lead the protagonist forward in his quest for Hoffman.

While studying the narrative technique of novels one cannot ignore the importance of endings. David Herman considers endings "privileged positions". The works of Rhys, Carter and Roberts are mostly open-ended and weaken the traditional concept of structure which lays down a rule for a proper beginning, middle and end. The open endedness of these texts leaves scope for the readers to develop the story in whichever way they like. The stories end with Antoinette jumping out of her patriarchal prison; Desiderio regretting the victory of reason; the Red Riding Hoods and Beautys learning the ways of the wolves and the Beasts as survival strategies; Mrs Noah waking up to a new dawn and promising herself to write daily; Josephine and Mary retiring and leaving their writings for their daughters to learn from and tamper with.

The ending of *WSS* is especially relevant. Antoinette narrates the last scene in which the dominant images in Rhys like "colour and greyness, heat and cold, her lover and the man who hates her" (Angier 98) come together. According to Simpson, the red dress has dual suggestivity. For Antoinette it represents "the potential warmth and light she may still achieve, the living truth of the fire that its colour suggests" whereas for Rochester the red dress symbolizes "her untoward and unclean sexual proclivities" (Simpson 131). The dull grey wrapper that Grace makes Antoinette wear signifies "death-in-life to which she has been assigned by her keepers" (131). Plasa notes that Antoinette's red dress "is a satirical comment on an English character which fears and so represses any outbreak of spontaneous warmth, joy, or colour, and which tries, like Grace Poole, to force others into its grey wrapper" (68).

Burning of the patriarchal mansion is a motif in feminist literature and symbolise women's toppling of that which restricts them. Mona Fayad asserts that "Antoinette jumps out of language, out of the book, into the world of the author" in order to re-enter the lost origins. The jump shows Antoinette's rejection of the symbolic and a leap into the unconscious desires, the most powerful of which is the death drive. Caroline Rody reads Antoinette's act as "resisting the self-sacrificial closure" of *Jane Eyre's* plot (217). Helene Carr agrees that "Antoinette has the last word" in the text and though Rochester's hate may have been colder and stronger the ending of the novel asserts the value of heat and light (88). According to Simpson, the fire in the end is only as an assertion of Antoinette's power and seizure of her own agency but also the enforcement of her identity as a victim. The fact that it happens in the text of Antoinette's dream with contradictory suggestions mimics the "illogical logic of a dream state" (Simpson 132) thus showing how dream could be used as a mode of narrating complex experiences. Helene Carr says that Rhys in her fictions shifts, bends, re-invents ways of using language "to open up fresh possibilities of being", "she recreates and reshapes language to map the unknown and uncharted world of ambivalence" (77) and uses language as a tool that makes "alternative sense of the world" (81).

The ending of *PNE* is a detailed description of Eve running away from both science and myth to a world free of myths, symbols and stereotypes. Edward J. Ahearn analyses the ending of the novel as a rebirth of Eve in eternity, "an uncertain and unspecified present" (8). In order to enhance the effect, Carter freezes the frame of the narrative about Eve's backward and inward movement through which she enters the womb and is reborn. The line with which the text closes uses repetition lending an incantatory effect: "Ocean, ocean, mother of mysteries, bear me to the place of birth" (*PNE* 191). Such rhythmic use of language is prescribed by linguists like Kristeva for opening the language to the feminine chora.

Roberts's works disrupt the traditional growth trajectory of sin, suffering and redemption based on the Christian doctrine. Her characters suffer and grow, but the possibility of redemption is replaced by an ongoing search for peace and contentment. Mary's, Mrs Noah's and Josephine's lives have been a quest which passes on to Deborah, Sarah and Isabelle. According to Rosie White, the novels of Michele Roberts "work beyond closure, revelling in the fluidity and free play of intertextuality", "produce the noise and volume of textuality and exceed the finitude and coherence of a whole, formal structure" (2). Lucy Sargisson calls *BMN* an open ended, fragmented and feminine text: "it is a text of multiplicity in terms of subjectivity and narrative; the female body is written into the text" (818). Commenting on the subversiveness of such texts she further asserts that "the problematization of the text is also a tactic of *ecriture feminine*, self-conscious and overtly transgressive writing that aims, amongst other things, to disrupt the symbolic order of representation" (822).

The gaps, silences and aporias in *WSS* symbolise the failure of language to communicate the reality of experience. Simpson says that "a striking feature of Rhys's narrative is its apparent dedication to broken phrases and lacunae, and the effects these aporias produce" (90). Silences rule the text both on Antoinette's and Edward's narration and mark their fears and distrust as well as their dilemma of expression. "Offline narration" (Herman 99) which includes dreams, hallucinations and visions, and are a prominent feature of *ecriture feminine* are more important than "online narration" or real life perceptions. In *Good Morning, Midnight* the features of unconscious and repressed are revealed through dreams and offline narration dominates the text. According to Emery Lou, Rhys's narratives "dispel the hegemony of prevailing ideologies, including that of the consolidated and privatized self, and counter them with 'other shapes' and 'other forms' that have their sources in West Indian history and culture" through what Bakhtin calls internal dialogization (170).

It could be concluded that these contemporary British women writers know that the main tool used by the imperialists is control over language. Therefore Rhys, Carter and Roberts try to break the mould of the manmade language through continuous revision and narrative experimentations. To solve the problem of the feasibility of a language based on the semiotic rhythms of the female body, Rhys uses a highly suggestive subtext in *WSS* formed of aporias, gaps in speech and silences in dialogue. She uses graphological devices to create ambiguity and makes her text dialogic in nature.

Carter chooses genres like magic realism, speculative fiction, fantasy and gothic to underscore the deconstructive powers of the imagination and weaken the strictures of the symbolic language. She uses a densely allusive and figurative style for the same purpose. Her thickly textured style aids the motive of defamiliarization which makes the improbable appear true and undermines the tyranny of realism.

Roberts like Rhys and Carter, introduces ambiguity in her works through syntactic innovations. Instead of merely demythologising the myths generated by the master narratives like Carter, she creates new myths to replace the old as suggested by Barthes. The Christian myths of Genesis, Flood and the Ark etcetera find new subversive versions in Roberts's novels and give women the right to exercise their sensuality and spirituality simultaneously.

The opening up of old texts for re-vision, using a style that is flexible and suggestive, calls for the reader's participation. The readers can co-create the "writerly" texts like *WSS, PNE, IDH, BC, BMN, SG* and *IS* with the author leading to what Barthes calls textual bliss or jouissance (*The Pleasure of the Text*). This textual jouissance and plurality, sources of liberation and joy according to Barthes, are manifest in the works of Jean Rhys, Angela Carter and Michele Roberts.

WORKS CITED

Ahearn, Edward J. "The Modern English Visionary: Peter Ackroyd's Hawksmoor and Angela Carter's *The Passion of New Eve*". *Twentieth Century Literature* 46.4 (2000): 453. *Questia*. Web. 18 Dec. 2010.

Angier, Carole. *Lives of Modern Women*: *Jean Rhys*. New York: Penguin Books, 1985. Print.

Ashcroft, Bill, Gareth Griffiths, and Helen Tiffin. *The Empire Writes Back: Theory and Practice in Post-Colonial Literatures*. 2nd ed. London: Routledge, 2005. Print.

Bakhtin, M.M. *Rabelais and his World.* Trans. Hélène Iswolsky. Bloomington: Indiana University Press, 1993. Print.

Barthes, Roland. *Mythologies*. New York: Hill and Wang, 1972. Print.

——. S/Z. Trans. Richard Howard. New York: Hill and Wang, 1974. Print.

——. *The Pleasure of Text*. Trans. Richard Miller. New York: Hill and Wang, 1975. Web. 14 Oct. 2010.

Bowers, Maggie Ann. *Magic Realism*. Abigdon: Routledge, 2007. Print.

Bronte, Charlotte. *Jane Eyre*. Noida: Mayoor Paperbacks, 1987. Print.

Carr, Helen. *Jean Rhys*. Plymouth: Northcote House Publishers, 1996. Print.

Carter, Angela. "Notes from the Frontline": *On Gender and Writing*. Ed. Micheline Wandor. Pandora, 1983. Web. 10 July 2011.

——. *The Bloody Chamber.* London: Vintage, 1995. Print.

——. *The Infernal Desire Machines of Doctor Hoffman*. London: Penguin, 1982. Print.

——. *The Passion of the New Eve*. London: Virago, 1982. Print.

Childs, Peter. *Contemporary Novelists: British Fiction since 1970*. New York: Palgrave Macmillan, 2005. Print.

Cixous, Helene. "*The Laugh of the Medusa*". Trans. Keith Cohen and Paula Cohen. *Signs*. 1(4), 1976. Web. 10 Feb 2012.

Clark, Robert. "Angela Carter's Desire Machines". *Women's Studies: An Interdisciplinary Journal* 14.2 (1987). Print.

Daly, Mary. *Gyn/Ecology: The Metaethics of Radical Feminism*. Beacon Press, 1978. Web. 12 Mar 2012.

Emery, Mary Lou. "Modernist Crosscurrents". Ed Judith L. Raiskin. Wide Sargasso Sea: A Norton Critical Edition. New York: W.W. Norton and Company, 1999. Print.

Fayad, Mona. "Unquiet Ghosts: The Struggle for Representation in Jean Rhys's Wide Sargasso Sea". *Modern Fiction Studies* 34 Fall (1988). Web. 16 April 2012.

Gamble, Sarah. *Angela Carter: A Literary Life*. New York: Palgrave Macmillan, 2006. Print.

——. ed. *The Fiction of Angela Carter: A Reader's Guide to Essential Criticism*. New York: Palgrave Macmillan, 2001. Print.

Gilbert, Sandra and Susan Gubar. *The Mad Woman in the Attic: The Woman Writer and the Nineteenth-Century Literary Imagination*. New Haven: Yale University Press, 1979. Print.

Herman, David. *The Cambridge Companion to Narrative*. Cambridge: Cambridge University Press, 2007. Print.

Irigaray, Luce. "When Our Lips Speak Together". Trans. Carolyn Burke. Signs 6.1, 1980. JSTOR. Web. 2 Jan 2011.

Jackson, Rosemary. *Fantasy: The Literature of Subversion*. London and New York: Routledge, 1988. Web. 1 Mar 2012.

Johnson, Daniel. "Books Barely Furnish a Room". *The Times*. 16 September, 1992. Web.

Jung, Carl Gustav. *Psychological Types*. Pantheon Books, 1962. Web. 12 May 2012.

Kaveney, Roz. "New New World Dreams: Angle Carter and Science Fiction". Ed. Lorna Sage. *Flesh and the Mirror: Essays on the Art of Angela Carter*. London: Virago Press, 1994. Print.

Kristeva, Julia. ""Nous Deux" or a (Hi)story of Intertextuality". *The Romanic Review* 93.1-2 (2002): 7+. *Questia*. Web. 15 May 2012.

——. *Revolution in Poetic Language*. New York: Columbia University Press, 1984. Print.

Lane, Richard J., Rod Maugham and Philip Tew eds. *Contemporary British Fiction*. Cambridge: Polity Press, 2003. Print.

Linnet, Maren. "New Words, New Everything: Fragmentation and Trauma in Jean Rhys". Literary Criterion, July 2006. Print.

Makinen, Merja. "Angela Carter's *The Bloody Chamber* and the Decolonisation of Feminine Sexuality". Ed. Alison Easton. *New Casebooks: Angela Carter*. London: Macmillan Press Ltd., 2000. Print.

Meaney, Gerardine. "History and Women's Time: *Heroes and Villains*". Ed. Alison Easton. *New Casebooks: Angela Carter*. London: Macmillan Press Ltd., 2000. Print.

Moi, Toril. *Sexual/Textual Politics*. Routledge, 2002. Web. 12 Dec 2011.

Morris, Pam. *Realism*. London: Routledge, 2003. Print.

Munford, Rebecca ed. *Re-Visiting Angela Carter. Texts, Contexts, Intertexts*. New York: Palgrave Macmillan, 2006. Print.

Olson, Tillie. *Silences*. Delacorte, 1978. Web. 1 May 2012.

Peach, Linden. *Modern Novelists: Angela Carter*. London: Macmillan, 1998. Print.

Plasa, Carl ed. *Jean Rhys: Wide Sargasso Sea – A Readers Guide to Essential Criticism*. New York: Palgrave Macmillan, 2001. Print.

Punter, David. *The Literature of Terror: A History of Gothic Fictions from 1765 to the Present Day*. Longman: 1980. Print.

Rhys, Jean. *Wide Sargasso Sea*. London: Andre Deutsch Limited, 1966. 6th impression 1983. Print.

Roberts, Michele. *Impossible Saints*. New York: Harcourt Brace and Company, 1999. Print.

——. Interviewed by Maria Soraya Garcia Sanchez. *Talking about Women, History and Writing with Michele Roberts. Atlantis*. 27.2 (Dec 2005). Web. 26 Oct 2011.

——. Interviewed by Patricia Bastida Rodriguez. *On Women, Christianity and History: An Interview with Michele Roberts*. Atlantis 25.1 (June 2003). Web. 13 Nov 2010.

——. *The Book of Mrs. Noah*. London: Metheun, 1987. Print.

——. *The Secret Gospel of Mary Magdalene*. London: Vintage, 2007. Print.

Robinson, Sally. *Engendering the Subject: Gender and Self-Representation in Contemporary Women's Fiction*. New York: State University of New York Press, 1991. Print.

——. "The Anti-Hero as Oedipus: Gender and the Postmodern Narrative in The Infernal Desire of Doctor Hoffman". Ed. Alison Easton. *Angela Carter: New Casebooks. London:* Macmillan Press Ltd., 2000. Print.

Rody, Caroline. "Burning Down the House: The Revisionary Paradigm of Jean Rhys's *Wide Sargasso Sea*". Ed Judith L. Raiskin. *Wide Sargasso Sea: A Norton Critical Edition*. New York: W.W. Norton and Company, 1999. Print.

Russo, Mary. *The Female Grotesque: Risk, Excess and Modernity*. London: Routledge, 1994. Print.

Sargisson, Lucy. *Contemporary Feminist Utopianism*. New York: Routledge, 1996. *Questia*. Web, 7 Mar 2011.

Showalter, Elaine. "Toward a Feminist Poetics". *The New Feminist Criticism: Essays on Women, Literature and Theory ed.* Showalter. New York: Pantheon, 1985. Print.

Simpson, Anne B. Territories of the Psyche: The Fiction of Jean Rhys. New York: Palgrave Macmillan, 2005. Print.

Spaull, Sue. *Gynocriticism: Feminist Reading*. ed. Sara Mills et all. New York: Harvester Wheatsheaf, 1989. Print.

Spender, Dale. *Man Made Language*. Routledge and Kegan Paul, 1980. Web. 7 May 2012.

Stockwell, Peter. *Cognitive Poetics: An Introduction*. London: Routledge, 2002. Print.

Swyt, Wendy. ""Wolfings": Angela Carter's Becoming-Narrative". *Studies in Short Fiction* 33.3 (1996): 315+. *Questia*. Web. 18 Dec. 2010.

Teslenko, Tatiana. *Feminist Utopian Novels of the 1970s: Joanna Russ and Dorothy Bryant*. New York: Routledge, 2003. *Questia*. Web. 7 March 2011.

Zipes, Jack. *Fairy Tales and the Art of Subversion*. London: Routledge, 1988. Print.

6
Conclusion

Narratives fulfil the basic human need of finding meaning in life. Narratives not only define the power relations that exist in the world but also condition people in social, cultural and religious behaviour by making them play the roles set for them. As these narratives themselves are governed by power equations, some narratives are chosen above the rest to represent gender, race and religion. Rhys, Carter and Roberts study how such powerful narratives, or master narratives, have trapped women in images from which they need to be rescued. In order to free women from false generalization, the contemporary women writers have chosen to rewrite and subvert the patriarchal myths, religious beliefs and historical tales from feminist perspectives.

Examining the gender status quo Rhys, Carter and Roberts analyze the outcome of norm formation and generalization. They study how the process of norm formation by those in power does severe injustice to those who do not fit in the straitjacket of their normative standards. Rhys looks at the problem from the point of view of the Creoles and their longing for acceptance by the people they live amongst. Carter highlights ways of breaking through the narrow walls of reason and moral hypocrisy through her aberrant characters like Tristessa, Mother, New Eve, Fevvers and Nora Chance. Roberts researches on the Christian era when the Popes were at the apex of the power structures and governed the society through punitive measures like the

Inquisition. Roberts scrutinises the history of Christianity and while pointing out at its patriarchal roots tries to envision an alternate religion based on the feminine principles of love, peace and equality.

Rhys subverts the notions about the genetic and cultural determination of the Jamaicans, Creoles and English, in the Caribbean islands, just before and after the abolition of slavery. Taking the postcolonial Jamaica as the backdrop, Rhys subverts the relationship between the victim and victimizer to show that both of them suffer as participants in the power game. Though all the three writers target those in power, Rhys is the only one who explicitly shows the weaknesses of the cruel. Rochester and Daniel cause Antoinette pain because of their psychological weaknesses. Antoinette burns Thornfield Hall only when she finds herself trapped and helpless.

Carter on the other hand targets the attitudes of bigotry and fanaticism. She takes up Western mythology for deconstruction because myths falsely come under "a semi religious coating". She also attacks myths about gender inherent in the western culture, in the form of fairy tales, psychoanalytic theories, philosophical doctrines etcetera, to free women from pedestals and bars, halos and horns. Roberts, unlike Carter, re-mythologizes along with de-mythologizing. She creates alternate myths to fill the gap left by the deconstruction of the old ones. Instead of creating one central narrative she fills her novels with multiple small narratives which create their own small gravitational spaces, none overruling the other. Thus, she celebrates multiplicity and heterogeneity.

Being an anti-essentialist feminist, Carter uses theatricality as a trope to show the performance of gender. Female grotesques like Mother in *PNE* and Fevvers in *NC* are used by Carter to show the malleability of human bodies and deconstruct the notion of biological determinism. Carter brings pornography too within her range of deconstructive mimicry. Pornography supports domination of women, and Carter visualizes the possibility of "a moral pornographer" who wouldn't distinguish between men and women while writing about sadomasochism and other pornographic practices. Carter, being one such "moral pornographer", criticizes female subjugation in pornographic culture by inverting the image of "angel in the house" and conceptualizes violent and sensual females like the female vampire in "The Lady of the House of Love" (*The Bloody Chamber*). Roberts targets the figures of the father and the mother as the pillar and the carrier of patriarchy respectively within the domestic space, as her main objects of subversion. As in Carter's works, liberation of female sexuality is a major concern in Roberts's novels too.

Roberts, while creating her feminist utopias, also pictures a new Adam instead of a new Eve, in the form of the figure of Jesus Christ (*SG*) and Walser (*NC*). These men cherish equality and are almost feminine in the way they feel. Roberts underscores the spiritual powers of women exemplified by their power to communicate telepathically, see visionary dreams, communicate with God through the body, which subverts the subordination of women by the Church in spiritual matters. Roberts takes pride in revealing how women have always been subversive and have tried to fracture the Catholic convention from within the walls of the convent. She takes Saint Theresa of Avila and Saint Therese of Lisieux as examples. Josephine, the protagonist of *IS* being a Carmelite, subverts the order from within by leading a double life, one for the inspectors and other for the free woman inside her. Her idea of the new convent as a double house and her secret autobiography beaded in the form of a rosary show how she knows to keep her secret hidden from those who cannot appreciate it. The metaphor of a rosary is also significant due to its religious connotation. Roberts draws parallels between holiness and (w)holiness. The most important trope in her writings is the quest for (w)holiness which one achieves as a result of successfully integrating the multiple aspects of self within one's personality.

Looking at the three writers together one can conclude that Carter and Roberts are more devotedly and enthusiastically feminist in their approach than Rhys. Roberts being a socialist feminist has a more pronounced homosocial element in her novels than either of her contemporaries. She is the one, who valorizes the image of woman as the creator, mother and writer.

She motivates women as mothers to take help from other women in child rearing and women as writers to learn from other women writers through collective writing and participating in writers' workshops. Mother is a figure that serves as the object of quest in most of her novels. Roberts also provides a positive vision of the future through her description of possible feminist utopias in *SG, IS* and *BMN*. Carter on the other hand, does not offer any brave new world to her protagonists like Melanie in *TMT*, Fevvers in *NC* or Eve in *PNE*.

Roberts envisions the likelihood of homosocial bonding between women and by depicting the practice of homoerotic and autoerotic sexualities. Carter mimicry of the Oedipal narrative creates space for the projection of successful relationships between women. Rhys also undermines the monologic nature of the Oedipal narrative through making her novels dialogic and open to multiple voices. She subverts the extremism, exclusion and prejudices of the Oedipal narrative by adopting moderation, inclusion and objectivity in her narrative structure. Instead of projecting Edward Rochester as a villain she shows the inherent flaw in such dichotomous portrayals of characters. She uses the principles of dialogism rather than closures in her art of characterization. Roberts and Carter, unlike Rhys, use a single narrative voice in their texts but make the reader doubt the reliability of the narrative point of view and open the text to reader's interference through the use of uncertain tone and double entendre. All the three writers leave their novels open ended for underscoring ambiguity and weakening the monologic conclusions. To sum up, one can say that Rhys, Carter and Roberts are trying to find ways for the survival of women as free individuals and autonomous writers.

Returning to the question posed in the introductory chapter, about the need and relevance of gender conscious literature in the post-feminist era, it is now possible to state that the status quo of gender relations is still detrimental to women's self-actualization. The change in society that Dominic Head (2002) and Richard Bradford (2007) speak of, in terms of gender relations, has partly been validated by Rhys, Carter and Roberts in their works. But these three creative writers also bring to the readers' notice that the "room" is still not available to many women even in the twenty first century. Though Carter treats masculinity and femininity as a result of one's placement in the power equation irrespective of one's biological sex, still her works depict that the position of the subjugated object is generally occupied by women.

The futuristic stories in the fiction of Michele Roberts and the speculative fiction of Angela Carter clearly show that technological advancement does not entail the liberation of women. Though living in highly developed futuristic societies, Roberts's and Carter's female protagonists are still exploited as sex toys. The cyborgian worlds of Carter, fitted with hi-tech equipments, are regulated by totalitarian myths. Carter also keeps recreating the zeitgeist of the 1960s in her novels which clearly demonstrates that the Cultural Revolution which opposed tradition, freed sexuality and liberated arts from convention was unable to liberate women as individuals.

As depicted in the novels of Carter and Roberts, even today, the options available to women for liberation from the societal and cultural norms are more theoretical than practical. The novels of Roberts, which were written chiefly after the 1990s, clearly depict that there is a gap between what women are, want to be and are expected to be in their families and societies. Even the economically independent Sibyls and Saints in Roberts's fiction are anxious about meeting the desirability standards set by men. The various dilemmas and fears about motherhood that torment Roberts's female protagonists show that women's biological capacity for reproduction still is a major factor in determining their role in society. Carter suggests in her speculative fiction that this mental colonization of women by patriarchy is made worse by the dissemination of media images which women try to imitate and perfect. Being trapped in the male gaze, they get further removed them from their goal of liberation.

After having studied the techniques of subversion used by the three writers under examination one can now review another issue raised in the introductory chapter about the effects of these techniques. The possibility that misoandry in subversive literature written by women would strengthen the case for misogyny is negated by a thorough investigation of the works of Rhys, Carter and Roberts. This study has revealed an absence of misoandry in the writings of these three women writers. If there is a comic and revolting caricature of Zero, the character of Mother is projected in a similar manner too. Carter even critiques societies like SCUM through the comic portrayal of the castrating Mother. Roberts's portrayal of men as the perpetrators of female exploitation is a plea against gender discrimination, not for strengthening it. She also gives benevolent portrayals of a good father and a good lover in the final stories in *IS* and *BMN*. Rhys is also equally empathetic towards Edward, Antoinette and Daniel. These writers are not misoandrists, and what they critique is the attitude of dominance and the misuse of power by both men and women.

One significant shift in the works of Carter is that her fictional works change from densely packed theoretical novels to Carnivalesque tales and from the portrayal of homme fatales to the conceptualization of the "new woman". The sharply satiric tone of Michele Roberts's novels appears to have mellowed down after confessing her complex feelings towards her father and the Catholic Church in *BMN* and *IS*. Roberts accepts that she has come to terms with her anger towards religion and patriarchy and now approaches these themes with more objectivity.

A Select Bibliography

PRIMARY SOURCES

Carter, Angela. *The Bloody Chamber.* London: Vintage, 1995. Print.

——. *The Infernal Desire Machines of Doctor Hoffman.* London: Penguin, 1982. Print.

——. *The Passion of the New Eve.* London: Virago, 1982. Print.

Rhys, Jean. *Wide Sargasso Sea.* London: Andre Deutsch Limited, 1966. 6th impression 1983. Print.

Roberts, Michele. *Impossible Saints.* New York: Harcourt Brace and Company, 1999. Print.

——. *The Book of Mrs. Noah.* London: Metheun, 1987. Print.

——. *The Secret Gospel of Mary Magdalene.* London: Vintage, 2007. Print.

RELATED STUDY

Carter, Angela. *Expletives Deleted.* London: Vontage, 2006. Print.

——. *Heroes and Villains.* London: Penguin, 1981. Print.

——. *Love.* New York: Penguin, 1988. Print.

——. *Nights at the Circus.* London: The Hogarth Press, 1984. Print.

——. "Notes from the Frontline": *On Gender and Writing*. Ed. Micheline Wandor. Pandora, 1983. Web. 10 July 2011.

——. *Several Perceptions*. London: Virago, 1995. Print.

——. *Shadow Dance*. London: Virago, 1995. Print.

——. *The Magic Toyshop*. London: Virago, 1996. Print.

——. *The Sadeian Woman*. New York: Penguin. 2001. Print.

——. *Wise Children*. London: Vintage, 1992. Print.

Rhys, Jean. *After Leaving Mr. Mackenzie*. London: Penguin, 1930. Print.

——. *Good Morning, Midnight*. London: Penguin, 1969. Print.

——. "Selected Letters". Ed Judith L. Raiskin. *Wide Sargasso Sea: A Norton Critical Edition*. New York: W.W. Norton and Company, 1999. Print.

——. *Smile Please*. London: Andre Deutsch, 1979. Print.

——. *Quartet*. London: Penguin, 1928. Print.

——. *Voyage in the Dark*. London: Penguin, 1969. Print.

Roberts, Michele. "A Maze of Magic". *The Guardian*. 18 March 2009. Web. 12 May 2009.

——. *Daughters of the House*. London: Virago Press, 1992. Print

——. *Delusion*. New York: Pegasus, 2008. Print.

——. *Flesh and Blood*. London: Virago, 1995. Print.

——. *Food, Sex and God: On Inspiration and Writing*. London: Virago, 1998. Print.

——. *Mud: Stories of Sex and Love*. London: Virago, 2012. Print.

——. *Paper Houses: A Memoir of the '70s and Beyond*. London: Virago, 2007. Print.

——. *Playing Sardines*. London: Virago, 2002. Print.

——. "Questions and Answers". Ed. M Wandor. On Gender and Writing. London, Boston, Melbourne and Henley: Pandora Press, 1983. Print.

——. *Reader, I married Him*. London: Virago, 2006. Print.

——. *The Looking Glass*. London: Virago. 2001. Print.

——. "The Little Flower". *New Statesman*. 12 Jan 2004. *Questia*. Web. 3 Mar 2011.

——. "The Novels of Colette". *New Statesman*. 27 Nov 2000. *Questia*. Web. 7 Mar 2011.

INTERVIEWS

Carter, Anna. Interviewed by Anna Katsavos. "An Interview with Angela Carter". *The Review of Contemporary Fiction* 14.3 (1994). *Questia*. Web. 18 Dec 2010.

——. Interviewed by Les Bedford. "Angela Carter: An Interview". Sheffield: Sheffield University Television, 1977.

Rhys, Jean. Interviewed by Hannah Carter. "Fated to be Sad". *Guardian*. 8 Aug 1968. Web. 2 July 2010.

Roberts, Michele. Interviewed by Jenny Newman. *An Interview with Michele Roberts*. Web. 12 Dec 2011.

——. Interviewed by Linda Richards. *January Magazine*. Web. 23 Jan 2011.

——. Interviewed by Maria Soraya Garcia Sanchez. *Talking about Women, History and Writing with Michele Roberts. Atlantis*. 27.2 (Dec 2005). Web. 26 Oct 2011.

——. Interviewed by Patricia Bastida Rodriguez. *On Women, Christianity and History: An Interview with Michele Roberts*. Atlantis 25.1 (June 2003). Web. 13 Nov 2010.

SECONDARY SOURCES

Abrams, M.H. and Geoffrey Galt Harpham. A Handbook of Literary Terms. New Delhi: Cengage Learning, 2009. Print.

Acheson, James ed. *The British Novel Since 1960*. New York: St. Martin's Press, 1991. Print.

Acheson, James, and Sarah C.E. Ross, eds. *The Contemporary British Novel*. Edinburgh: Edinburgh University Press, 2005. Print.

Adams, Robert M. ed. and trans. *Utopia*. London: Norton and Company, 2003. Print.

Alexander, Flora. *Contemporary Women Novelists: Modern Fiction*. New York: Edward Arnold, 1989. Print.

Allen, Graham. *Intertextuality*. London: Routledge, 2007. Print.

Andrews, Virginia. *Flowers in the Attic*. London: Harper Collins, 1993. Print.

Angier, Carole. *Lives of Modern Women: Jean Rhys*. New York: Penguin Books, 1985. Print.

Anzaldua, Gloria. *Borderlands: The New Mestiza*. San Francisco: Aunt Lute Books, 1987. Print.

Aristotle. *On the Generation of Animals*. Trans. Arthur Platt. eBooks@Adelaide. The University of Adelaide library. 25 Aug 2010. Web. 10 May 2012.

Armitt, Lucie. *Contemporary Women's Fiction and the Fantastic*. New York: Macmillan Press Ltd., 2000. Print.

Armstrong, Nancy. *Desire and Domestic Fiction: A Political History of the Novel*. Oxford: Oxford University Press, 1987. Print.

Ashcroft, Bill, Gareth Griffiths, and Helen Tiffin. *The Empire Writes Back: Theory and Practice in Post-Colonial Literatures*. 2nd ed. London: Routledge, 2005. Print.

Bakhtin, M.M. *Rabelais and his World*. Trans. Hélène Iswolsky. Bloomington: Indiana University Press, 1993. Print.

Bakhtin, M.M. *The Dialogic Imagination: Four Essays*. Ed. Michael Holquist. Trans. Caryl Emerson and Michael Holquist. Austin and London: University of Texas Press. 1981. Print.

Baldick, Chris. *The Oxford Book of Gothic Tales*. Oxford: Oxford University Press, 1993. Print.

Barthes, Roland. *Mythologies*. New York: Hill and Wang, 1972. Print.

——. *S/Z*. Trans. Richard Howard. New York: Hill and Wang, 1974. Print.

Baudrillard, Jean. *Screened Out*. Trans. Chris Turner. London: Verso, 2002. Print.

——. *Simulacra and Simulations*. Trans. Sheila Faria Glaser. US: The University of Michigan Press, 1994. Web. 17 May 2012.

Beauman, Nicola. *A Very Great Profession: The Woman's Novel*. London: Virago, 1983. Print.

Beauvoir, Simone de. *The Second Sex* trans. and ed. H.M. Parshley. Harmondsworth: Penguin 1982. Print.

Beebe, John ed. *Jung: Aspects of the Masculine*. Trans. RFC Hill. London: Routledge: Macmillan, 1997. Print.

Beer, Gillian. "Representing Women: Re-presenting the Past". Eds. Catherine Belsey and Jane Moore. *The Feminist Reader*. London: Macmillan Press, 1997. Print.

Benjamin, Jessica. *Shadow of the Other: Intersubjectivity and Gender in Psychoanalysis*. New York: Routledge, 1998. Print.

Bhabha, Homi K. *Nation and Narration*. London: Routledge, 1990. Print.

Boddy, Kasia. Ali Smith and Sarah Wood eds. *Brilliant Careers*: The Virago Book of Twentieth Century Fiction. London: Virago, 2000. Print.

Booker, M. Keith. *Techniques of Subversion in Modern Literature: Transgression, Abjection, and the Carnivalesque*. Gainesville, FL: University of Florida Press, 1991. Print.

Bollas, Christopher. *The Shadow of the Object: Psychoanalysis of the Unthought Known*. New York: Columbia University Press, 1987. Print.

Bowers, Maggie Ann. *Magic Realism*. Abigdon: Routledge, 2007. Print.

Bradford, Richard. *The Novel Now: Contemporary British Fiction*. USA: Blackwell Publishing, 2007. Print.

Braithwaite, Edward Kamau. *Contradictory Omens: Cultural Diversity and Integration in the Caribbean*. Kingston, Jamiaca: Savacou Publications, 1974. Print.

Bronte, Charlotte. *Jane Eyre*. Noida: Mayoor Paperbacks, 1987. Print.

Butler, Judith. *Bodies that Matter: On the Discursive Limits of Sex*. London: Routledge, 1993. Print.

——. *Gender Trouble: Feminism and the Subversion of Identity*. London: Routledge, 1990. Print.

Cameron, Deborah. *Feminism and Linguistic Theory*. New York: Palgrave, 1985. Print.

Carr, Helen. *Jean Rhys*. Plymouth: Northcote House Publishers, 1996. Print.

Chodorow, Nancy J. *The Reproduction of Mothering: Psychoanalysis and the Sociology of Gender*. Berkley, Los Angeles, London: University of California Press, 1978. Print.

Childs, Peter. *Contemporary Novelists: British Fiction since 1970*. New York: Palgrave Macmillan, 2005. Print.

Cixous, Helene. "Sorties: Out and Out: Attacks/Ways Out/ Forays". Eds. Catherine Belsey and Jane Moore. *The Feminist Reader*. London: Macmillan Press, 1997. Print.

——. "The Laugh of the Medusa". Trans. Keith Cohen and Paula Cohen. *New French Feminisms*. Ed. Elaine Marks. New York: Schockin, 1981. Print.

Connor, Steven. *The English Novel in History 1950-1995*. London: Routledge, 1996. Print.

Berger, John. *Ways of Seeing*. Penguin Group, 1972. Web. 7 Jan 2012.

Craig, Amanda. *The Mistressclass: Michele Roberts*, 2003. Web. 20 Jan 2012.

Creed, Barbara. *The Monstrous Feminine: Film, Feminism and Psychoanalysis*. London: Routledge, 1993. Print.

Curtis, Jan. "The Secret of Wide Sargasso Sea." *Critique*. 31.3 (1990). *Questia*. Web. 18 Dec. 2010.

Daly, Mary. *Gyn/Ecology: The Metaethics of Radical Feminism*. Beacon Press, 1978. Web. 12 Mar 2012.

——. *The Church and the Second Sex*. Harper and Row, 1968. Web. 16 Oct 2009.

Deleuze, Gilles and Felix Guattari. *Anti-Oedipus: Capitalism and Schizophrenia*. Trans. Robert Hurley, Mark Seem and

Helen R. Lane. London and New York: Continuum, 2004. Web. 18 Jan 2012.

Derrida, Jacques. "Of Grammatology as a positive Science". *Of Grammatology.* Trans. Gayatri Chakravorty Spivak. Baltimore and London: Johns Hopkins University Press, 1976. Print.

Drake, Sandra. "Race and Caribbean Culture as Thematics of Liberation in Jean Rhys' Wide Sargasso Sea". *Jean Rhys: Wide Sargasso Sea—A Norton Critical Edition* ed. Judith L. Raiskin. New York and London: W.W. Norton and Company, 1998. Print.

Dunne, Gullian A. *Lesbian Lifestyles: Women's Work and the Politics of Sexuality*. London: Macmillan, 1997. Print.

Dworkin, Andrea. *Our Blood: Prophecies and Discourses on Sexual Politics*. The Women's Press (1982). Print.

Eagleton, Mary. *A Concise Companion to Feminist Theory*. UK: Blackwell, 2003. Print.

——. ed. *Feminist Literary Criticism*. New York: Longman, 1991. Print.

Eagleton, Robert. "The Fiction of Angela Carter". *Contemporary British Fiction* ed. Richard J. Lane. Cambridge: Polity Press, 2003. Print.

Easthope, Antony. The Unconscious. London. Routledge, 1999. Print.

Easton, Alison. "Introduction: Reading Angela Carter". *New Casebooks: Angela Carter*. London: Macmillan Press Ltd., 2000. Print.

Emery, Mary Lou. "Modernist Crosscurrents". Ed Judith L. Raiskin. *Wide Sargasso Sea: A Norton Critical Edition.* New York: W.W. Norton and Company, 1999. Print.

Eisentein, Hester. *Contemporary Feminist Thought*. London: Unwin Paperbacks, 1984. Print.

Erwin, Lee. "History and Narrative in *Wide Sargasso Sea*". Ed Judith L. Raiskin. *Wide Sargasso Sea: A Norton Critical Edition*. New York: W.W. Norton and Company, 1999. Print.

Evans, Kim (dir). *Angela Carter's Curious Room. Omnibus. BBC* 2. 15 Sep 1992. Web. 21 Oct 2010.

Fairbain, W. Ronald D. "The Repression and the Return of Bad Objects". *An Object-Relations Theory of the Personality.* New York: Basic Books, 1954. Print.

Farwell, Marilyn. *Heterosexual Plots and Lesbian Narratives.* New York: New York University Press, 1990. Print.

Felman, Shoshna. "Women and Madness: The Critical Fallacy". Eds Catherine Belsey and Jane Moore. *The Feminist Reader.* London: Macmillan Press Ltd., 1997. Print.

Felski, Rita. *Beyond Feminist Aesthetics: Feminist Literature and Social Change.* London: Hutchinson Radius, 1989. Print.

Feng, Pin-Chia and Kate Lui. *World Literature in English,* 1966. Web. 3 Aug 2011.

Feral, Josette. "Powers of Difference". eds. Hester Eisentein and Alice Jardine. *The Future of Difference.* New Brunswick. 1989. Print.

Filmer, Kath ed. *Twentieth Century Fantasies.* London: Macmillan, 1992. Print.

Fiorenza, Elizabeth Schussler. *In Memory of Her: A Feminist Theological Reconstruction of Christian Origins.* New York: Crossroad, 1983. Web. 30 April, 2009.

Firestone, Shulamith. *The Dialectic of Sex: The Case for Feminist Revolution.* New York: William Morrow and Company, 1970. Print.

Foucault, Michel. *Madness and Civilization: A History of Insanity in the Age of Reason.* Trans. Richard Howard. New York: Vintage, 1988. Print.

——. *The History of Sexuality.* Vol 1. London: Penguin, 1990. Print.

Francis, Anne Cranny. *Feminist Fiction: Feminist Uses of Generic Fiction.* Oxford: Polity Press, 1990. Print.

Freud, Sigmund. *The Ego and the Id.* Ed. James Strachey. New York: W. W. Norton and Company, 1989. Print.

——. *Three Essays on the Theory of Sexuality.* Trans. James Strachey. New York: Basic Books, 1962. Print.

Gamble, Sarah. *Angela Carter: A Literary Life*. New York: Palgrave Macmillan, 2006. Print.

Gamble, Sarah ed. *The Fiction of Angela Carter: A Reader's Guide to Essential Criticism*. New York: Palgrave Macmillan, 2001. Print.

Gandhi, Leela. *Postcolonial Theory: A Critical Introduction*. New Delhi. Oxford University Press, 1998. Print.

Gasiorek, Andrzej. *Post-War British Fiction Realism and After*. New York: Edward Arnold, 1995. Print.

Gilbert, Sandra and Susan Gubar. *The Mad Woman in the Attic: The Woman Writer and the Nineteenth-Century Literary Imagination*. New Haven: Yale University Press, 1979. Print.

Gilligan, Carol. *In a Different Voice: Psychological Theory and Women's Development*. USA: Harvard University Press, 1982. Print.

Gilman, Charlotte Perkins. *The Yellow Wallpaper*. Electronic Text Center: University of Virginia Library. Feb 1997. Web. 29 May 2012.

Girards, Rene. *Vision and Difference*. trans. Patrick Gregory. London: Continuum, 2005. Print.

Glen, Heather ed. Jane Eyre. *New Casebooks: Contemporary Critical Essays*. London: Macmillan Press, 1997. Print.

Gramsci, Antonio. Ed. David Forgacs Lawrence. *A Gramsci Reader: Selected Writings 1916-1935*. London and Wishart, 1999. Print.

Greaney, Michael. *Contemporary Fiction and the Uses of Theory: The Novel from Structuralism and Postmodernism*. New York: Palgrave Macmillan, 2006. Print.

Grimm, Jacob and Wilhelm Grimm. *Grimm's Fairy Tales*. Trans. Edgar Taylor and Marian Edwardes. *Public Literature.org*. Web. 18 May 2012.

Habib, MAR. *A History of Literary Criticism*. Oxford: Blackwell, 2005. Print.

Haraway, Donna J. "The Promises of Monsters: A Regenerative Poetics for Inappropriate/d Others". Grossberg et al, eds. *Cultural Studies*. New York: Routledge, 1992. Print.

Harris, Wilson. "Carnival of Psyche: Jean Rhys's *Wide Sargasso Sea*". Ed. Judith L. Raiskin. *Wide Sargasso Sea: A Norton Critical Edition*. New York: W.W. Norton and Company, 1999. Print.

Hassan, Ihab. *The Dismemberment of Orpheus: Toward a Postmodern Literature*. New York: Oxford University Press, 1971. Print.

Head, Dominic. *The Cambridge Introduction to Modern British Fiction 1950-2000*. UK: Cambridge University Press, 2002. Print.

Herman, David. *The Cambridge Companion to Narrative*. Cambridge: Cambridge University Press, 2007. Print.

Hermans, H.J.M. and Kempen, H.J.G. *The Dialogical Self: Meaning as Movement*. San Diego: Academic Press, 1993. Print.

Hermans, H.J.M. and Dimaggio, G. Eds. *The Dialogical Self in Psychotherapy*. New York: Brunner & Routledge, 2004. Print.

Hill, RFC trans. *Jung: Four Archetypes*. London: Routledge, 2003. Print.

Hixon, Martha. "New Wine in Old Bottles". Ed Elizabeth Wanning Harries. *Twice Upon a Time: Women Writers and the History of the Fairy Tale*. Princeton: Princeton University Press, 2001. Print.

Humm, Maggie. *Border Traffic: Strategies of Contemporary Women Writers*. Manchester and New York: Manchester University Press, 1991. Print.

Hunt, Anna. "'The Margins of the Imaginative Life': The Abject and the Grotesque in Angela Carter and Jonathan Swift". Ed. Rebecca Munford. *Re-Visiting Angela Carter. Texts, Contexts, Intertexts*. New York: Palgrave Macmillan, 2006. Print.

Hutcheon, Linda. *A Poetics of Postmodernism: History, Theory, Fiction*. New York and London: Routledge, 1988. Print.

Huyssen, Andreas. *After the Great Divide: Modernism, Mass Culture, Postmodernism*. Bloomington and Indianapolis: Indiana University Press, 1986. Print.

Irigaray, Luce. *Je Tu Nous: Towards a Culture of Difference*. NY: Routledge, 1993. Print.

——. *The Sex which is Not One*. Trans. Catherine Porter and Carolyn Burke. Ithaca: Cornwall University Press, 1985. Print.

Jack, Ian. Ed. *Best of Young British Novelists*. London: Granta, 2003. Print.

Jackson, Rosemary. *Fantasy: The Literature of Subversion*. London and New York: Routledge, 1988. Web. 1 Mar 2012.

Jager, Ronald. Ed. *Essays in Logic from Aristotle to Russell*. Englewood Cliffs, NJ: Prentice-Hall, 1963. Print.

Johnson, Heather. "Textualising the Double-gendered Body: Forms of the Grotesque in *The Passion of New Eve*". Ed. Alison Easton. *New Casebooks: Angela Carter*. London: Macmillan Press Ltd., 2000. Print.

Johnson, Heather L. "Transgressive Symbolism and the Transsexual Subject in Angela Carter's The Passion of New Eve". Joseph Bristow and Trev Lynn Broughton eds. *The Infernal Desires of Angela Carter: Fiction, Femininity, Feminism*. London: Longman, 1997. Print.

Jones, Ernest. *Sigmund Freud: Life and Work Vol. 1: The Young Freud 1856-1900*. London: Hogarth Press, 1953. Print.

Jung, Carl Gustav. *Psychological Types*. Pantheon Books, 1962. Web. 12 May 2012.

Kafka, Franz. *The Metamorphosis*. New York: Bentam Dell, 1972. Print.

Kaveney, Roz. "New New World Dreams: Angle Carter and Science Fiction". Ed. Lorna Sage. *Flesh and the Mirror: Essays on the Art of Angela Carter*. London: Virago Press, 1994. Print.

Keenan, Sally. "Angela Carter's *The Sadeian Woman*: Feminism as Treason". Ed. Alison Easton. *New Casebooks: Angela Carter*. London: Macmillan Press Ltd., 2000. Print.

Kenyon, Olga. *Women Novelists Today: A Survey of English Writing in the Seventies and Eighties*. Brighton: Harvester, 1988. Print.

King, Karen L. "Women in Ancient Christianity". *The New Discoveries. Frontline: The First Christians*. Web. 2 Nov 2009.

Klein, Melanie. "Early Stages of the Oedipus Conflict". Contributions to Psycho-Analysis, 1921-1945. London: Hogarth Press, 1950. Print.

——. "Notes on Some Schizoid Mechanisms". 1946. Developments in Psycho Analysis. London: Hogarth, 1952. Print.

Kristeva, Julia. *Revolution in Poetic Language*. New York: Columbia University Press, 1984. Print.

——. *Powers of Horror: An Essay on Abjection*. New York: Columbia University Press, 1982. Print.

Lacan, Jacques. *Ecrits: A Selection*. UK: Tavistock Publications, 1977. Print.

——. *The Ego in Freud's Theory and in the Technique of Psychoanalysis*. Ed. Jacques-Alain Miller. New York: Norton, 1988. Print.

Lakoff, Robin Tolmach. *Language and Woman's Place: Text and Commentaries*. Ed. Mary Bucholtz. Oxford: Oxford University Press, 2004. Print.

Lane, Richard J., Rod Maugham and Philip Tew eds. *Contemporary British Fiction*. Cambridge: Polity Press, 2003. Print.

Lessing, Doris. *The Golden Notebook. The Golden Notebook Project*. 10 Nov 2008. Web. 30 May 2012.

Lewis, Liz. *Charlotte Bronte and Jean Rhys*, Dec. 2001. Web. 2 Aug 2012.

Linnet, Maren. "New Words, New Everything: Fragmentation and Trauma in Jean Rhys". Literary Criterion, July 2006. Print.

Look Lai, Wally. "The Road to Thornfield Hall: An Analysis of Jean Rhys's *Wide Sargasso Sea*". Ed. John La Rose. *New Beacon Reviews: Collection One*. London: New Beacon Books, 1968. Print.

Lyotard, Jean-Francois. *The Postmodern Condition: A Report on Knowledge*. Trans. Geoffrey Bennington and Brian Massumi. Minneapolis: University of Minnesota Press, 1984. Print.

Mackean, Ian. *Literature in English Post-1914*. London: Hodder Arnold, 2005. Print.

Madsen, Deborah L. *Feminist Theory and Literary Practice*. London: Photo Press, 2000. Print.

Makinen, Merja. "Angela Carter's *The Bloody Chamber* and the Decolonisation of Feminine Sexuality". Ed. Alison Easton. *New Casebooks: Angela Carter*. London: Macmillan Press Ltd., 2000. Print.

Manlovw, Colin. "In the Demythologising Business: Angela Carter's The Infernal Desire Machines of Doctor Hoffman (1972)". Ed. Kath Filmer. *Twentieth Century Fantasies*. London: Macmillan, 1992. Print.

Massie, Allan. *The Novel Today: A Critical Guide to the British Novel 1970-1989*. New York: Longman, 1990. Print.

Matus, Jill. "Blonde, Black and Hottentot Venus: Context and Critique in Angela Carter's 'Black Venus'". *New Casebooks: Angela Carter*. London: Macmillan Press Ltd., 2000. Print.

Meaney, Gerardine. "History and Women's Time: *Heroes and Villains*". Ed. Alison Easton. *New Casebooks: Angela Carter*. London: Macmillan Press Ltd., 2000. Print.

Miles, Rosalind. *The Female Form: Women Writers and the Conquest of the Novel*. London: Routledge, 1990. Print.

Mill, John Stuart. *The Subjugation of Women. Modern History Sourcebook*. Fordham University. Web. 25 May 2012.

Miller, Jean Baker. *Toward a New Psychology of Women*. Massachusetts: Beacon Press, 1976. Print.

Miller, Karl. *Doubles: Studies in Literary History*. Faber Find, 2009. Web. 30 Mar 2012.

Miller, Nancy K. *Subject to Change*. New York: Columbia University Press, 1988. Print.

Millet, K. *Sexual Politics*. New York: Doubleday, 1969. Print.

Moi, Toril. *Sexual/Texual Politics*. Routledge, 2002. Web. 12 Dec. 2011.

Morgan, Robin ed. *Sisterhood is Powerful: An Anthology of Writings from the Women's Liberation Movement*. New York: Random House, 1970. Print.

Morris, Pam. *Literature and Feminism: An Introduction*. Oxford: Blackwell, 1993. Print.

——. *Realism*. London: Routledge, 2003. Print.

Morrison, Iago. *Contemporary Fiction*. New York: Routledge Taylor and Francis Group, 2003. Print.

Munford, Rebecca. "Angela Carter and the Politics of Intertextuality". *Re-Visiting Angela Carter. Texts, Contexts, Intertexts*. New York: Palgrave Macmillan, 2006. Print.

Naipaul, V.S. *The Enigma of Arrival*. London: Penguin Books, 1987. Print.

Neu, Jerome. Ed. *The Cambridge Companion to Freud*. Cambridge: Cambridge University Press, 1991. Print.

Nicol, Bran. *The Cambridge Introduction to Postmodern Fiction*. UK: Cambridge University Press, 2009. Print.

Nietzsche, Friedrich Wilhelm. *Beyond Good and Evil*. Trans. Marion Faber, Oxford: Oxford World's Classics, 1998. Print.

——. *The Gay Science*. Trans. Walter Kaufmann. New York: Random House Inc., 1974. Print.

Norris, Christopher. *Deconstruction*. London: Routledge, 2005. Print.

Olson, Tillie. *Silences*. Delacorte, 1978. Web. 1 May 2012.

Osland, Dianne and Marea Mitchell. *Representing Women and Female Desire from Arcadia to Jane Eyre*. New York: Palgrave Macmillan, 2005. Print.

Osborne, Richard. *Freud: For Beginners*. Illus. Maurice Mechan. Chennai: Orient Longman, 2000. Print.

Owen, Craig. "The Discourse of Others: Feminists and Postmodernism". Ed. Hal Foster. *The Anti-Aesthetic: Essays on Postmodern Culture*. Port Townsend, Wash: Bay Press, 1983. Print.

Page, Eimer. *Jean Rhys Biography*, 7 May 1997. Web. 21 Oct 2011.

Palmer, Paulina. *Contemporary Women's Fiction: Narrative Practice and Feminist Theory*. Hertfordshire: Harvester Wheatsheaf, 1989. Print.

——. "From Coded Mannequin to Bird Woman: Angela Carter's Magic Flight". *Women Reading Women's Writing*. New York: 1987. Print.

Patmore, Coventry. "The Angel in the House". *The Victorian Web*. Web. 17 May 2012.

Palumbo, Donald ed. *Erotic Universe: Sexuality and Fantastic Literature*. New York: Greenwood Press, 1986. Questia. Web. 18 Dec 2010.

Parker, Emma ed. *Contemporary British Women Writers*. Cambridge: D.S. Brewer, 2004.

Parry, Benita. "Two Native Voices in *Wide Sargasso Sea*". Ed Judith L. Raiskin. *Wide Sargasso Sea: A Norton Critical Edition*. New York: W.W. Norton and Company, 1999. Print.

Peach, Linden. *Modern Novelists: Angela Carter*. London: Macmillan, 1998. Print.

Perrault, Charles. *The Tales of Mother Goose. Ciff Ciaff: Old Tales*. Web. 18 May 2012.

Phillips, Caryl. *Cambridge*. New York: Vintage International, 1991. Print.

Pitchford, Nicola. *Tactical Readings: Feminist Postmodernism in the Novels of Kathy Acker and Angela Carter*. Lewisburg: Bucknell University Press, 2002. *Questia*. Web. 18 Dec 2010.

Plasa, Carl ed. *Jean Rhys: Wide Sargasso Sea—A Readers Guide to Essential Criticism*. New York: Palgrave Macmillan, 2001. Print.

Plato. "Phaedrus". Trans. Alexander Nehamas and Paul Woodruff. *Plato: Complete Works*. Ed. John M. Cooper. Web. 14 Feb 2010.

——. *The Republic*. Trans. Benjamin Jowett. *ebooks @adelaide*. 29 Aug 2010 Web. 26 Nov 2011.

——. *Timaeus*. Trans. Benjamin Jowett. *The Internet Classics Archive*. Web. 10 Aug 2012.

Pollock, Griselda. *Vision and Difference*. London: Routledge, 1988. Print.

Poston, Carol H. *A Vindication of the Rights of Woman: Mary Wollstonecraft*. London: Norton and Company, 1988. Print.

Price, Janet, and Margrit Shildrick. *Feminist Theory and the Body-A Reader*. New York: Routledge, 1999. Print.

Punter, David ed. *A Companion to the Gothic*. Oxford: Blackwell Publishers, 2000. Print.

——. *Postcolonial Imaginings: Fictions of a New World Order*. New Delhi: Atlantic Publishers and Distributors, 2000. Print.

——. *The Literature of Terror: A History of Gothic Fictions from 1765 to the Present Day*. Longman: 1980. Print.

Raiskin, Judith. "England: Dream and Nightmare". Ed. Judith L. Raiskin. *Wide Sargasso Sea: A Norton Critical Edition*. New York: W.W. Norton and Company, 1999. Print.

Ramchand, Kenneth. "The Place of Jean Rhys and *Wide Sargasso Sea*". Ed Judith L. Raiskin. *Wide Sargasso Sea: A Norton Critical Edition*. New York: W.W. Norton and Company, 1999. Print.

Rai, Sudha. "*The Book of Mrs Noah*: Theory and Practice in Feminist Rewriting". Eds Santosh Gupta and Preeti Bhatt.

Contemporary British Fiction: History and the Present. Jaipur: Rawat Publications, 2007. Print.

Rice, Philip and Patricia Waugh. *Modern Literary Theory: A Reader.* London: Hodder Arnold, 1989. Print.

Rich, Adrienne. *Of Woman Born: Motherhood as Experience and Institution.* 1977. *History is a Weapon.* Web. 17 May 2012.

Roberts, Adam. *Science Fiction.* London: Routledge, 2000. Print.

Robinson, Sally. *Engendering the Subject: Gender and Self-Representation in Contemporary Women's Fiction.* New York: State University of New York Press, 1991. Print.

——. "The Anti-Hero as Oedipus: Gender and the Postmodern Narrative in The Infernal Desire of Doctor Hoffman". Ed. Alison Easton. *Angela Carter: New Casebooks. London:* Macmillan Press Ltd., 2000. Print.

Robson, Mark and Peter Stock Well. *Language in Theory: A Resource Book for Students.* London: Routledge Taylor, 2005. Print.

Rody, Caroline. "Burning Down the House: The Revisionary Paradigm of Jean Rhys's *Wide Sargasso Sea*". Ed Judith L. Raiskin. *Wide Sargasso Sea: A Norton Critical Edition.* New York: W.W. Norton and Company, 1999. Print.

Rogers, Katharine M. *The Troublesome Helpmate: A History of Misogyny in Literature.* Seattle: University of Washington Press, 1968. *Questia.* Web. 18 Dec. 2010.

Rosso, Jeana Del. *Writing Catholic Women.* New York: Palgrave Macmillan, 2005. Print.

Ruether, Rosemary Radford. *Sexism and God-Talk: Towards a Feminist Theology.* Beacon Press, 1993. Web. 17 May 2010.

Russo, Mary. "Revamping Spectacle: Angela Carter's *Nights at the Circus*". Ed. Alison Easton. *New Casebooks: Angela Carter.* London: Macmillan Press Ltd., 2000. Print.

Russo, Mary J. *The Female Grotesque: Risk, Excess and Modernity.* New York: Routledge, 1994. Print.

——. *The Female Grotesque: Risk, Excess and Modernity.* London: Routledge, 1994. Print.

Sade, Marquis de. *Juliette*. Trans. Austryn Wainhouse. New York: Grove Press, 1968. Print.

——. *Justine or Good Conduct Well Chastised. Scribd*. Web. 18 May 2012.

Sage, Lorna. *Angela Carter*. Plymouth: Northcote House, 1994. Print.

——. "Death of the Author". *Women in the House of Fiction: Post War Women Novelists*. London: Macmillan, 1992. Print.

——. *Women in the House of Fiction: Post War Women Novelists*. London: Macmillan, 1992. Print.

Said, Edward. *Orientalism*. London: Penguin Books, 1978. Print.

Sanders, Julie. "Bubblegum and Revolution: Angela Carter's Hybrid Shakespeare". Ed Rebecca Munford. *Re-Visiting Angela Carter. Texts, Contexts, Intertexts*. New York: Palgrave Macmillan, 2006. Print.

Sargisson, Lucy. *Contemporary Feminist Utopianism*. New York: Routledge, 1996. *Questia*. Web, 7 Mar 2011.

Scott, Bonnie Kim. "The Gender of Postmodernism". Ed. Dennis Walder. *Literature in the Modern World: Critical Essays and Documents*. 2nd ed. Oxford: Oxford University Press, 2004. Print.

Scott, Joan Wallach. *Gender and the Politics of History*. New York: Columbia University Press, 1988. Print.

Sedgwick, Eve Kosofsky. *Between Men: English Literature and Male Homosocial Desire*. New York: Columbia University Press, 1985. Print.

Sellers, Susan. "Becoming Gods and Umblical Wordbows: The New Hagiography of Michele Roberts". *Myth and Fairy Tale in Contemporary Women's Fiction*. New York: Palgrave, 2002. Print.

Sengupta, Jayita. *Refractions of Desire: Feminist Perspectives in the Novels of Toni Morrison, Michele Roberts and Anita Desai*. New Delhi: Atlantic Publishers and Distributors, 2006. Print.

Shattock, Joanne. *The Oxford Guide to British Women Writers*. Oxford: Oxford University Press, 1994. Print.

Shelley, Mary. *Frankenstein; or, The Modern Prometheus*. Ed. Susan J. Wolfson. New York: Pearson Longman, 2007. Print.

Showalter, Elaine. *A Literature of Their Own: British Women Novelist from Bronte to Lessing*. London: Virago, 1978. Print.

——. "Feminist Criticism in the Wilderness". *Modern Criticism and Theory: A Reader. ed. David Lodge*. London: Longman, 1988. Print.

——. *The Female Malady: Women, Madness and English Culture 1830-1980*. London: Virago, 1985. Print.

——. "Toward a Feminist Poetics". *The New Feminist Criticism: Essays on Women, Literature and Theory ed.* Showalter. New York: Pantheon, 1985. Print.

Simons, Ion ed. *Contemporary Critical Theorists: From Lacan to Said*. New Delhi: Atlantic Publishers and Distributors, 2004. Print.

Simpson, Anne B. *Territories of the Psyche: The Fiction of Jean Rhys*. New York: Palgrave Macmillan, 2005. Print.

Smith, Barbara. "Toward a Black Feminist Criticism" in *The New Feminist Criticism: Essays on Women, Literature and Theory*. ed. Elaine Showalter. London: Virago, 1986. Print.

Spaull, Sue. *Gynocriticism: Feminist Reading*. Ed. Sara Mills et all. New York: Harvester Wheatsheaf, 1989. Print.

Spender, Dale. *Man Made Language*. Routledge and Kegan Paul, 1980. Web. 7 May 2012.

——. *Mothers of the Novel: Hundred Good Women Writers Before Jane Austen*. London: Pandora Press, 1986. Print.

——. "Women and Literary History". Eds. Catherine Belsey and Jane Moore. *The Feminist Reader*. London: Macmillan Press, 1997. Print.

Stevenson, Randall. *A Reader's Guide to the Twentieth Century Novel in Britain*. Hertfordshire: Harvester Wheatsheaf, 1993. Print.

Stockwell, Peter. *Cognitive Poetics: An Introduction*. London: Routledge, 2002. Print.

Sturken, Marita and Lisa Cartwright. *Practices of Looking: An Introduction of Visual Culture*. Oxford University Press, 2009. Web. 3 May 2012.

Sturrock, John. *Structuralism*. Oxford: Blackwell, 2003. Print.

Suleiman, Susan Rubin. *Subversive Intent: Gender, Politics and the Avant-Garde*. US: Harvard University Press, 1990. Print.

Telford, William R. "Jesus and Women in Fiction and Film." Ed. Ingrid Rosa Kitzberger. *Transformative Encounters: Jesus and Women Re-Viewed*. Boston: Brill, 2000. *Questia*. Web. 19 Feb 2011.

Teslenko, Tatiana. *Feminist Utopian Novels of the 1970s: Joanna Russ and Dorothy Bryant*. New York: Routledge, 2003. *Questia*. Web. 7 Mar 2011.

Tew, Philip. *The Contemporary British Novel*. London: Continuum International Publishing Group, 2004. Print.

Thomas, Sue. *The Worlding of Jean Rhys*. Westport, CT: Greenwood Press, 1999. *Questia*. Web. 18 Dec. 2010.

Thorpe, Michael. "The Other Side: Wide Sargasso Sea and Jane Eyre". Ed Judith L. Raiskin. *Wide Sargasso Sea: A Norton Critical Edition*. New York: W.W. Norton and Company, 1999. Print.

Tiffin, Helen. "Post-Colonial Literatures and Counter–Discourse". *The Post-Colonial Studies Reader*. Ed by Bill Ashcroft, Gareth Griffiths and Helen Tiffin. London: Routledge, 1995. Print.

Todd, Janet. *The Sign of Angelica*. London: Virago Press, 1989. Print.

Tonkin, Maggie. "Albertine/a the Ambiguous: Angela Carter's Reconfiguration of Marcel Proust's Modernist Muse". Ed. Rebecca Munford. *Re-Visiting Angela Carter. Texts, Contexts, Intertexts*. New York: Palgrave Macmillan, 2006. Print.

Trible, Phyllis. *Texts of Terror: Literary and Feminist Readings of Biblical Narratives*. Philadelphia, PA: Fortress Press, 1984. Print.

Verdonk, Peter and Jean Jacques Weber eds. *Twentieth Century Fiction: From Text to Context*. London: Routledge, 1995 Print.

Voragine, Jacobus de. *The Golden Legend or Lives of the Saints*. Trans. William Caxton. Ed. F.S. Ellis. Temple Classics, 1900. Web. 12 May 2012.

Walia, Rajni. *Women and Self: Fictions of Jean Rhys, Barbara Pym and Anita Brookner*. Delhi: Books Plus, 2001. Print.

Warner, Marina. *Alone of All Her Sex: The Myth and the Cult of the Virgin Mary*. London: Picador, 1976. Print.

Waugh, Patricia. *Literary Theory and Criticism*. New Delhi: Oxford University Press, 2006. Print.

——. *Metafiction: The Theory and Practice of Self-Conscious Fiction*. London: Routledge, 1984. Print.

Webb, Kate. "Seriously Funny: *Wise Children*". *New Casebooks: Angela Carter*. London: Macmillan Press Ltd., 2000. Print.

Webster, Roger. *Studying Literary Theory: An Introduction*. 2nd Edition. London: Arnold, 2001. Print.

Werlock, Abby H.P. Ed. *British Women Writing Fiction*. London: University of Alabama Press, 2000. Print.

Wilson, Elizabeth. *Hidden Agendas: Theory, Politics and Experience in the Women's Movement*. London: Tavistock, 1986. Print.

Wollstonecraft, Mary. *A Vindication of the Rights of Woman with Strictures on Moral and Political Subjects*. London: Joseph Johnson, 1792. Print.

Woolf Virginia. *A Room of One's Own*. London: Penguin, 1945. Print.

——. "*Jane Eyre* and *Wuthering Heights*". The Common Reader. Ed Andrew Mc Neillie. London, New York, San Diego: Harcourt Brace and Company, 1925. Print.

——. "Women and Fiction", *Virginia Woolf: Women and Writing* ed. Michele Barrett. London: Women's Press, 1979. Print.

Yeats, W.B. "The Second Coming". *PotW.org*. Aug 1996. Web. 18 Apr 2009.

Zipes, Jack. *Breaking the Magic Spell: Radical Theories of Folk and Fairy Tales*. Kentucky: The University Press of Kentucky, 2002. Print.

——. *Don't Bet on the Prince: Contemporary Feminist Fairy Tales in North America and England.* Aldershot: Ashgate, 2001. Print.

——. *Fairy Tales and the Art of Subversion*. London: Routledge, 1988. Print.

——. *The Trials and Tribulations of Little Red Riding Hood: Versions of the Tale in Sociocultural Context*. Heinemann, 1983. Print.

ARTICLES IN PERIODICALS, REVIEWS, SEMINARS AND NEWSPAPERS

Adams, Mars- Jones. "Women Beware Women". *New York Review of Books* 31 Jan 1985. Print.

Adjarian, M. M. "Between and Beyond Boundaries in Wide Sargasso Sea". *College Literature* 22.1 (1995): 202-209. Web. 3 March 2012.

Ahearn, Edward J. "The Modern English Visionary: Peter Ackroyd's Hawksmoor and Angela Carter's *The Passion of New Eve*". *Twentieth Century Literature* 46.4 (2000): 453. Print.

Alvarez, Alfred. "The Best Living English Novelist". *New York Times Book Review*. 17 March 1974: 6-7. Print.

"Aristotle." *Wikipedia: The Free Encyclopedia*. Wikimedia Foundation, Inc. 22 July 2004. Web. 20 July 2011.

Armstrong, Isobel. "Choosing What to Know". Rev. of A Closed Eye. *Times Literary Supplement*. 23 Aug 1991. Print.

Bamzai, Kaveree. "Map of the Heart". Rev. of *Visitors*. *Indian Express Sunday Magazine* 15 June 1997. Print.

Barker, Paul. "The Return of the Magic Storyteller". *The Independent on Sunday*. 8 January 1995. Web. 4 May 2009.

Brown, Kevin. "'Tis Pity She's a Whore: The Revision of Mary Magdalene in Contemporary Fiction". *Papers on Language and Literature* 42.3 (2006). Print.

Castro, Joy. "Jean Rhys". *The Review of Contemporary Fiction* 20.2 (2000). Print.

Clark, Robert. "Angela Carter's Desire Machines". *Women's Studies: An Interdisciplinary Journal* 14.2 (1987). Print.

Cummins, Marsha Z. "A Fairy-Tale Neurotic". Rev. of *Wide Sargasso Sea. Times Literary Supplement* 17 Nov. 1966. Print.

Duncer, Patricia. "Re-Imagining the Fairly Tales: Angela Carter's Bloody Chamber," *Literature and History*, 10:1 (*Spring*, 1984). Web. 23 May 2008.

Fayad, Mona. "Unquiet Ghosts : The Struggle for Representation in Jean Rhys's *Wide Sargasso Sea*": *Modern Fiction Studies* 34 (Autumn 1988). Print.

Fitzpatrick-Hanly, Margaret Ann. "Feminism as Facilitation and Resistance: the Question of Penis Envy". *Canadian Journal of Psychoanalysis* Vol. 2 (1994): 29-45. *Questia*. Web. 20 July 2010.

Haffenden, John. "Magical Mannerist: John Haffenden Talks to Angela Carter". *The Literary Review* (November, 1984). Web. 5 Nov 2008.

Hassan, Ihab. "Making Sense: The Trails of Postmodernism". *New Literary History*. 18.2, (1987). Print.

Hardy, Barbara "A Cindrella's Loneliness". Rev. of *Hotel du Lac. Times Literary Supplement* 14 Sept. 1984. Print.

Hegi, Ursula. "The Curse of Being a Good Woman". Rev. of *Fraud. New York Times Book Review* 10 Jan. 1993. Print.

Howard-Laity, Elizabeth. "Rewriting the Body in Michele Roberts' *Impossible Saints*". Web. 10 Feb 2012.

Irigaray, Luce. "When Our Lips Speak Together". Trans. Carolyn Burke. *Signs* 6.1, 1980. *JSTOR*. Web. 2 Jan 2011.

Johnson, Daniel. "Books Barely Furnish a Room". *The Times*. 16 September, 1992. Web. 11 July 2007.

Kaiser, Mary. "Fairy Tale as Sexual Allegory: Intertextuality in Angela Carter's The Bloody Chamber". *The Review of Contemporary Fiction* 14.3 (1994). *Questia*. Web. 21 May 2011.

Kristeva, Julia. ""Nous Deux" or a (Hi)story of Intertextuality". *The Romanic Review* 93.1-2 (2002): 7+. *Questia*. Web. 15 May 2012.

Lacan, Jacques. *The Seminars of Jacques Lacan*. Web. 18 May 2012.

Lawtoo, Nidesh. "Hybridity, Dialogism and Identity in Jean Rhys's *Wide Sargasso Sea* and Tsitsi Dangarembga's *Nervous Conditions*". *Portals: A Journal in Comparative Literature*. San Francisco State University, 2010. Web. 10 June 2010.

Lopez, Sania Villegas. "Telling Women's Lives: Vision as Historical Revision in the Work of Michele Roberts". *Atlantis*. Vol xxiii. 1(June 2001). Web. 10 Dec 2011.

Mac Arthur, John. "The Resurrection of Jesus Christ—Part 2". Web. 26 March 2010.

Meer, Jeff Vander. *The Scriptorium*. Web. 9 April 2007.

Monday, Ralph. "Adam and Lilith: Thanatos and the Resurrection of the Archetype". *The Mystica*. 7 May 2012. Web. 18 May 2012.

Milne, Andrew. *Spiders and Threads: The Angela Carter Website*, 4 February 2006. Web. 6 Sep 2009.

"Neurotic Women". Rev. of *Voyage in The Dark* and *Good Morning, Midnight*. *Times Literary Supplement* 20 July 1967. Print.

Ozer, Sevinc. "Women's Body as Colony: Impossible Saints". *Gale: Cengage Learning* (2008). Web. 3 Jan 2012.

Rich, Adrienne. "When We Dead Awaken: Writing as Re-Vision". *College English: Women, Writing and Teaching. National Council of Teachers of English* 34 (1), 1972. 11 Sep 2008. Web. 18 Sep 2011.

Rowland, Susan. "Michele Roberts's Virgins: Contesting Gender in Fictions, Re-writing Jungian Theory and Christian Myth". *Journal of Gender Studies*. 8.1 (1999). *Taylor and Francis Online*. Web. 12 May 2012.

Rubin, Andrew N. "Edward W. Said". *Arab Studies Quarterly*. Vol 26. 2004. Print.

Rushdie, Salman. "Angela Carter, 1940-92: A Very Good

Wizard, a Very Dear Friend". *New York Times*. 8 Mar 1992. Web. 3 Dec 2010.

Sage, Lorna. "A Savage Sideshadow". *New Review* 4 (July 1977). Web. 3 March 2012.

Salat, M.F. "Sub-versions and Contra-dictions". Ed. Shirin Kudchedkar. *Postmodernism and Feminism: Canadian Contexts*. Delhi: Pencraft International, 2005. Print.

Sheets, Robin Ann. "Pornography, Fairy Tales and Feminism: Angela Carter's *The Bloody Chamber*". *Journal of the History of Sexuality* 1.4 (1991). *Questia*. Web. 21 May 2011.

Smith, Jules. *Michele Roberts*. 2002. Web. 18 Oct 2009.

Spivak, Gayatri Chakravorty. "Three Women's Texts and a Critique of Imperialism". *Critical Inquiry*. 12.1. (1985) 243-261. *JSTOR*. Web. 20 Aug 2008.

Swyt, Wendy. ""Wolfings": Angela Carter's Becoming-Narrative". *Studies in Short Fiction* 33.3 (1996). *Questia*. Web. 18 Dec. 2010.

"The 50 Greatest British Writers since 1945". *Times*. 5 Jan 2008. Web. 21 July 2011.

Walter. "Bertha the Doomed". Rev. of *Wide Sargasso Sea*. *New York Times Book Review* 18 June 1967. Print.

White, Rosie. "Permeable Borders, Possible Worlds: History and Identity in the Novels of Michele Roberts". *Studies in the Literary Imagination* 36.2 (2003) *Questia*. Web. 18 Dec. 2010.

Wiseman, Zipporah, et al. "Roundtable Discussion: Is Subversion Subversive?". *Texas Journal of Women and the Law* 13.1 (2003). *Questia*. Web. 18 Dec. 2010.

Zeitkowitz, Richard E. "Writing a Feminine Paris in Jean Rhys's Quartet". *Journal of Modern Literature* 28.2 (2005) 1-17. Indiana University Press. Web. 1 Aug 2011.

Zivin, Alexander. Jean Rhys: An Overview, 2004. Web. 9 Jan 2011.